EVERY WHICH WAY

Calia Read

Chapter 1

Everything in life came down to choices.

It was always a general thought that the larger decisions held greater consequences, but if you really thought about it, so did the small ones.

The fresh scent of coffee dominated the room. Severine took a deep breath and leaned back into the couch with a smile. The aroma always offered her a sense of comfort and left her feeling warm and sated.

She placed her cup onto the table in front of her and looked down at the textbook in her lap. The quiet environment merged with the soft music playing, helped Severine tune everything out and focus on her never-ending studies.

The leather across from her creaked and she looked at her friend Lily, who was slithered deeper into the chair. It looked like the world's most awkward position.

"Umm...what are you doing?" Severine asked with a smirk.

Lily's dark blue eyes bulged. "Are they gone?" she mouthed slowly.

Severine looked around the coffee shop, at the people sitting around them. There were only two other customers. One was some emo dude in the corner, brooding over a notebook, probably writing heartbreaking poetry over the turns in his life.

The other, a middle aged woman, sat in the center of the coffee shop and pretended not to be reading the romance novel in front of her. It was highly doubtful Lily was hiding from them.

"Who are you talking about?" Severine asked. She placed her books next to her on the couch and leaned closer to her friend.

Lily made a frustrated noise and motioned with her eyes for Severine to turn around. "You idiot," she said through clenched teeth. "Look. At the cash register."

"If you can see them then why are you asking me if they've left?"

Lily ignored her and shifted in her seat. Her entire face was covered with the nearest magazine. Too bad she picked up the one titled Maxim. The cover featured some gorgeous, pouting actress. Her fingers were hooked around her lacy underwear, and somehow her white blouse was magically open, showing off her cleavage.

Keeping it classy for the world.

Severine, ignoring her friend's request to act nonchalant, simply turned around to stare curiously at the three males ordering drinks. The trio was unaware of the gawking. Severine kept it that way and turned back to Lily with her eyebrows cocked high in confusion.

"I made out with the buff one last year," Lily whispered.

Severine's mouth formed a perfect O. She quickly slid closer to Lily, away from the guys at the register. Lily kept her face buried in the magazine, and Severine yanked it away. "Talk. Now."

Lily shrugged like it was no big deal. She was still hunched in her seat like a paranoid escapee. "I was really drunk. I think I spent the evening trying to get his friend, Thayer's, attention but I ended up with Chris instead.

Not a bad second place if I do say so myself." Her eyes danced impishly.

Severine gawked at Lily with surprise. The sweet, gentle blonde sitting across from her never got drunk and certainly never made out with random males, no matter how yummy they looked. But then again, the girl in front of her now wasn't the same one that grew up in a strict, religious family. Naïve Lily was shed the minute they slammed the trunk of her car and drove out of their small Iowa town. This was her time to be free and she was coming into herself. Severine was glad they were on this journey together.

"Which one is Chris?"

She went to turn around, but Lily grabbed her arm quickly. "Don't turn around," she warned.

"Come on! I need to see this random dude that my shy Lily made out with."

"That's just it. He's a random dude. Nothing much to say about it." Quickly, she glanced up, her eyes drifting past Severine. "But Thayer isn't random. That dude's a freakin' legend."

"Legend? So he's a thing of the past? How long has he been in college?" Lily stared at her blankly. "Oh God, don't tell me we have a Van Wilder on our hands!"

"Not that kind of legend! He's amazing at sports, came here on a basketball scholarship—"

"I stopped listening at sports," Severine said dryly. "For being a 'legend,' I've never heard of him."

Lily threw her hands in the air in a gesture that said, 'how's that my fault?' "Maybe you've never heard of him because you were absorbed in some other dude that week, or month, or whatever the hell you were doing."

Severine ignored her friend's words. "Am I allowed to look at him? I need to see how good-looking this Chris and Thayer are. My hot-guy tracking system has never steered me wrong." Lily nodded her head in defeat.

Severine anxiously turned, not caring if she looked

like a stalker. She glanced at 'Thayer the God,' and it became obvious why he was here on a basketball scholarship.

If any guy stood over six feet she was elated, and this guy seemed to surpass her height requirement easily. She could wear any Jimmy Choo heel available and still feel tiny. Severine glanced at his faded, dark green shirt. It embraced his shoulders perfectly, showing just how much muscle was withheld from sight. Truthfully, even if he were wearing a cut-off with creepy pictures of wolves on the front and a fanny pack wrapped around his waist, it wouldn't matter. She'd still think he was drool worthy.

His head moved up and down as he spoke with the server. Severine watched as he reached toward his back jean pocket. A feeling of warmth consumed her body and quickly spread throughout.

There was something teasingly dangerous about watching him. He could turn around and catch her red-handed, and Severine secretly wanted him to do just that.

Her eyebrow rose as she watched him reach for his wallet, his actions inciting the muscles cording up his arm to spring against his skin. Even from where she sat, she could see the rough appearance of his hands. It shaped quality for any guy, showing just how active he was in life. This guy looked good—better than good.

She turned back toward her friend and was met with a smug grin. "Am I right? Or am I right?"

Severine gave a brisk nod. "Not bad." She tried to character someone uninterested. If she was even remotely believable, she should consider changing her major to creative arts.

"Not bad? The hot Calvin Klein models we taped in our lockers in high school were not bad." Lily inclined her head in Thayer's direction. "That's look-at-the-sky-and-scream, 'Thank you God,' as loud as you can!"

Severine grinned at Lily's example. "So is the dude a man slut?"

Lily sipped her coffee. "I have no clue. I don't remember much about that night, but I'm pretty sure I almost vomited all over his shoes."

"Charming."

"Now do you understand why I kept that night to myself?"

"I can see how that might be marginally embarrassing. How have I not seen this crazy, wild side of you until now?" Severine asked with raised brows.

"It was a one time thing. Honestly. If only my life was that exciting."

"Was I with you?" Severine asked.

Lily frowned over at Severine and tightened her loose ponytail. "Of course, but you were dancing with some guy."

"I just don't know if I can trust you anymore," Severine said, faking a sad voice. "What else are you hiding from me? When you say you're going to the library, are you really meeting up with these gorgeous hunks?" Severine glanced at Lily mischievously.

"Please. You know if I was meeting up with any gorgeous guy at the library I'd flood your inbox with texts."

Severine nodded solemnly. "I'd expect nothing less."

Lily once again hid her face from view. Only this time, she actually read the titles on the magazines before grabbing one. Severine ignored the books around her and spun back toward the front counter. Her name would be the first listed underneath the group, 'Gawkers and Proud!' It was more than rude, but if her name were written down first, Thayer's name would be listed next because he was staring right back, carefully scrutinizing her.

To Severine, his expression was blank—spotless and clean. She wondered what it would be like to create a mess in his eyes, to leave an imprint. She was willing to lay money down that she'd be the first.

Her thoughts bolted in different directions, but all she wanted was to focus on the unspoken challenge between the two of them.

A muscle in his jaw ticked and Severine smirked. She knew what he'd be like. Being near him would start out as a rollercoaster ride—her nerves would be frayed and she'd be completely terrified. With every inch toward the sky, Severine would want to be back on the ground.

Then the ride would take off. She'd have no time to think. The ride would direct her body which way to go, and her stomach would drop at the rush of speed. Her eyes would be clenched tightly because she'd be too afraid to look around. At the end, everything would slow, and it would all be over.

With her pulse racing, and a high running through her system, she'd walk away, swearing she'd never return. But she would come back again, and again. Anyone would.

His name was called and he turned. Their gaze was broken, and Severine felt victorious.

Lily was texting on her phone, completely lost in her own world. Ignoring the pile of massive textbooks sitting next to her, Severine picked up the newest Marie Claire instead. Every few pages she'd pause long enough to flick a glance over her shoulder. During the fifth glance, she spied Thayer walking through the door, followed by two guys—one who looked like he had more muscles than brain—probably Chris.

The third male, his hair covered with a baseball cap, looked familiar. Severine was positive he was in her Lit 105 class. He sat near the front and never talked to anyone. She watched as he turned around and held the door open for a stranger. His face was nothing but sharp angles, and the dark stubble scattered around his chin and cheeks intersected any ability of his face being too pretty.

His back was pressed against the glass door as he

looked at Severine. His focus was centered at her eyes, and his gaze seemed to spotlight every hidden secret she kept private. His lips kicked up in a grin, and her heart came to a grinding halt.

The bell attached to the door jingled loudly, announcing she had lost that round. Her high from Thayer had vanished. Severine now knew what it was like to feel cold and hot at the same time. The sensation was consuming. She looked down at the couch and blankly followed the cracked lines of the leather.

"The guy wearing the baseball hat? That's Thayer's brother, Macsen."

Of course he was.

Lily smiled ruefully. "Are you regretting your decision to study here?"

Severine shook her head and grabbed her laptop from the table. "How many cute guys are on campus?" Lily stared at her blankly. "Too many to count. They're forgettable."

Severine glanced at Lily and saw her repeatedly banging her pencil against her notebook. "Macsen's in his second year like us."

Her nod was brief as she stared at the jumbled words before her. "Good for him."

Lily nodded her head and lifted her eyebrows slightly before she went back to taking notes. The conversation was closed. Within the last five minutes, Severine's emotions had been twisted and warped dry. The confusion she was experiencing was foreign to her. Unconsciously, Severine rubbed between her eyes and re-read the paragraph she had been working on for the last five minutes.

Chapter Two

Severine stood in the middle of the doorway to her class. There were more chairs open than usual, maybe that's because Severine had arrived earlier than everyone else. Today was different from every other day because now she knew who else was hearing the same lecture as her and who had been in her view the entire time without her knowing.

Since yesterday, her mind kept replaying her encounter with the Sloan brothers. She wasn't going to encourage a conversation with Thayer Sloan. She knew his game and had no interest in playing it. But Macsen Sloan, he might be a different story.

Her eyes scanned the room, and she wasn't surprised to find a large body hunched over, reading a book. Confidently, Severine walked down the steps toward the front of the room. Around Macsen all the chairs were open. Severine could've chosen a seat a few chairs away from him, but she picked the one closest to him, on his right.

When she dropped her bag onto the floor, Macsen looked sharply at her. Finally, see could see his eyes. Everyone in the world had something special about his or her eyes. Everyone.

Macsen's eyes were unrivaled. They reminded her of

chartreuse. The rare times she saw her dad, he would have a bottle of French liqueur that was almost identical in color. Until now, it annoyed the hell out of her when he sat around drinking like a connoisseur of alcohol.

Looking straight at Macsen, she'd buy ten cases of that damn liqueur, just because.

Severine shifted in her seat to face him. "I'm Severine." She used the introduction as an excuse to stare him in the eyes.

"I know." His eyes zeroed on her face. Severine swore she was getting a slight buzz.

"So you know me, and I don't even know your name. Why is that?"

He gave her the same dull expression as before. "We've had this class together for the last eight weeks. You're just now magically noticing who I am?"

Severine smirked. He looked down at her lips and swallowed. In reaction to his reaction, her pulse started to race. "You seem really upset about that."

His lips fought to stay in a firm line, and those damn chartreuse eyes twisted with amusement. They were going to kill her before this class was over.

When he grabbed his book and went back to reading, Severine flicked an annoyed glance at the paperback in his hand. "Who's Terry Goodkind?"

Macsen pushed his face away from the book, his expression annoyed. Even as he tried to look put off, a small smirk formed on his lips. Now Severine knew why she couldn't stop thinking about Macsen Sloan last night. The reason was clear.

People like Severine—the restless kind—couldn't help but gravitate near the composed and peaceful. He placed his book—face down—and folded his arms in front of him. "He's an author."

She nodded her head, ready to say more, but their professor walked into the room. Severine looked around and finally realized the seats were filled around them.

Before she could respond to Macsen, his focal point went from her and to the front of the room.

Severine tried to focus on the lecture, but her thoughts were off in all directions. Basically, skipping this class would've been more beneficial. She could've gotten a good nap, at least.

Class wrapped up and she watched Macsen grab his backpack, shoving all his belongings inside. He was in a rush. Severine couldn't help but think she was the reason for his quick pace. Did she make him nervous?

No matter what he was feeling, she was still going to talk to him. Of course she was. It made complete sense, considering the intelligent part of her brain had skipped town and left her all alone. Severine was impulsive all the time but this was more—it was spontaneous and hurried. She wanted to know more about this person that was so categorically her opposite.

"Do you go the coffee shop with your brother a lot?" Severine blurted out.

He rolled back on his heels and slowly smiled. "So that's why you're talking to me."

Severine frowned and grabbed her bag off the table. It was her turn to look at him skeptically. "You saw me with Thayer and thought I'd somehow lead the magical way into my brother's bed." Macsen provided with the same smile on his face.

She hated assumptions, especially when they were directed at her.

Pushing her hair over her shoulder, Severine grabbed her bag and moved toward the door, knowing full well that Macsen was behind her, hot on her heels. "Why is it your first assumption— that I'm trying to get with your brother?"

"You're kidding, right?"

"Do I look like I'm kidding?" Severine shot back and quickly sighed. "Listen, if I'd wanted to talk to your brother, I would've yesterday."

He stared at her with confusion, as if she was an impossible equation he could never figure out. People pushed around them and a guy bumped into Macsen, jerking him out of staring at Severine. With his hands in his jeans, he finally spoke. "I'm Macsen. But just call me Mac."

It was all wrong. Severine could never call him by this nickname. "You don't look like a Mac," Severine admitted as they started walking with the students around them.

He glanced at her as they stepped out of the building. The sunlight glinted onto his hair and his eyes. They now looked yellow as he smiled at her. Skip the slight buzz; she was full on drunk from those irises. "And you really don't keep your thoughts to yourself, do you?"

Severine shrugged, but a smile started to form on her face. "It's one of my many charms."

One of his hands reached out and stopped her from moving. His grip was gentle, but it got Severine's attention. The lust running rampant through her veins told her she liked his hands on her. She knew for a fact it would happen again. "How many charms do you have?"

"Is this like my online dating profile, and I have to lure you in with eight attributes that make me, me?"

His head kicked back and he laughed. It was raw. It completely saturated the air around them and made Severine smile in return. "It is," he finally said. Severine shrugged her shoulder and tried to appear elusive. "Oh, so now you're suddenly shy?"

Her mouth opened up to respond but someone else beat her to it.

"Macsen!"

Severine turned at the same time as Macsen and watched a girl come running toward them. When she stopped in front of them, Severine took her in. Her hair ended at her jaw. Severine could catch a fellow hair dyer instantly, and it was clear that the girl standing inches from her loved to dye her hair four shades darker than her natural shade. The blonde shade peeking around the roots made it obvious. Dyed hair girl was slightly interesting, but it had nothing to do with her choice of blue jeans and plain black, long sleeved shirt. It was the quirky glasses that made her seem perky and bright. But as she narrowed her eyes at Severine's presence, Severine knew she was far from optimistic. *Lord. Not one of those girls.*

"Haley, I just got out of class." Macsen said as he leaned down to quickly hug her. He towered over Haley's medium sized frame. It was like watching a poodle beg his or her owner for a treat. "I've been looking for you everywhere," she answered back. I'm-so-different-than-the-rest-of-you girl pointedly glared in Severine's direction.

He laughed with enjoyment and patted her arm. Severine watched every touch and action closely.

"You wanna get some lunch?" Haley asked.

If Haley were an animal, this would be about the time she'd start peeing around Macsen to claim her territory. Severine wasn't going to stick around for her second act of tricks.

Macsen looked over at Severine with uncertainty in his eyes. Severine's eyes gleamed as he looked over Haley's head and held her stare. "See ya later, Macsen," Severine called out as she slowly walked away.

Her smile was attractive—a smile that could slay a guy—and walked away. Severine didn't look back. She already knew Macsen would be staring, and Haley would be launching invisible switchblades her way.

Her conversation with Macsen answered the question her mind had been asking the minute she saw him. There was something to Macsen Sloan. Severine wanted to know more than something, though, she wanted to know everything.

*   *   *   *   *

"So it's been a whole week, eh?" Lily ripped open a package of chips and leaned back in her chair with a smug grin.

Severine stabbed her fork at a large chunk of lettuce. Her salad was far from healthy. The cafe they went to for lunch had a salad buffet, and Severine always piled the pieces of lettuce with cheese, bacon bits, an unhealthy amount of ranch and anything else available. "You make it seem like I'm marking every day not spent talking to Macsen on a calendar."

"I wouldn't doubt it," Lily muttered.

A week, a whole week and Macsen still hadn't said more than a few words to her. Last week, when they talked, she was assured that it wouldn't be the last time. She worked her anger away by stabbing a tomato with her fork.

"What are you thinking about?" Lily asked cautiously.

Severine answered as she reached for her drink, "Nothing. Why?"

"You look like you're constipated," Lily blurted out. "So that shows me you're thinking about something that you shouldn't."

Lily knew Severine almost too well. "I'm good."

"So," Lily said in between chews, "you're telling me that you're gonna leave this dude alone?"

"What? I can't make a friend?" Severine asked innocently.

"Have you had a 'guy' friend? Ever?" The skeptical look on Lily's face made Severine laugh.

"Yes! There's Benji. He's cool."

"Well, he's not the norm," Lily said sternly and looked away with a blush on her cheeks.

Severine threw her hands up in the air. "Whoa. Are you kidding me—do you like him?"

The look Lily gave her was enough to know she was right. She squirmed slightly in her chair and finally responded, "Is this grade school?"

"Yes," Severine said deadpan.

"In that case, yes, I do. I was playing a mean game of M.A.S.H., and well, his name came up last. He had the mansion. We had two kids and a pet lizard. It seemed like the most viable option."

Severine smiled across the table at Lily. "You're so lucky."

Lily picked up the lone piece of lettuce sitting on the table and threw it at Severine. While Severine picked the piece out of her hair, she saw the object of Lily's affection looking for a place to sit. "Hey there, Benji!" Severine called out loudly.

"Sever-ineeee!" Lily whined out and gripped the sides of the table in a panic.

Severine was an only child. While she grew up creating imaginary friends to stay entertained, Lily had four other siblings to drive her insane. Lily was the only person close enough to her, Severine considered her to be a sister. All she wanted was for someone to see how amazing Lily was on sight.

But expressing her feelings wasn't exactly Severine's strongest suit. Most times things just burst out of her mouth without thought. With a shrug, Severine dropped her fork and leaned closer. "Lily, I'm just trying to nudge you toward him. I'm helping you get someone, someone you know you'll probably never talk to otherwise!"

"Hey, what the hell? I'm not mute, you know!"

Lifting an eyebrow, Severine looked doubtfully at her best friend. "To me, or anyone else close to you, you're not. But come on, you turn mute around any dude you've ever salivated over!"

Lily slouched forward and rubbed her forehead. "I know," she groaned loudly. "That's never gonna change, is it?"

Severine shrugged. "How am I supposed to know? That's like asking if I'll ever stop being a serial dater. Doubtful, but you never know. Things could always change for us."

Lily snorted and took a long gulp of her Coke. "Why? Because we're in college and this is the time for self-discovery and liberation?"

"Sure...why not. Now shut it, Ben's close." She scooted over and allowed him to take her chair. "Hey."

Severine glanced at her best guy friend—maybe her only guy friend—and all but did a happy dance at the thought of him getting together with Lily.

Ben sat loudly and ripped the wrapping around his burger. He slid a glance at Severine. "What's up with you?"

"Nothing! Why does everyone keep asking me that?"

He answered her as he attacked the fries on his tray. "You look like you're thinking something."

"He's right. You're thinking something," Melissa confirmed next to Lily.

Melissa shared a class with Lily and with her glasses and preppy outfits that consisted of peach cardigans, layered with a white polo, Melissa looked like she belonged on a debate team. Severine thought she had her pegged, but she was completely wrong. When they'd go out, Melissa would show a different side outside of school. The girl could drink with the best of them and didn't vomit all over the place. Severine was a guarded person, but she let Melissa in instantly.

"Melissa! You're too sweet to be agreeing with Ben!"

Melissa shrugged and adjusted her glasses. She glanced up at Ben and quickly blushed. She turned red at the sight of anyone she didn't know.

"He's right. What are you thinking?" Melissa asked.

"I was thinking," Severine said slowly, "that we should do something tonight."

Across from them a dude belched loudly. Severine

looked up at the noise and crinkled her nose. Ben followed her gaze with a frown. "Tim? Are you interested in him?"

Severine gave Ben a look and slowly shook her head no. "Did you see my face? That wasn't an 'Oh my gosh, I need to be near that dude' face. No, my face was, 'Ugh. I can smell his lunch from here.'"

"I'm not deaf, Blake!" Tim called out.

Severine gave him a short wave. "Don't belch like a sumo wrestler then."

He had a good sense of humor and laughed loudly as he moved his chair closer to their table and smiled at Lily and Severine. "There's a party this weekend. Are you girls going?"

Severine glanced at Lily and shrugged her shoulder. When she looked across the table at Ben, an idea started to slowly form. "Depends...are you going, Benji?"

"Stop calling me that," Ben gritted out.

Honestly, she couldn't help it. She took one look at him during freshman orientation and knew that with his low-key demeanor, he'd be an instant friend. With his blonde hair and blue eyes, he looked like an All-American boy. After that, Benji just kind of stuck.

"Fine, Benjamin," Severine pronounced slowly. "Are you going to the party? Lily, Melissa and I might go."

"I'm not going," Melissa put into the conversation quietly.

Severine pointed the tip of her fork in Melissa's direction. "Yes, you are."

"Do you remember what happened the last time we went to a party? I kept giggling at some dude because he was brooding. I kept calling him Gabriel."

"Why did you call him that?" Lily asked.

She shook her head. "Because he looked like one? I don't know, I can't remember."

"Oh yeah!" Severine snapped her fingers and leaned across the table. "Didn't you tell him he looked like the guys on the romance novels you read?"

"Okay. Don't make it sound like I'm the only one who reads them. They're underneath your bed just like they are for me."

"Not really. When the eReader came into my life, my books were hidden from sight. Literally."

"Yo!" Tim waved his hand in the air. All three girls looked at him, forgetting he was still waiting for an answer. "You ladies coming?"

"Just sit there and look pretty, will ya?" Severine patted his arm and focused on her food. Her fork was inches away from her mouth when she heard a voice behind her.

"Does she always snap out orders to you, Tim?"

Severine's sat up straight. The low-toned voice came from behind her, but close enough that Severine knew whomever it was, they were sitting close by. Close enough to hear everything she was saying. She turned around quickly, partially out of fear that it was Macsen.

Instead of those chartreuse eyes that Severine fell over, it was eyes a shaded color of gray that stared back at her with untamed energy. Thayer waited for her to answer, and when she only gave him a dark look, a smug expression crossed his face.

Sure enough, he sat right behind her. Depending how long he had been there, he had probably heard everything she and Lily talked about. Severine had no time to be embarrassed, she wanted to punch that conceited little grin off his face.

She ignored everyone at his table and placed her elbow on the top of her chair. Her expression was serene as she leaned closer to Thayer. "Tim's smart. Any brilliant guy knows that the key to success is to always follow my directive." Her smile brightened her features as Thayer backed further toward his table. She knew he was probably thinking of something biting to say back to her. Severine had thrown a gauntlet his way when she shouldn't have. "Besides, you're just pissed that it isn't you I'm dragging by the shirt."

She should've stopped while she had the chance. She was like a kid near a candy jar. There was no way she was just going to take one piece, she needed more than that. From the slow blaze in Thayer's eyes, she knew that her jab was completely worth it.

A low whistle came from the guy sitting across from Thayer, and Severine glanced in his direction. Thayer's gaze was still on Severine, and she felt giddy, like she could do twenty cartwheels in a row, giddy.

"That might be the first time a girl's ever given you shit, Thayer. I think I'm in love."

Severine recognized the muscular dude as the same one with Thayer and Macsen at the coffee shop, Lily's make-out buddy. He grinned deviously at Severine. She smiled back and leaned forward. Her movement caused her shoulder to brush against Thayer's arm. Energy zinged between the two of them. Ignoring the feeling, she placed her hand out to Chris. "Severine Blake."

He raised a brow and shook her hand. "Chris." She moved her hand back, but stayed close to their table.

"So, how do you know my good buddy, Thayer, here?"

Severine glimpsed a look at Thayer's profile. He sat forward and chewed his food slowly. "I don't know him."

Chris slapped his hands together, and his shoulders shook with laughter. "Oh, this is fucking great! I love you Say-vuh-reen," he pronounced her name slowly.

Severine cringed. "Not Sayvuhreen, not Sever-reen...it's Seh-vreen."

Chris gave her a funny look. "There's no way I'm gonna remember that."

"Carry on then," Severine said dryly. "Everyone says it wrong."

"So how come I've never seen you around?" Chris asked.

Severine took a glance at the girls sitting at their table and raised her eyebrows. "Maybe because you surround yourself in a sea of bleach?" Chris laughed even louder the second time.

He stabbed a finger in the air, right in her direction. "Next party I hear of, you're coming with us."

Thayer's shoulders stiffened slightly over Chris's declaration, and Severine smiled brightly. "Sounds amazing!" It was doubtful that she would go. Severine just wanted to piss Thayer off.

She turned back toward her table. Melissa had left and now it was only Lily and Ben. Apparently, while she was volleying barbs back and forth with Thayer, Lily had decided that, in fact, she could talk and struck up a conversation with Ben.

"I gotta go to the library. I'll see you later, Lily." Her friend barely gave her a glance. "Lily? You there?"

Finally, Lily looked her way, nodded her head and practically shooed her away.

Before she left to go to her next class, Severine glanced at Thayer's table one last time. The girls she'd insulted earlier were dressed like they were about to catch a flight to Cabo. Severine stopped a groan from emerging from her throat. There should be a shirt for all girls like them. Not even that...maybe a club. Their slogan: Destroying the impression of girls everywhere since the word 'tramp stamp' was invented.

Chris called out her name, and she didn't have to look far to find his wide smile. But from his shout everyone in the room stopped to look in her general direction. *This isn't awkward at all,* Severine thought. "Yeah?"

"There's a party tomorrow. You coming?"

Severine quickly glanced at Thayer. He stared sharply at her and looked her up and down. It wasn't a leer that creepy dudes always seemed to achieve.

His eyes bore through her in a way that she couldn't

describe, maybe because she had never been looked at that way. Thayer's eyes connected with the pale pink, sequined cardigan that ended around her knees; she paired it with a skinny belt that was wrapped around her mid-section. He hardly glanced at her jeans before he stared her straight in the face. He looked pissed and frustrated as hell.

"So, you going?" Chris called out again.

Severine nodded her head instantly and kept her gaze connected with Thayer's. "Lily and I just might have to show up."

It didn't surprise her when he turned his back and started talking to the blonde seated next to him.

Chapter Three

"Hey!" Lily shouted over the blow dryer. "Is Anne here yet?"

Severine looked up from putting her socks on long enough to shout out, "She'll be here in like five minutes. So hurry!"

Anne lived in the same dorm as them and was the perfect friend to bring along to any party. It was all about the buddy system. And when that didn't work, Severine made Ben tag along. Tonight she had both options coming with her.

That should've made her relax, but her nerves were cinched together and refused to loosen up. As it was, she already knew what, or rather, who, had her emotions so distorted right now. Thayer.

After her encounter with Thayer, she had a headache the size of Russia. It was long gone, but she was still stressed out and edgy. The two of them around each other would equal complete chaos. She wanted to sweep through and triumph over him. Severine knew that the feeling was mutual—he wanted the same thing.

She had always had a streak of competitiveness in her blood. But Severine wasn't used to it going to this level. It was bizarre, completely unnatural. All that feeling told her was that his brother, Macsen, was where she should place her focus.

A black silk shirt was thrown at her head. She snatched it away impatiently. "Lily!" Severine shouted and sifted through her way-too-small closet.

Between the two of them they were stuck in a room with not enough space...closet space. Cubbyholes in kindergarten were bigger than the square footage of their closet. Severine could handle the tiny room. It was a given, living in a dorm. Both she and Lily decorated their sides with personal touches that defined who they were. It was a miracle the two of them hadn't butted heads when it came to their room.

Lily gravitated toward bright colors. Sometimes when Severine woke up in the morning, she'd get an instant headache if she gazed over at Lily's side, probably because Severine preferred dark and muted tones. All her side of the room consisted of was a dark blue, floral comforter, gray sheets and a bunch of pictures in frames on top of her desk.

Clutter made her stress out. If her side of the room was clean and organized, she could take a deep breath of relief. With the entire room clean, she was on cloud nine. But with Lily, that never happened. Severine could come to terms with never having an organized room, but one thing she couldn't accept was a tiny closet. When your clothes were piled on top of one another and you were in a rush, all you wanted to do was cuss out the poor, innocent space. "That's your sixth shirt! Chill out, okay?"

"I can't chill!" Lily quickly straightened her hair near the mirror on her side of the room. It was the fifth time she had straightened that particular piece of hair. Severine kept her mouth shut and dug around their clothes to find a shirt. A brown low cut cross-front shirt was the only thing hanging up. It was the winner for tonight. "Here."

Lily caught it with one hand and put it on quickly. "Are you sure this is okay? It doesn't look like I'm getting an interview for Hooters?"

"Not really." Severine leaned over Lily and quickly put on her lipstick. Her breath slightly fogged up the mirror, but her reflection would be the same as it had always been. Clear or blurry, her green eyes would still be shining. The freckles scattered across her nose and cheeks would always be a reminder of summers spent in the sun. The dark slant of her eyebrows would constantly give her the appearance of haughty superiority. And her lips would always appear plump.

A strand of her dark brown hair fell over her shoulder and curved around the underside of her breast. If Severine could be the girl on those Pantene Pro-V commercials, she'd die a very happy lady. Instead, she was stuck with hair that couldn't decide between straight and wavy.

Severine referred to it as "stravy."

Her hair was a daily battle, but it was one that her mom taught her to win at a young age. When she was twelve, her mom handed Severine two items and told her: *"These two things will be your secret weapons to prevail over all the waviness. The serum will never let you down. The curling iron I gave you will sometimes be the best invention out there, and sometimes you'll curse its existence. Welcome to womanhood."*

Severine smirked at the words running through her head and tilted her head so her hair could fall over her shoulder. Tonight she had won the hair battle. These moments were hard to come by.

"Yo!" Lily snapped her fingers and tugged her shirt down. "What do you think?"

Severine pulled back from the mirror and looked her friend up and down. "You're showing enough, but not enough to say, 'Hey look! The girls are out tonight!'"

Lily looked down at her chest. "In my case, I think it's bee stings. Tonight they're just getting help from the Miraculous. God bless Victoria."

Severine spritzed perfume on her wrist and grinned,

"I second that. Now, are we ready to go?"

"Aren't we waiting for Anne?"

Severine walked to her closet and yanked on her fall jacket. "We can meet at her room."

"Wait." Severine turned back to Lily. "You're covered up." Lily's eyes bulged out in concern. "Are you sick?"

Severine looked down at her brown suede boots, holey jeans, and lace turtleneck. "We're going for you. I'm simply the messenger who finds out where the parties are so you can see lover boy."

A weird expression crossed Lily's face. "You sure?"

Holding up two fingers, she smiled at her closest friend. "Girl Scout honor. Now, come on. Let's go!"

Lily grabbed her coat and followed. Severine shut the door behind her and wondered just how long she'd keep telling that lie to herself.

*   *   *   *   *

People poured out of the frat house in front of them, some already plastered and staggering with the help of their friends.

Lily, Anne and Severine stared at the sight. "It looks like we're the first ones here," Anne said dryly. Looking at Anne in all her petite glory, you'd never know she had the mouth of a soldier, and the humor to go with it. Her black hair was pushed back with the help of a headband, and her dark eyes scanned the grass like a predator looking for its first prey.

Anne was gorgeous, completely striking in her own right, but she was intense. It scared the hell out of most guys. And that made her the perfect party buddy. She had your back.

Severine let go of a deep breath and looked at Anne and Lily. "Okay. Before we go in, let's reiterate: if we lose sight of one another that doesn't give any of us the right to go all depend-a-ho."

Anne pulled away with a funny look. "Dependa what?"

Lily smirked, and Severine stared solemnly at Anne. "Depend-a-ho is a female that sits around, waiting for a dude. She often scours the room, adjusts her dress constantly, and stutters around a guy because she thinks it's cute."

Lily nodded her head. "It also includes lip biting and constantly twirling your hair."

Severine snapped her fingers. "Shit. I forgot those two points. Just don't be 'that girl,' Anne."

Anne snorted. "Don't insult me. I get the picture. We stick next to each other."

Severine looped both arms between her friends and walked up the stairs with them by her side. Fall was spreading throughout campus, and they huddled tightly together. This wasn't her first party. It was freezing, but coats remained in the car. The chances of them getting 'lost' at this party were extremely high.

They walked across the porch and music was already blasting through the open windows. Severine squinted as they walked in. She used her height to her advantage and peered over the girls around them. She spotted a body that towered over everyone else and her eyes narrowed at Thayer.

She practically grunted in objection when she saw that Ben stood next to him. Instantly, she grabbed Lily's hand, and Lily grabbed Anne's. The three of them made their way through the heavy crowds of laughter, dancing, and people practically having sex on the open wood floor.

They were steps away from Ben when Tim's voice boomed above the music, "HEY! It's you!" His words were slurred, and Severine was pretty sure that half of his drink landed on the dude next to him.

"It's me! Figure that!" She called back.

He laughed like she'd said the funniest thing in the world. "Come over here. Are these your friends?"

Severine glanced at Anne and Lily and acted shocked. "No, they're two homeless people I found on the street. Instead of food, they wanted to go to a party—something about a bucket list..."

"Ah, cool, cool."

Lily snorted on her laughter, and Severine smiled. Tim blocked their way to where Ben stood, and she nudged Lily. "Lover at twelve o'clock."

"My twelve o'clock or yours?"

"What are you guys talking about?" Anne asked confused.

Severine ignored Anne's question and gave Lily a funny expression. "Lily, what other twelve o'clock would there be? He's in front of us, you dumb ass!"

She jumped slightly and smiled widely. "Oh!"

"What are you guys talking about?" Anne asked louder. She was sharp, but the girl couldn't hang onto a conversation if someone paid her to.

"One word," Lily shouted across Severine, "Benjamin."

Anne looked confused. "Who?" Her eyes registered quickly, "Ohhh...I know him."

Severine wrapped an arm around her closest friend. "Lily's interested in him, if you haven't noticed her drooling all over herself."

A bored look crossed Anne's face as she looked at the people around them. "So this is why we're here?"

Severine looked around with her. "Exactly why."

"And we're gonna have to make Lily dance with him or at least talk to him?"

"Yep," Severine confirmed.

Anne nodded her head. Her task had been handed out, and she was on a mission.

"Gotcha."

"You sure you wanna dance with Ben?" Tim asked Lily with a wink.

Her friend was branching out of her comfort zone,

but that didn't mean she was going wild with the best of them. With a red face and bugged out eyes, Lily shook her head. She looked at Tim slowly, taking in his high and tight haircut and blue polo. "Yeah. I'm sure."

"Tim!" Severine shouted out. "You're gonna give her a heart attack."

College was a minefield of freakishly good-looking guys. Severine was just now getting used to it. Lily would sometimes relapse and drool like an idiot. Now was one of those times.

Thayer sauntered up to the circle they were slowly starting to form. "Dude, where have you been?" Tim asked him.

Two twins were underneath each of his arms. That's where he had been.

A clumsy grin was on his face as he nodded at Severine. "I've been busy."

God, two minutes around this dude, and she already needed to start breathing treatments to control her anger. He took his arm away from one of the girls to tip his head back and take a drink of his beer. His eyes stayed on Severine the whole time.

She watched his fingers latch around one of the redhead's shoulders. It looked like it was more out of support. With both arms around the girls, it made his black v-neck shirt ride up slightly, enough for Severine to see the gray line of his boxers and the block writing of Calvin Klein. When her eyes reached his face, he was waiting. His gray eyes were void. She'd never be able to construe his thoughts. That's what probably drew every girl to him.

"So, what do we have here?" Tim asked Thayer. His arm was still around Lily, but he smirked at whore one and whore two.

One of the perky redheads answered for the two of them. "Oh, I'm Farrah," she pointed toward her twin, "and this is Faith."

"A few of my brain cells just fizzled out," Anne muttered into Severine's ear before she broke their circle and shouted out, "I'm getting a drink!"

So much for the buddy system. Severine didn't blame her, though. You could have fun without your crotch hanging out. Obviously, Farrah and Faith didn't receive the memo. Severine cocked her leg out and crossed her arms. Thayer followed the action with his eyes. "Wow, this is just awesome. Two future Playboy bunnies in the making, standing right in front of me!"

The two dummies in front of her smiled, clearly not catching onto Severine's sarcasm. Thayer grinned, and she wanted to punch that deprecated look off his face.

"SAVE-uh-Reen!" her name was boomed across the room as Chris barreled toward her. It came out of his mouth, always in syllables, and always pronounced differently. "Dammit, I'm fucking happy to see you!"

"Yeah?"

"Of course." He nodded his head and smacked Thayer on the shoulder. "My buddy here thought you wouldn't show up."

"Why would you think that?" Severine directly asked Thayer.

"Yeah, why would you think that?" Chris crossed his massive arms and smiled widely.

Thayer remained silent, but his body language showed just how tense he was. He lifted a wide shoulder. "You don't seem like the party type."

It was a barb. Instead of walking away or ignoring his bait, she stood taller. With heels, she towered over every girl here, but next to him she didn't even come close to doing the damage she wanted. He looked down at her and smiled. "Do I go to parties? Yes. Do I go to parties to find my next hook up? No. That might be why I'm not on your radar."

Chris laughed loudly and clapped his hands together. "Shit. Mac needs to hear this."

Severine was in a standoff with Thayer. She could hear Chris shouting, "Hey! Anyone know where Mac is?" She taunted him to respond. Her feet shifted forward slightly, not even enough for anyone to notice. Thayer's eyes dilated somewhat, and she grasped the fact that she could cause a reaction out of him.

Thayer reached out and grabbed Chris from walking away. "Who said you weren't on my radar?" With his arm still holding Chris, he waited for her to answer.

She pointed to her chest, waiting for him to take a look. His gaze rested on her face. "The girls aren't out to play. I've never said the phrase, 'Like, who does that?!' and my Facebook status doesn't have some annoying quote saying, *'To the world you may be one person. To one person, you may be the world.'*"

Chris nudged her and laughed, but she was burnt raw. Her emotions were chafed, barely holding onto the rope that was keeping her from saying something callous.

His lips contorted in a smile, and her gut clenched tightly. He was doing it again.

Severine waited impatiently for him to respond. All he did was draw the girls closer to his body. "Ladies, why don't we go dance?" The three of them turned, and Thayer left Severine's sight.

She forgot the pain and smiled in Lily's direction. "I need a drink, you?"

"Uh," Lily watched Severine's movements. She was unsure of how to respond. "Yeah?"

"Great." Severine grabbed her friend's hand and snatched it from Tim's. She left both guys behind, and walked toward the kitchen. Her emotions were in possession of her actions. You better believe it found the alcohol in seconds.

"What. The. Hell." Lily stated.

Severine walked across the old kitchen tile floor and sidestepped the spills from previous drinks. Out of the entire kitchen, there was only one counter that was semi clean. Severine chose that spot, gripped the counter behind her and rolled her neck in a circle. "I'm gonna lose it around that dude." Lily's eyes gleamed like two bright stars. Curse her. "I'm serious! You know, it's not even the fact that he's clearly a douche. The problem is, he knows he's a douche."

Lily took a sip out of her cup and scrunched her face up in pain. "So many douches in the world."

Severine nodded. "He's king of Doucheville."

Lily snorted on her drink.

"He owns Douchedome. All assholes compete in the douche form of the Olympics at Douchedome."

"He must be busy then," Lily remarked with a smile.

"You're not helping," Severine gritted out. "You're supposed to agree with me!"

Lily finally gave up and dumped the liquid from her drink into the sink, "I do agree with you. But what do you want me to say? The guy gets to you. I think on a perverse level, you kind of like it."

It was perverse. Gross. Wrong. All of it was sick and twisted. Right now, it was Severine's state of mind.

"Can we keep playing this game? It's fun. I wanna see how many phrases we can come up with." Lily clapped her hands together, and Severine smirked. It was nice to have a friend who had a jacked up sense of humor like she did.

"Wasn't the mission to have Lily dancing with Ben, or, ah, whatever the hell his name is?" Anne asked as she walked into the kitchen and snatched an unopened beer out of a random dude's hand.

"You're kidding, right? You left my side to get a drink. Where was my wing man when I needed her?!"

Anne snorted darkly, "You were hardly alone. I saw you talking to Thayer."

Severine threw her hands up in the air. "Am I the only one who didn't know him up until a few days ago?"

Both Lily and Anne nodded in agreement. Finally,

Anne spoke up. "If you think about it, it's kind of understandable."

Severine jumped up onto the counter. "Oh, I have to hear this."

"The ego on the two of you is enough to make the windows shatter. So you're in Severine-land, and he's chilling in all his hot dude glory. You are like two magnets repelling each other. The magnetic field is too much."

Lily nodded her agreement. Severine flicked her gaze between the two of them. "That's the worst example, ever. Please tell me, why are we friends again?"

Anne squeezed Severine's cheeks together and cooed. "Because I give you the world's cheesiest examples, and I'm gonna find Ben. Then I'm gonna make him dance with Lily. That's why we're friends." She grabbed Lily's hand and stomped towards the front room.

"I hate you!" Severine shouted.

"You freaking LOVE ME!" Anne screamed back.

She rotated on the counter-top and stared at the people dancing. For once, she wasn't out there. She wasn't in bliss. Her mind wasn't content.

Severine felt like shit.

Thayer glanced across the room at her. She wanted to look anywhere else. Her mind whispered that it'd be incredibly weak of her to turn away first. But she did anyway.

Her feet touched the wood floor. She needed some air.

"Mac, I think we should leave. I hate-"

Severine heard the name Mac, and her ears perked up. The voice that was speaking was high-pitched and annoying. It was Fran Drescher on a bad day.

Macsen and Haley stood huddled together in the tight hallway. She didn't know what was going on between the two of them. Truthfully, Severine didn't really care. Macsen was here, and it perked her mood up slightly.

Her lips turned up in a smile. There was something about this guy. He had on a baseball cap, and even in a shaded, dark hallway, it fit him. He stood tall, leaning against the wall. His arms were crossed as he listened to Haley talk. His eyes were focused on her, but they looked vaguely bored.

"Macsen, oh, Macsen!" Severine sang out.

His head snapped in her direction, and recognition showed in his eyes. Her confidence was back. It made her movement fluid, her smile secure. Unlike his, which was hesitant as she came closer. "Hey."

Severine leaned against the wall. She attempted to stare at his eyes, but it was too dim. "What are you doing here?"

His expression was dull, almost uninterested. "It's a party. What do you think I'm doing here?"

"I mean literally. Why are you here?" She made a face and tapped the wall behind him. "You're standing in a creepy, dark hallway that looks like the set for the next Freddy Krueger movie."

He smiled widely, and Severine's heart escalated into a never-ending hammer. It was wrong that she could amass so much satisfaction from their encounters. But it was a good kind of wrong.

"So what are you doing here? Thayer's..." He flung his hand toward the sounds of people. "Well, he's somewhere. Shouldn't you be with him?"

Did he still think she was after him? It was Severine's turn to give a dull expression. "If I wanted to get in his pants, don't you think I'd be with him now, close enough to be a second skin?"

Macsen's cheeks colored. It seemed like every time Severine talked to him, she always managed to take him off guard. And when she did, his face showed his shock. His eyes widened before they flicked down to the ground.

He scratched at the black stubble on his face and rubbed his neck. He didn't hide anything: annoyance, anger or happiness. Severine could read his emotions. It sent a feeling of euphoria through her body.

He shook his head back and forth and slowly grinned. "Do you ever not say what you're feeling?"

Severine smiled mischievously. "Do you want me to?"

Briefly, his eyes glanced behind her. His eyes were deep in concentration, almost callous. Before Severine turned to look behind her, his eyes drew back to her face. With a light smirk on his face, he leaned closer. "No, I don't think I do."

Someone coughed loudly behind Macsen, and he jumped at the sound. He was lost in her. But, then again, she had also forgotten Haley was there.

"I need to go to the restroom," Haley bit out sharply.

Severine watched as he nodded and smiled a friendly smile. Friendly. She stored that away in her head.

The bathroom door slammed. Severine cringed and moved toward the opposite wall. "Are you two together or something?"

Macsen dug his hands deeply into his jean pockets. His expression was amused as he looked at her. "No."

"Not together, but she acts like she owns you." Severine tsked lightly. "Sounds like there's something there."

He shrugged. "We've known each other since high school. We're just good friends."

"Ooo-kay," Severine drew out slowly.

"She's just a protective friend," Macsen admitted.

"That's what the passive dumb girl says about her abusive relationship with her boyfriend."

He remained silent and Severine continued, "So all this time we've had the same class together..."

"And two others," Macsen said quickly.

Severine gave him a look and said, "No, we don't."

"Yeah, like, we totally do," Macsen said in a girl's voice.

"Fine, name them."

"Psychology 101 and Literature. And if you don't believe me, you usually slip in before class begins and sit near the back with your friends."

"So you watch me? Are you one of the quiet, stalker types that silently keeps watch of all the girls in the room?"

"What kind of predator description is that?"

Severine looked up at the ceiling in thought and snapped her fingers. "Ted Bundy! Hah!"

"No, that's a serial killer," Macsen smiled widely. "You compared me to a serial killer. Nice."

"You never know, it could happen."

"All right. Okay, fine. If I become a serial killer all because of this conversation, I am bringing you down during my trial."

"An accomplice?"

"Precisely." His expression showed his amusement. She finally realized that she didn't know where Lily was, Anne could be in a fight with some dude, and her mind hadn't thought about Thayer in...a while. It felt good.

"I think this is the most messed up conversation I've ever had," Macsen said slowly.

Severine schooled her features into shock. "What? You usually don't talk about your ambitions? I'm honored to be the first."

His laughter came out choked. "I think my ambitions are directed toward a different road."

"Oh yeah? Where..."

"Mac, I'm ready to go," a voice snapped out. It cut their moment in two.

Haley locked her hands firmly on her hips. She pierced Severine with a harsh stare, eyes flared with a challenge. Severine arranged a smile on her face, one that showed just how relaxed she was with this girl. There was nothing to prove against Haley.

"You okay?" Macsen asked her with concern.

Haley shook her head. "You're my ride, and I don't feel good."

"Oh." Macsen glanced at Severine with conflict in his eyes before looking at Haley. "Yeah, come on. I'll take you home."

"I'll see ya later, Macsen," Severine called out.

He nodded his head slowly. It was like he was recognizing her for who she really was. "I'll definitely see you later."

He brushed past her and walked down the hall. Severine waited. Whatever was coursing through her, she wanted more. There could be substance between them; a level of interest with Macsen that she didn't expect. Before she had walked into this house, Severine knew the element that held her the most was curiosity. It was eager and intense. But how much of her interest was inquisitive? And when did it morph into something more?

No one would ever know where Severine truly came from. No one would know that her dad was a magician that never seemed to stop disappearing.

Anyone who looked at Severine would see a girl that was confident and strong.

Her mom's voice flashed into her head, along with the memory of her mom wiping away the tears from her face." *You should never show your emotions. Someone will steal them away, and you'll be left with nothing, Severine..."*

Severine didn't want to be crumbled into nothing. But she wanted to have that feeling. Severine wanted to know if she was really missing out—was there something to relationships that she just wasn't seeing? Was it truly worth it?

But Macsen might be. He seemed like a risk she wanted to try to take.

She walked back to the island next to the kitchen and leaned in the same spot she had been in before.

Tim slid up beside her and pointed at Ben and Lily. They danced close together, and Severine watched her friend with a smile that was genuine, yet pensive.

"They're really hitting it off," Tim stated.

"Yeah, they look good together." Severine grabbed his beer and took a long drink. She was over-thinking everything. Why was she building a situation up that wasn't even there?

Severine turned and placed the empty bottle on the counter behind the two of them and yanked his hand. "Come on, let's dance."

Chapter Four

"How much do you want?"

"Everything you have."

"Do you wanna get your stomach pumped?"

Severine groaned and held out her hand. "Whatever. Just give me some. I'm dying over here."

Lily shook out four Tylenol and dumped them into Severine's outstretched hand. "Why did you drink so much?"

Severine held up a finger and quickly swallowed the pills down. They needed to kick in. Fast.

She looked like shit. Her eyes were bloodshot, her face pale. The first thing she did when Lily woke her up was grab her sunglasses. Lily was determined to keep up with their Saturday routine, whether Severine was hungover or not.

That's how Severine ended up at IHOP, staring at the menu until her eyes crossed. "This is your fault," Severine muttered.

Lily rolled her eyes. "Right. I forced you to sit in front of the Jager-train, held your mouth open, and shoved the liquid down your throat."

Severine adjusted her glasses and leaned further back in the booth. "I'm glad that you can at least admit it."

Lily's food came, and Severine sipped from the coffee in front of her. Last night she acted stupid. Did she regret getting drunk? Hell, yes. Who wouldn't? The side effects made Severine want to boycott parties altogether. More than anything, she regretted the reason why she drank.

When her vision settled on the dark liquid in front of her, Macsen's face swirled in the cup. She blinked once, and his face was gone. She was falling apart over a guy—a guy she had only spoken to twice.

Severine grabbed a napkin and picked it apart. Pieces fell to the slightly clean table. She used this as a distraction from the nausea brewing in her gut and the confusion in her head.

Lily's fork dragged across her plate, and Severine scrunched her face up in pain. "You're eating like a pig."

Lily bit into her pancake and made a face of bliss. "Seems like someone's a little jealous they can't enjoy all my yummy food."

"Blech," Severine grumbled and laid her face on the table.

"Stop. You're ruining my perfect breakfast. And besides, I have Ben news."

Severine moved her head and smiled across the table at her friend. "Yeah? Was it a love connection?"

Her fork clanked loudly onto her plate as she leaned forward. This time, the noise was an accident. "He's amazing! I swear, we talked for hours last night. Ben's just...so...sweet, attentive." Lily paused and quickly shook her head. "Okay, now I'm rambling like an idiot."

"It's okay." Severine's smile was tiny, but she was so happy for her friend. "You're happy. You deserve to be. So, when are you gonna see him again?"

Lily's face was blank, "Uh...in class?"

"Oy!" Severine wanted to clasp her head in frustration but that would only bring more pain. "Lily, did he say he wanted to?"

"Yeah."

"It's Benji, so he probably will. But you need to keep going, no more being shy! And if all else fails, lure him in with pizza."

"What if he doesn't like pizza?" Lily asked.

"Then he's a cyborg robot and needs to be executed immediately!"

The waitress came and took away Lily's food. When she left, Lily drummed her fingers repeatedly on the table. "Why did you drink so much last night?"

"Lapse in judgment. It won't happen again."

Lily's laugh came out in a short burst. "I'm not judging. It's just not like you to do that."

It wasn't like her to be this confused either. But apparently her mind wanted to travel down a different direction lately.

"What's going on with you?"

Severine stood up straighter. Lily narrowed her eyes. She couldn't hide anything from Lily, and even when she could, it didn't last long. She'd better make it last. "Nothing is wrong. I'm still seeing double. Other than that, I'm fine."

"I should make you take those damn sunglasses off," Lily finally muttered.

"But you won't, because you love me."

The waitress came back with their bills and handed Severine a to-go box with food.

Lily gave her a strange look. Severine placed her money on the table and slid out of the booth with her food in one arm. "I'm hung-over, not stupid. You better believe I'm getting food to go."

*   *   *   *   *

Being early to class wasn't for Severine. Showing up late wasn't exactly either. If she arrived with a few minutes to spare, it was perfect—enough time to settle down and not waste time.

Today she was late. She'd slept through her alarm and was forced to rush around her room like a psychopath. The first thing in sight was put on her body.

As she ran across campus, Severine looked down at her yellow sweater, jeans, and ballet flats. They weren't her first choice. Her routine had been thrown off kilter, and it left her pissed off. The rest of the day she would feel unprepared.

Her body was already begging to curl underneath her sheets. The option to skip class was there. It wasn't the most important one to attend, and it made the truth all the more apparent. Severine knew the real reason for her rushed pace. Green eyes flashed in her mind, and she instantly stopped running.

Slow. It. Down.

A deep breath escaped her mouth as she finally walked into her first class and moved toward the front of the room. An open seat was next to Macsen, and she smiled and placed her bag on the table.

Macsen looked up from his book and grinned widely. He shoved the sleeves of his gray zip-up toward his elbows and leaned back in his chair.

"Taken?" Severine asked.

"You wanna sit next to me again? I think dear Severine Blake is the stalker of the school."

She smirked. "You could only dream I was stalking you."

Macsen leaned closer. Severine smelled the scent of his cologne. She busied herself with her bag but she could still smell him.

"How was the rest of the party?"

"Oh!" Severine turned from her laptop and stared at him with shock. "You don't know, do you?"

"Know what?" Macsen leaned closer. Severine's gut clenched over the action. Those gorgeous eyes that she couldn't see Friday night were clear and bright and right in front of her.

"Everyone danced around, and a few girls cried their hearts out over a boy feud and looked like raccoons with mascara running everywhere. It was epic."

Macsen whistled, "I missed all that?"

"Yes, but don't worry. I'm sure somewhere, somewhere, a YouTube video of the whole thing will pop up. Until then, I will hold it above your head."

He smirked and went back to his book. Severine slid a notebook from her bag and flipped through the pages. She was searching for nothing; it just gave her something to do. "So, how is Haley and her I.B.S.?"

A book held between his hands dropped to the table. He stared at her with wide, shocked eyes. "Her what?"

Severine flipped her braid over her shoulder. "You know, Irritable Bowel Syndrome? By how quickly you guys left the party, I figured that was what she had. She was in the bathroom for a really long time."

Severine continued and smiled at his open mouth. "My Uncle Allan had it." Severine shuddered and kept speaking. "He had to constantly keep laxatives around the house. Needless to say, I never stayed long at his house during family gatherings."

Macsen slowly shook his head. A smile was hidden. It was barely there, but Severine saw it. "She doesn't have that."

"Are you sure?" Severine asked with raised brows.

"Yes, I'm sure!" He abruptly stopped speaking. His lips kicked up in a small grin. "I can't believe we're talking about shit this early in the morning."

"You seem tired. Chances are, you got more sleep than me."

"Rough weekend?"

Severine kept her voice evasive. "You could say that."

"I heard you had a lot of fun after I left the party."

"Checking up on me, Macsen?"

"My brother was there." Macsen shifted closer and

let his statement hover in the air. She took her fill of his eyes, noticing the light green etched around his pupils.

Severine gave his shoulder a friendly pat. Just from observing him, she could tell that he was lean. Muscles didn't define his sleeves. But underneath her hands, there was more strength than she thought there would be. Briskly, she moved her hand, placing it on her thigh. "Funny, once you left I wondered what your ambitions actually were!"

"Yeah, sure." He didn't sound convinced. "You danced your life away."

"Your stalker tendencies are showing again. You gotta control it."

He laughed loudly. And there it was—that emotion Severine couldn't pinpoint, singed throughout her body. It burned.

"I'll do my best," Macsen responded back.

Severine watched him tap his fingers on his knee to an invisible song. He glanced at her and looked away. His expression was almost shy. "I want to be a journalist." His gorgeous, genuine eyes looked at her once again. "Are you happy now?"

He had just confided something personal to her. She could tell from his tense shoulders and cautious stare it was something he didn't disclose to many people. "I'm not surprised. You have that look about you."

For a moment, his eyes grew slightly. "I think that's probably the biggest compliment you could ever give me."

"That you have that look about you?"

Macsen nodded.

"Well, I never lie," Severine stated confidently.

"How can you tell?"

"I just can," Severine tried to appear annoyed. She failed when she saw Macsen's slow grin. "Stop pestering me. I can't concentrate, and you're agitating my psychic vibes."

"You have psychic vibes?"

"No. But I can tell you it's been a full five minutes since you've looked down at your book."

He scrutinized her closely. "You sound accomplished."

"I am." Severine appeared confident, when inside, she was coiled tight with skittish nerves. "Can you even tell me who the main characters are?"

He remained silent.

Class started minutes later. Severine's mood morphed into happiness. She couldn't school her facial muscles into any other expression. Talking to Macsen just did that. He diligently listened to the professor and seemed to practically absorb every word.

But a few times he'd fix a stare in her direction, and it made half her body prickle with awareness. Severine knew that when his attention was on her, he had no idea what was being said in front of them.

For the first time, the minutes in class rushed past. She was almost sad to leave. Slowly, Severine gathered her stuff.

Macsen stood back and patiently waited for her. While she took her time, he finally spoke up. "So what's going on? Why are you really sitting next to me?"

Severine frowned and walked through the door. Macsen followed. "Uhh...because I want to?"

"Really, what's the truth? This whole semester you've sat in the top row and flirted with every male in the classroom. So what's your gain?"

Her happiness deflated instantly, but she still kept her smile in place. "No gain, Macsen."

He rejected her answer instantly and frowned. "Please, you're *that* girl."

Macsen's words were a punch she would've never expected. It was a blow. The guy could strike with his words better than most girls. "What girl?"

Did she really want to know the answer to that? He

didn't notice her glare and slashed his hand through the air. "The girl that flirts from guy to guy and does it just because she can."

Severine kept her anger at bay and took a deep breath. "That's a bad thing because...?"

"You don't deny it?"

Their shoulders touched, and Severine discreetly moved away. She wanted to leave this conversation and go her own way. Pride could be painful sometimes. And right now, hers was suffocating. "What would I deny?" Severine stopped in the middle of the hallway and turned to Macsen. "That I do what every single guy does?" He halted his steps and turned to her with an angry guise.

Funny, that should be her expression.

He stepped closer. There was no giving or taking when he was around. Severine couldn't pick what she wanted to feel. If that were the case, then right now she wouldn't be so bothered by his statement.

Macsen was robbing her of everything.

"Maybe I'm seeing you differently." He uttered his words firmly, with finality. "Why show them something you're not?"

There were no words to shut him down, to protect her. She opened her mouth, but all that escaped was a deep breath. He nodded his head toward her once, accepting her silence for what it was. Her shock was bright enough for anyone to notice.

Severine watched him walk away. She was beginning to doubt herself. Bodies shifted past her, going in every direction. She followed them blindly. His opinion shouldn't matter, but it did. Her shelter, the one that she used at every turn, felt yanked from her fingers.

At the thought, her fingers reacted and gripped her bag tightly. She was still Severine. She was still herself. She was secure with her actions.

But you're not. Her thoughts jeered back in response.

She crossed her fingers that he didn't notice her struggle. It was the worst, thinking he might know how much his words truly bothered her.

Now, right now, she was feeling like *that* girl. It pissed her off and carried a deep amount of shame with it.

"Severine! Wait up!" Lily caught up with her and squealed loudly. "I did it!" She proudly announced.

Severine's mind wasn't really focused enough to have a conversation with anyone. She repeated back Lily's words to herself, but her eyebrows still formed a tight v. "What?"

Lily rolled her eyes and looped her arm through Severine's. "I took your advice and walked up to Benjamin. I suggested we get together and hang out or something."

"That's great, Lily!" Severine meant it. Her sullen thoughts were bumped down to a lower shelf. They were still there, waiting for a quiet time to sneak their way to the top.

"He wants to hang out tonight."

"I completely approve," Severine stated.

"Really?"

Severine bumped her hip against Lily's. "Uh, duh. You grabbed your confidence, slapped it around a little and look what happened! You're meeting up with him later!"

"I thought you'd be pissed a little," Lily confessed.

"Because?" There was always a because.

Lily shrugged and made no eye contact. "He wants me to meet him at the Sloan's apartment. I told him you'd come with me."

Her hand made contact with her forehead the minute she heard the last name of Sloan. "I'm not going!"

"It's a study thing," Lily quickly said.

"None of us share the same class," Severine whined. "How would it be a study thing?"

"Ben and I do!"

"Yes," Severine said slowly. "But I don't. You see the trifecta? Oh wait, we don't make one!"

"But I want you there. Look, I'm not comfortable enough to go there myself. Hell, I'm lucky I even approached him today. Baby steps, Severine, baby steps."

Severine was proud of Lily, but that didn't mean she was going.

"So, will you come?" Lily prodded gently.

Severine's lips dropped down in thought. "If I hear the name Sloan one more time, I'm gonna cut my ears off. I'm not in the mood to deal with them."

Lily glanced at Severine thoughtfully. "I thought you were fine with Macsen?"

"I'll tell you later."

"When, later?"

"When we're on our way to their place, and you swing by a coffee shop to get me a pumpkin spice frappe." Severine was weak. That should make her cringe. But for her best friend, she'd do just about anything to see her happy. Being weak sometimes wasn't the worst thing.

Lily bounced around and hugged Severine tightly. "Oh I love you, chica! I do!"

Severine's lips remained tight. "I love you too. This will be great." She was going to hell. She didn't mean anything she had just said.

"Great? It will be freakin' amazing."

There was nothing to really say to that. Severine nodded her head and kept her lips sealed tightly shut.

Chapter Five

"You know, this is ridiculous," Lily hissed out into the cold night air.

Severine adjusted her bag and hurried across the parking lot. "You said you needed to study, right?" Her friend barely nodded her head. Severine gestured behind her with both hands. "Well, look no further!"

"I don't think anyone had the library in mind."

Severine sighed. It wasn't a pretty sigh. "I'm with you, like you asked me."

Lily adjusted her winter hat. She was pissed, but she'd get over it. "What's the problem with going over to the Sloans' apartment?"

Because one of them would be there. Because it's too much. Because I'm terrified.

She was still trying to recharge her emotions from her conversation with Macsen. Seeing both Sloan brothers at the same time just seemed like a giant disaster waiting to explode around her. Severine took her time answering, toying with the straw of her frappe, and trying to form the right words—anything to portray how perfectly in control she was. "Lily, going over to their apartment? Really?"

Lily scrutinized Severine and finally gave up the fight before she sighed loudly. "Ben suggested it."

Severine wrapped her arm around Lily and squeezed her tightly. "I know that. But stick with me, there's no reason why we should go there."

"Why does it bother you?"

"Uh...it just spells trouble." She was a much better liar than this. A part of her wanted Lily to call her out on her bullshit.

"You realize it's a get-together, not an orgy, right?"

Severine kept silent and held the door open. Lily stayed rooted on the sidewalk and pinned a sneaky smile in Severine's direction. "Are you scared to go over there?"

"Yes," Severine admitted slowly before she let go of the door and moved closer to the warmth inside. "I'm also scared of the dark, snakes, and the movie, *The Ring*. All for good reasons."

"Well, the freaky girl in that movie is creepy," Lily pointed out as they entered the library. "Snakes freak anyone out, and the dark thing...well, that explains why you slept with a nightlight in high school." Lily tried to laugh lightly, but instead it came out with a gust of energy. She was done being mad.

Severine unraveled her scarf from her neck as she quickly scanned the inside of the campus library. It was quiet, minus the silent beep of librarians scanning books being checked. The first floor mostly held fiction reads. It was a place people could voluntarily read. Upstairs, where they were heading, that's where noise was completely unacceptable. A pen dropping was liable to have someone kicked out. For tonight, it was the perfect place.

They bypassed the elevator, and the two of them walked up the brick steps toward the second floor. Lily finally spoke again in a hushed voice. "I can't figure out why they freak you out so much. Tell me, what's your good reason?"

Severine swung her head toward Lily. "Ah! I thought we were done talking about this!"

"When you're freaked about something, it's not just something. The two individuals you fear are only guys. You could stomp across them with a beautiful pair of Manolo Blahniks and walk away like it was nothing."

Severine wanted to, but somehow she knew if she made that attempt, she'd be the one with the marks. It was her conscience that whispered they'd walk away scrape-free.

"It just doesn't feel right around them," her answer was vague. But it was all Severine could say.

"Wow," Lily commented dryly as they walked in between the rows of books. Save the elderly lady standing at the reference section, not a soul was upstairs. "It's a rager," Lily said sarcastically.

Rows of books were scattered throughout the area around them. Lined in perfect order, in the middle of the room were six tables. All of them were empty.

"I love it up here," Severine said in a hushed voice. "You look out the window, and it's perfect in the fall. The color of the leaves relaxes me."

Lily's eyebrows rose. "Yeah, sure thing, Thomas Kinkade. Where's your easel?"

Severine snapped her finger and pointed at the chair across from her. "Zip it, and sit down."

"You're a buzz-kill, you know that?"

She made a sound through her nose and dug out her books. "I've been called some unique things, but buzz-kill has never been one of them." Severine settled into her seat and looked down at her phone. "What time are they supposed to get here? Remember, my time is precious."

"Relax, re-runs of *Roseanne* will still be on when we get back to the dorms."

Severine draped the strap of her bag on the back of her chair and looked around the room. "Well, while they're taking their sweet time, I'm gonna go pee."

Lily shrugged out of her jacket and stared at the screen of her phone. She barely nodded her head.

Severine stalled in the bathroom. She took the world's longest pee and stared at the writings around her. It turns out you can learn a lot from a bathroom stall. A girl named Tiffany was a whore. Severine scrunched up her nose. If you're going to write the information out, at least have the consideration to carry enough nail polish to finish the message. Selfishness was what it was.

She took extra time to wash her hands. They were cleansed so well, they could pass any inspection. When Severine glanced at herself in the mirror, inches from her face, her cheeks were flushed bright red from the outdoors. With the cold weather came pale skin. Her freckles along the bridge of her nose and upper cheeks had faded. If anyone was to really look, they'd notice they were still there, still peppered across her face.

Severine didn't want to look too long at her reflection, because if she stared any longer, she'd notice the change of emotions in her eyes. She stepped away from the mirror, straightened out her shirt and left.

Who would want to waste their time sitting around at a library? Unless you wanted to read or study, there was no way you'd willingly volunteer to tag along. She was hoping that was Thayer and Macsen's mindset.

When she saw Lily and Ben sitting around the table, Severine almost broke out in the Irish jig. The down funk she was in earlier instantly lifted.

"Hey," Severine breathed out. "I'm back. Not that you care or anything."

"Did you fall into the toilet? You were gone a long time," Lily stated.

Severine's eyes sparkled as she grabbed a notebook. "Yep, I totally fell in. That's exactly what happened." She ignored Lily's eye roll and turned towards Ben. "So Ben, no one came with you? That's too bad."

Ben opened his mouth and quickly shut it.

"At a distance, I thought you were talking about me." The voice came to her right, and a scent of shampoo and soap cloaked itself all around her. Severine almost broke the pen in her hand as more words were spoken close to her ear. "Now I know you were."

So freaking close.

Severine leaned her elbow on the table and circled her face around to stare up at Thayer. His hands were hidden in the pockets of his hoodie and a pair of track pants hung on his hips. The dirty blonde hair that almost bordered on brown was messed around in complete chaos. It was ruthless to see him look so good without making an effort. Yet, there was nothing better than a guy that didn't try. Any male that just was made her nerves tingle in appreciation.

"Sorry I'm late." Thayer sat down next to Severine. He glanced at her briefly. "Practice went over."

Great. Severine rubbed the bridge of her nose. Now all she could picture was that he just came from the shower, from practice. He probably wore one of those practice jerseys that were created to show amazing biceps and make a girl's jaw unhinge all the way to the ground.

His gray eyes gleamed brightly, like he knew exactly what she was imagining. "I can tell you were waiting anxiously for me," Thayer said, his tone hushed.

Severine mashed her teeth together and wrote firmly on the paper in front of her. Maybe if she pressed down hard enough, she could get the picture of Thayer sweating out of her head. It wasn't a bad scene to envision.

Justifying the thought only showed Severine that she needed some serious help.

"I didn't think you'd show," Severine blurted out.

Normally, she could say what she wanted, whenever. It was controlled. She knew exactly what was coming out of her mouth. Around Thayer, there was no filter. Everything just burst through the nonexistent dam.

His lips quirked up, "I know."

"Now that we're all here, we can study."

"You know Macsen's coming." He shifted close enough for her to smell his clean scent; close enough that Severine could count the flecks of black in his eyes. But she didn't do that...

Five. There were five little flecks.

Severine nodded her head like an obedient bobble head and gave a one-word answer. "Cool."

Tonight was going to hell. It wasn't as if she walked into the library convinced they wouldn't be here, but before she heard Thayer, she was well on her way to that feeling.

Right now, she felt a fucked up mixture of excitement and panic. The dynamic between the two brothers was strained. Sometimes, like right now, she didn't care. Later on, she would, later was when the panic would set in.

He grunted. "I'm sure that doesn't bother you at all."

Severine laid her pencil down. All her attention was on him. It was easy now that she wasn't fighting the urge. "Enlighten me. Tell me why you think that."

"Are you searching for ways to be pissed at me?" Thayer asked.

It was her fault for being piqued into the conversation. Severine couldn't blame anyone but herself. "When you make a statement like that, I'm curious."

He leaned back in his chair—to the point that it was dangling on two legs. She wanted to kick it out from underneath his feet. "It's just obvious which Sloan brother you prefer to be around."

"I prefer talking to him," Severine mumbled. They both knew which brother. No need to elaborate.

Thayer didn't buy anything she was saying. "That's it?"

"What else would there be?" Her thoughts and feelings felt uncovered and completely bare. It made Severine move back slightly.

Thayer's seat dropped firmly on the floor, and he shifted his body toward her. He was thinking something bad. It shone in his eyes. And his smile...it was almost artful. He skillfully perfected the devious grin: a slow smirk of the lips that never touched his eyes. "I think you prefer me more in a lot of different ways."

Show no reaction. Keep your expression neutral.

Severine opened her mouth to retort. He beat her to the finish line.

"This might be sweeter than I thought. You can't think of anything to say back."

Sparks were seconds away from shooting out of Severine's ears. She gave him a hard look. "I've thought about many things to say, unfortunately, all of them start with Fuck. And end with you."

Nothing. Not a look of surprise, not a look of amusement. He stared at her a second longer than she was comfortable with and folded his fingers atop his stomach. "So your dark side is out to play?"

They both stared at each other. Neither one retreated first. It was Lily's voice that finally made Severine look away.

"Oh look!" Lily said with forced enthusiasm. "Macsen's here."

Thayer pulled away, and Severine took a deep breath. It didn't help her much; she was still breathing him in.

"Macsen. Come sit. So great to see you!" Lily hopped out of her chair and quickly grabbed a chair from an available table.

Severine smirked at Lily's attempt to keep everything calm and evenhanded. She glanced over at Macsen as he caught her eye. From his expression, she knew he was curious about what he had interrupted.

If she tried hard enough, she could create her perfect Eden. It'd be far away from here—maybe on a beach. Her paradise didn't include being caged in between the Sloan brothers. Severine wanted out of this room. If she could sprout wings, she'd have taken flight.

"Sit down, brother," Thayer said, his tone completely flat.

Macsen barely acknowledged Thayer and set his book bag on the floor. "How are you, Severine?"

"Much, much better." She pointedly looked at Thayer at her last word. Her smile was genuine when she directed her attention back to Macsen.

Flicking his green eyes in Thayer's direction, Macsen leaned closer to Severine. "What did I miss?"

"Nothing," Ben muttered. "Just the world's most incredibly awkward conversation. Ever."

Macsen nodded his head in understanding. "If you were talking to Thayer, that sounds about right."

Severine grinned and went back to studying. At the rate she was going, she'd be on this page for the next hour. Her mind was a sphere that never seemed to stop spinning. After a while, she gave up and shut her book. Slowly, she traced the words on the exterior of the book.

Everyone was quiet. It wasn't the silence that was accompanied by calm energy. All five of them sat with their backs straight. They were runners at the starting line. One of them was going to bolt.

Macsen shifted loudly in his seat. Severine looked up on instinct. He gave her a pointed look and nudged his head toward the shelves of books on the right side of the floor. Severine gave him a brief nod.

He wanted to talk to her. She got up to follow him, and she swore that with each step her legs were calling out, *don't talk about it, don't talk about it.*

When they were settled in the back, Macsen turned around and sighed loudly.

"I think I offended you earlier."

"Hmm?" Severine couldn't materialize indifference. She could at least try.

"Let me rephrase. Earlier, in class, I upset you."

Severine's face remained neutral, and he narrowed his eyes. "I'm sorry if I did," he said sincerely.

"You didn't, though." To her ears, it sounded good enough. "There's no reason to apologize for something you didn't do, right?"

He looked doubtful. It seemed he wanted to say more, but finally, he nodded. "You sure?"

"Positive."

"If you're positive, then let's go back." He swept his hand in front of himself for her to go first.

"You felt the tension. Do you really wanna go back to that?"

He dug his hands into his pockets and leaned against the shelf behind him. "What did I interrupt earlier?"

"You interrupted nothing."

"Really? It looked like something." Macsen's lips quirked, "Is my brother getting to you?"

"He's been giving me a headache since the minute I met him," Severine admitted.

Macsen laughed. He didn't keep it restrained like everyone else would. It was carefree and easy. The soothing reverberations subdued all the anxiety that came from talking to Thayer.

"Most of the time, he's not such a douchelord."

Severine laughed dryly. "So I bring out the worst in him?"

He mulled over her question and reluctantly nodded his head. "For reasons you won't ever understand, yeah, you do."

"Perfect."

He pressed his shoulder against her, and she moved closer. All she needed was a barrier to lean against, and his was impenetrable.

They stood in a congenial silence. Severine was afraid to break the moment. It was the most at ease she had been around the Sloan brothers. God, this was a requisite for her emotions.

"Is this why you lured me here? So you could talk about Thayer?"

"I'm not blind. I could see how tense you were."

Severine was rigid because she was trying to keep hold of herself. She was close to yielding, which was almost ridiculous. How could she disinherit feelings that were never there?

"Let's not talk about your brother."

"After tonight, are you ever gonna voluntarily see me again?"

Severine walked forward and looked over her shoulder to smirk at him. "Outside of class?"

"Yeah."

"You guys are strange," Severine noted.

Macsen nodded instantly. "It comes with the last name."

"There's a lot of weird tension between you guys."

"There always will be."

"So I probably shouldn't," Severine said finally.

"Are you wanting me to beg to see you?"

Severine wagged her finger in his direction. He reached out to grab it. "I think you're begging to beg."

"Do I need to ask you?" Macsen asked with a playful grin. His light-green eyes were bright. They were going to raze her until there was nothing left. Severine was okay with that. He could get as close to her as he wanted. There was no need to run from him.

"Yes," Severine said in a hushed tone.

"See me outside of class, apart from all this bullshit. I want to see just you."

Her smile slightly dimmed over his words. Macsen grinned, grabbed her fingers, and held them loosely within his grasp. His words took her off guard. Something furled around in her belly. It spread and reached for her heart, each time never quite grabbing on.

"Yeah," she said slowly. "I'd like that."

Something was languidly forming between them.

They were starting to fit together. She was going to remember this moment. It was going to stay with her.

The two of them walked back to their table. Thayer's eyes seemed to be waiting for her before she had rounded the corner. They always seemed selected in her direction.

Call it vicious, but she held his eyes. Right now, she was involved in the world's longest staring contest. She was going to win. All of her attention was on Thayer. When Macsen's palm touched her lower back, she barely registered the contact.

What was worse than being around two Sloan brothers? Having one physically touch her skin, and the other's gaze sear her to her very origin. He was too far to know or realize, but his gaze felt more real than skin-to-skin contact.

Thayer's eyes flicked away from her body and back to his computer screen. He repeated the process five times. Each time she felt it rattle her body.

By the time she and Macsen reached the table, her legs were wobbling worse than an infant learning how to take their first steps. She sat and re-opened the textbook she had given up on minutes—or maybe it was hours—ago.

Macsen's knee brushed against her. Severine's neck snapped up.

"So you asked me, but I never got the chance to ask, what's your ambition?"

Her eyelids moved quickly as she tried to focus on his question. "Uh. To spotlight at all major strip clubs."

Thayer coughed loudly. Macsen's laughter was abrupt as he glanced at her with round eyes. "Come on, be serious."

"Ah, well, seriously?" Severine paused and looked over at him. "I want to be a dermatologist."

"Really?" he asked with wide eyes.

It wasn't the most typical major. She knew that. People's reactions would never get old. "What? Did you think I was majoring in, like, beerology?"

"No," Macsen grumbled. "I just didn't expect that answer."

Severine held her hands in the air. "I take it back! I really wanna major in nursing. So when Halloween comes around, I'll save money on my costume."

"Now that is fucking genius," Thayer commented.

Everyone turned his way. It was hard to tell what exactly was running through his head as he stared fixedly at his laptop.

All he wanted was to get under her skin. It would irritate her, and it would drive him only further to provoke.

"Anyway," Macsen drew out slowly. "I have to know. What makes you wanna be a dermatologist?"

This was okay territory. She could talk about her goals all day long. "The question should be, why wouldn't I want to be a dermatologist?" Both Thayer and Macsen stared at her like a third eye had grown between her eyebrows. "Stop looking at me like that! It's fascinating to me, the body's hormones, how our bodies deal with stress, lifestyles. I really want to specialize in Dermatopathology. It's more along the lines of acne, or any skin diseases, but cosmetic dermatology is something I've thought about for a while." She stopped talking to finally realize that she was rambling. More than rambling, she was telling them her dreams. It was more than she really wanted to relay to anyone.

Thayer whistled loudly. "Wow."

Severine shrugged self-consciously. "My major could still change, so you never know."

"Sounds likes you have it all planned out, though," Thayer commented.

When she looked at him, she saw understanding in his expression. Admiration was written clearly in his gray eyes. "I do."

Thayer paused to look at her a little longer before his

head turned to Macsen. His expression showed he knew a secret that no one else knew. "So how was Haley's?"

Lily made eye contact with Severine and quickly looked away.

"I didn't go to Haley's, dumbass."

"Seriously though, you better watch the fuck out. She'll make a voodoo doll of you," Thayer warned. "If you wake up screaming tonight, I'll know why."

"Dick," Macsen responded back instantly. How many times did they bite each other's heads off like this?

"Oh, this is sweet," Severine said with false happiness. "Have you guys always been this close?" The words poured out of her mouth. She couldn't really help it. Things were starting to get awkward. Quick.

"So, Severine," Thayer said her name sharply, and she flinched.

Her expression was cautious while his was harsh. She felt like a child caught doing something wrong.

"Yeah?"

"Have you and Mac known each other long?"

Severine quickly glanced at Ben. He shrugged his shoulder. She leaned close. "I've known him the same amount of time as I've known you."

"So you don't know him." He turned away. A muscle along his jaw ticked. Severine was starting to see that it was an action he did when he was pissed. His mouth opened and snapped shut tightly. Thayer wanted to say something. Severine didn't know if she was grateful or so curious she was pissed.

"Well, I'm done studying," Lily pronounced slowly.

Thank God. Severine gave Lily a grateful smile from across the table. They couldn't leave at a better time.

Everyone moved out of their seats, gathering their books. Severine hefted her bag up and over her shoulder and made a dramatic groan.

"Give it here." Thayer reached out and plucked her bag from her shoulder. "It looks like a lot of pressure."

It was a simple statement, a statement that anyone could have said. That was the difference between Thayer and everyone else. Nothing that came out of his mouth was simple, and it sure as hell wasn't innocent. He said it to provoke.

Severine took it seriously. Every space in between his words scared the shit out of her.

There would never be a truce between them. The two of them had too much pride.

He walked ahead of everyone else, leaving Severine to stare at his retreating form. No one heard the exchange. She lost that round.

*   *   *   *   *

"What was that?" Lily asked the minute Severine shut the car door.

Severine messed with the radio station. "What you just witnessed was me being a total idiot. And why I was right."

Lily pulled away from the library, a smirk firmly planted on her lips. If anything good came out of tonight, it was Lily opening up to Ben. "So did you have fun with Ben?"

"Nuh-uh." Lily shook her head back and forth. "You better tell me what that was back there!"

Severine's fingers combed through her dark strands. She gripped the strands tightly before letting loose. "That was an epic disaster."

"Maybe for you; Ben and I were entertained."

"He wasn't even supposed to show up," Severine muttered. They didn't have much further to go until they reached their dorm. She didn't care and uncoiled her legs to rest on the dashboard. Her mind felt worn. It had just been down the most twisted, warped hole. All it wanted was a break.

Lily drummed her fingers loudly on her steering

wheel. "Okay. You wanna know something?"

"If it goes along the lines of 'Thayer's transferring schools,' then sure!"

When Lily bit her lip, Severine knew it wasn't good. That was Lily's sign that she was going to admit something she didn't want to share.

"IknewThayerwascoming." Her words came out as one word. Severine still heard it loud and clear.

"Ahh!" Severine groaned. "Why?"

"I know you don't like the dude!" Lily held her hands briefly in the air to show her innocence. "But he asked Ben if he could come. Besides, weren't you the one that said nothing bad can happen in a library?"

That was when she was certain he and Macsen wouldn't show up. Leave it to the Sloan brothers to tarnish the one place Severine never thought they could. Everything was up for grabs now. Was she next? "Well, I'm a compulsive liar. You should never listen to me."

Lily rolled her eyes but grinned at the same time. "If you really wanna know, I-"

"I don't," Severine chimed in dryly.

"Watching you guys is kind of..." Lily appeared out of words.

"Hellish, wrong. Something a friend shouldn't do?" Severine provided.

They parked near their dorm. The engine shut off, and Lily finally looked at Severine. "It's fun to watch."

"Lily! My pain is fun to watch?"

"I can't help it!" Lily said delightfully. "I like that he dares you with practically everything."

Of course Lily could like that he dared Severine; she wasn't the one being challenged.

"People that are too much alike? Yeah, they usually blow up around each other," Severine finally admitted. They were the same. Severine was sure he knew the truth too.

"Where did you and Macsen flounce off to?" She

moved her eyebrows up and down.

Severine was beginning to loosen up over the change of subject. "We just talked in some corner."

"Sounds so romantic." Lily fluttered her eyes repeatedly. Severine whacked her shoulder and opened her door.

"It was better than sitting at the table of torture."

Lily slammed her door and hopped up onto the sidewalk. "If you call that torture, then I'm game."

Chapter Six

Every day had a theme song, each one different from the last. Lily swore upon it. Most times, Severine thought it was crap, but today she was starting to think that her friend might be right.

Sometimes, the shit that came out of Lily's mouth made sense. Severine trudged up the stairs humming, "Bad Day." Although, her day was far past bad; it sucked.

"Annneeee," Severine dragged out. She was too lazy to even talk right.

"Yes?"

"You look like you could be a really fast typist..." Severine trailed off and wiggled her eyebrows.

"I'm not typing your paper."

"I'll pay you a thousand dollars," Severine said as she dug for her keys.

Anne smiled and walked over to Severine. "Bad day?"

"Yeah. I have decided that I truly am going to drop out and become one of those crazy coupon ladies. I could make a killing off that."

"But you'd also be the world's most organized hoarder..."

"Thanks for the encouragement. I saw a three-legged cat outdoors, maybe you can steal its cat food later."

Anne barely smirked at Severine's barb. "Change.

We're going to the gym."

"Why would I start going now? I don't even know where the campus gym is located."

"Get rid of some steam." Anne made herself at home and dug through Severine's closet. "I'm not saying that you have to run five miles, but I promise you'll feel so much better."

"I'm not going." With that statement, Severine dropped onto her bed, and rolled into a comfortable position.

"Yes." Anne stood up and threw a pair of workout clothes at Severine. "You are. How many times have I gone to some lame-ass party with you?"

Severine lifted her head to lazily look at Anne. She had a point.

Anne knew she was close to talking Severine into it and quickly went in for the kill. "Besides, there is a crap-load of tasteful dudes to stare at."

Her eyes busted wide. Anne smiled. Severine wasn't thinking about any tasteful dudes, except Thayer. There was a slight chance he'd be there.

Last night materialized back into her mind. It had driven her nuts all day and was somehow making another appearance. Severine wasn't going to pretend she didn't want to see him. She did. That's what disgusted her.

"It's our personal Hunk du Jour," Anne offered with an artful smile.

*   *   *   *   *

Sweat dripped down her neck. Severine wiped the perspiration away and focused on the dummy in front of her. All her frustration went into the next kick. Her legs backed away, and she repeated the process.

Anne was right. This was a great way to blow off steam. Before she had started harassing the blameless dummy, she was liable to snap on an innocent bystander. And so far, she hadn't seen Thayer. She lifted her leg and kicked as hard as she could.

"Uhh, you okay there? I think Bill's head is ready to fall off." Anne looked at the dummy they had lovingly named Bill.

Severine took a deep breath and stepped away. Her legs burned, and her muscles felt like jelly. "Your turn."

Anne gave the dummy a skeptical look. "Uh, I don't think there's much left for me kick."

"Okay, well let's use the treadmill next."

"We've already done that," Anne pointed out, as she silently offered Severine a bottled water. "Besides, we've been here for almost two hours. I think I'm gonna have to use a wheelchair tomorrow to get to class. Can we please go back to the dorms? Please?"

Severine wasn't in control of her feelings. Her breath came out in pants, and she concentrated on poor Bill in front of her. She didn't want to talk about it, but what other choice did she have?

"I think I like someone I shouldn't."

It was hard to shock or surprise Anne. She spun the cap of her bottle quickly and practically ran to Severine's side. "Who? Details!"

"Macsen Sloan," Severine stated quietly. It was a lie. She meant the other Sloan brother. Thayer.

Anne looked at her, confused. "Mac? You like Mac?" She rested her hands on her hips and peered at the people around them before glancing back at Severine. "That's a good thing, right?"

Severine nodded before going back to kicking the dummy repeatedly.

"Then why shouldn't you like him? Macsen's not off-limits. He's a great guy."

"I know that," wheezed out Severine. Her heart wasn't pounding from the exertion that was pouring out of her body. It came from an internal struggle. The truth was hard to keep in when it was begging to be set free.

"You should go for it," Anne winked.

There was nothing else to do but nod. Severine knew he was the safer route. He made her laugh. Being around Macsen gave her a calmness that normally never stuck. It made sense. For once, Severine needed to follow her logic and gut.

"I can't take it," Anne declared with fatigue shading her words. "I'm going to walk to the locker room, while I still can."

A short burst of laughter escaped Severine. "Go. I'll be there soon." She picked up her water and took a long gulp.

"I feel like I'm gonna see you on *Cops* in a few years."

At the sound of the voice, Severine bit into the plastic rim of the bottle. Thayer was behind her, watching her with a mixture of respect and interest. This wasn't Severine's top place to hang out. Ever.

For him, it evidently was.

Severine pulled the bottle away from her lips. Thayer followed the motion almost eagerly. This wasn't good for the stress that Severine had just chased out of her body. "It's my self-defense practice. You know, from all the douchebags out there."

Thayer grinned. It didn't crook on one side. There was nothing half-hearted with him. When he smiled, it was all consuming. "Well, I'm a guy, and I'll officially be standing two feet away from you."

Severine panted out a laugh, still trying to get the remainder of her breath back. With him here, it officially became ten times harder. He leaned against the wall, dressed in a cut off and basketball shorts. One thing could be checked off her giant list of never-ending questions. He looked just as she imagined after working out.

Maybe she was wrong about the whole sports being the devil's playground theory. If everyone looked this good after a workout, she'd buy front row tickets to their male basketball team. Clearly, she was missing out.

"If you stay two feet away at all times, then we might end up being B.F.F."

"How would I enjoy that?" Optimism glinted off of him. Severine had never seen him this way. She whacked her almost empty water bottle over and over against her thigh. Mischief danced in his eyes. It would cause catastrophic damage for anyone.

"Two feet away? I think that's two feet too fucking far."

"God, are you kidding me? You just wasted a really good line on me."

He stepped away from the wall. "Severine, I have no 'good lines,'" he said with air quotes. "That would mean I was using someone else's words. Whatever I say is all mine."

Her hand stilled, and the bottle paused in mid-swing. If he was kidding, he had the world's best poker face. She hated not knowing what he was really thinking. It made it impossible to keep up with him.

"So, are you coming over tonight?"

Severine quirked an eyebrow, "Uh. No. If I haven't gone to your apartment before, why would I be coming over tonight?"

"Macsen was talking about having you over." He lifted his gym bag over his shoulder and motioned for Severine to follow. She was too curious to tell him that the girl's locker room was the other way, opposite of where he was walking.

"Well, obviously not tonight," Severine repeatedly calmly. But internally, her blood rushed from the intense workout. She should feel sated and calm, but she didn't. She only felt worse—like a Red Bull mixed with sleeping pills. Her body wanted rest, but her mind was too amped up to follow orders.

"Macsen will be crushed," Thayer said

conversationally.

"You sound way too happy about me not coming over. Do I bother you?"

"Do you get under my skin?" They walked down the tight hallway. Thayer scooted closer, to let people walk past them, and his arm pressed firmly against hers. Her heart plunged ahead, and without her consent, she was on the rollercoaster she never wanted to ride. "Yeah, you definitely get under me."

Strength was embedded in her blood, but Severine was beginning to think that she had little to no self-control around him. Right now, she knew how it felt to be the girls she hated.

It was routine for her to rent sappy movies with Lily, bust out the popcorn and watch the corny plot play out in front of them. "*That would never happen,*" Severine would always say.

Real life just didn't play out like that. Her heart thundered loudly, and tingles pricked her skin like sharp needles. All it proved to her was that those feelings could be true.

"What are you really trying to say to me?" Severine finally asked.

"Why does what I think bother you?" Thayer shot back.

"It doesn't," Severine said unhurriedly.

"Good," Thayer repeated back, just as slowly.

"Well, if we're done, I'm gonna go." Severine stepped around him and clenched her iPod tightly in her hands.

"How come I always seem to piss you off?" Thayer called out.

Severine turned around. "Huh?"

Thayer grinned and kept the distance between them. "I don't think I've ever gotten someone worked up as much as you."

He said it loud enough for anyone walking by to hear, and a few idiots that passed by whistled loudly.

Severine's face turned red in anger. Nothing irked her more than when she was given a hard time.

Severine yanked his hand and pushed him toward the stairwell door. "Will you shut up? Everyone's staring."

"Is this better?" Thayer whispered.

Severine shifted back from him and groaned. He didn't know what was bothering her—that she liked him when she really, really shouldn't. Finally she ground out, "I'm close to having a hemorrhage because of *YOU!*"

"That's the sexiest thing I've heard all day."

"Oh f-" Severine veered off. She was completely losing her calm demeanor. Who was she kidding? She never really had a good hold on her patience when he was around. "You're driving me crazy."

Thayer laughed and moved to stand in front of her. He was way too close. "At least I'm driving you toward something."

Severine stared at the dirty ceiling above her as she spoke. "Toward the road of insanity?"

"Why ask me? That's for you to figure out." His hands possessed her arms. It was enough to make Severine want to jump out of her skin. He officially had all of her attention. "Tell me, what do you see in my brother?"

Her spirits crashed. Instantly, a picture of Macsen came into her head. Severine quickly ducked her head and moved out of Thayer's hold. "Why are you bringing him up?"

Thayer's expression slammed into her gut. His eyes looked divided. Indecision and eagerness showed as he studied her carefully. "Normally, I'm not this gracious, but right now, I'm choosing to give you heads-up on Mac and me." Severine said nothing. Maybe finally someone would shed some light into the dark room where these brothers kept their secrets. "Things appear simple with us, and they're not. You wanna date my brother? That's fine." He came to a standstill and stared distractedly at the stairs behind Severine. "You just need to know, things in our family have never been manageable. It's all a giant clusterfuck of mistakes and let downs."

Severine swallowed. "I didn't ask for a background story of your family. Macsen's just a friend."

His eyebrow cocked skeptically. "That's it?"

"Yeah, it is," Severine said. An edge outlined her words.

"Know what you're getting into," Thayer warned as he backed away near the exit. Somehow it sounded more like a plea. "Everyone has baggage, Blake, even the good ones."

"And yours?" Severine asked to his retreating back.

Thayer's back tensed. He turned around. With his arms still crossed, he leaned down close to her body and spoke to her profile. "What do I have to reserve? Everything is in front of you, Severine."

His words snatched her interest, and she couldn't look away. His cloudy gray eyes were intense and alert as he gauged her reaction.

She couldn't give him one. How could she? Severine finally understood the truth.

Thayer didn't find her snarky, strong backbone as a put off. He found those qualities a challenge.

When she glanced back at Thayer, his face was still solemn. His countenance was one of victory.

She knew the truth. And now, there was an unspoken agreement between them. The two of them no longer had to perceive what was true and what was complete bullshit.

Silently, he left the stairwell. Severine moved back to the wall and pressed her head against the wall in front of her. Her eyes were clenched tightly as she lightly banged her forehead on the wall.

"Oh shit," she finally muttered.

*   *   *   *   *

Fresh air seemed like the best idea.

Anne left after Severine promised that she was okay walking. Honestly, she needed to be alone. How many times was Severine ever really by herself to reflect over her thoughts? Answer: Never.

But instead, she called her mom. Talking over her issues with her mom was something that would never get old, no matter what age she was. It always took off the weight of life that reality consistently seemed to press onto her shoulders.

It took a few rings before her mom, Clacy, answered. Severine may have some heavy conversations with the only stable parent in her life, but she always had to be the one to call first.

Clacy had some secret aversion to the phone. It was up to everyone else in the family to keep in touch with her. She avoided the phone like the plague. She was a telemarketer's nightmare. After a few rings, Clacy answered. For her mom, that was considerably fast. "How are you sweetie?"

Severine breathed out deeply, "Ehh, pretty good. I'm walking home from the gym."

"What? Are you nuts? Tell me you have your pepper spray with you."

Not only was her mom a top-notch phone tease, she always believed everyone in the world was being stalked by a predator. Clacy had watched way too many *Lifetime* movies.

"Yes, Mom," Severine responded patiently. "I also have my brass knucks on. And if that doesn't work, then I braided my hair and shoved knives in between each braid. I'll swing my hair around like a plane blade. While I'm defending myself, I'll make sure that the song, "Whip My Hair" is playing. Trust me. I'm safe."

"Severine," Clacy warned, "you're too much of a

smart ass. You need to be prepared for all the creep rotters in the world."

"Stop watching reruns of *Oprah*. I'm good, okay?"

"Moving on," her mom grumbled. "How are your classes going?"

"Dragging along at a snail's pace."

"Sounds promising."

"Oh I know, right?" Severine laughed.

"So, how's Lily doing?"

The subject of Lily immediately opened Severine up. "Right now she's floating on clouds, because of a guy."

"Well, she's happy, good for her."

"His name is Ben, and he's a great guy."

"Good, good," her mom said distractedly. "She needs a good guy. And how have *you* been?"

"Okay I guess..." Severine's words trailed off. The point of calling her mom was to open up to someone about what was really bothering her. She cut to the chase. "I met two brothers."

"Brothers, Severine?"

Severine groaned, "I'm not dating them together, at the same time."

Over the phone, a crinkly noise was heard. Her mom was moving around. "Clearly, you like one of them."

"Yeah..."

"So tell me about these boys."

Severine sighed and took a big breath of air. "They couldn't be more opposite of each other. Macsen, he's really funny, talkative and even a little nerdy."

"Interesting."

"I have a few classes with him, and I swear he reads a different book each time."

"The other brother?" Clacy asked.

Here it was, the part Severine wanted to avoid, but couldn't wait to talk about. "The other one is sarcastic, a little quiet. I guess Lily said he's here on a basketball scholarship."

"And the quiet brother?"

"Thayer," Severine provided.

"Yes, this Thayer guy. Is he bad news?"

Yes, he's bad for me and terrible for my heart. "No, not really."

"And you like which one?"

"I have no idea," Severine answered quickly.

"Good luck. Honestly, they both sound intriguing. I think it would be interesting to see you with the 'nerdy' brother," her mom paused, "although, the other brother is a lot like you. It'd be funny to see you get a taste of your own medicine."

"Thanks a lot."

Clacy laughed over Severine's irritated voice. "I'm sorry, sweetie. But it's just a known fact that every girl, no matter what she says, is drawn by the idea of transforming the unattainable guy. It's addicting."

"Yesss," Severine drew out. "But we both know how that works out."

Clacy scoffed, "Nonsense. I have you, don't I?"

Severine's dad had been in her life shorter than a carton of milk sitting in a fridge. There wasn't a reason to be bitter about it. She couldn't miss something she'd never had. "Touching, Madre, you should put that in a Hallmark card."

"I'm serious, Severine! But it'll be fine. You're a smart girl."

"How's Grandma doing?" Severine finally asked. Not that she wanted to. Every week it seemed her strong, efficient grandma, who had always been a constant in her life, was fading away. Grandma was more forgetful, would lose sight of what was going on around her and even dressing "down." For someone who was always so put together, it was shocking to see.

Clacy took a deep breath. When was that ever a good thing? "She's Grandma, honey. I'll talk to her on the phone and sometimes she's her normal self, but the next minute she forgets your cousin's newest baby."

"You mean Kadyn...who is now two?"

"That's the very one."

"And...has she gone to the doctor?"

"Of course she goes!" Her mom's voice rose. Severine held the phone away from her ear. "But it's never for the reasons she really needs to go."

They all knew it was Alzheimer's. Maybe her grandma knew it too, but she refused to acknowledge it. Instead, she focused on the pains in her feet, or how her tomatoes were growing. It was frustrating. How could you help someone who refused any help?

"I'm meeting her tomorrow to go shopping with her."

"One of her favorite pastimes—she'll enjoy that," Severine joked lightly.

"Alrighty, honey, I need to get off here. I have to pick her up early."

"Lemme guess, Hardee's for breakfast?"

"That's the first thing she wanted to do, like always."

"Love ya, Mom."

"Love you, too."

Instead of feeling at peace, Severine felt even more stressed. She should probably call her grandma, but she didn't want to. You couldn't deal with something if it didn't exist, right?

She needed that mantra for everything happening in her life right now.

Chapter Seven

"We need to do something this weekend." Severine said as she leaned her elbows against the step behind her.

"Whatcha have in mind, chickadee?" Lily moved toward Severine. This was one of the rare times Lily wasn't with Ben. Over the course of the last few weeks, they'd been together constantly. Lily walked around with a perma-grin. Severine watched Ben with a stealth that would make any ninja jealous. The smile on Lily's face needed to remain a fixture. Severine wanted to be sure that Ben wanted the same thing.

If only Severine could have the same solid grin on her face. She was tired of being moody and desperately needed to get away from her thoughts.

"I don't know, a leisurely trip to Target? Road trip to Cali?"

"There's a new bar down by The Ville. Everyone's going."

It wasn't exactly what Severine had in mind. She stared down at her shoes and tried to figure out why she felt so restless. She wanted to do something, but then she changed her mind seconds later. Nothing seemed good enough lately. That was what she deserved for talking to Macsen and Thayer. Severine sat up and dramatically sighed. "Why are we still outside?"

"I'm waiting for Ben to get here."

"Okay." Severine stood and brushed the dirt off her jeans. "No guy is worth me freezing my ass off."

"Oh! There he is!" Lily jumped away from the concrete stairs and into Ben's arms. Right on the sidewalk, she practically humped him. Behind the humping couple stood Thayer.

He was a nightmare that never seemed to go away. She couldn't escape him. Over the last few weeks, she had seen him around campus. After their talk at the gym, they'd barely said two words to each other. A glance from him was enough. He expected answers from her, when she had no idea what the question was to begin with.

One thing would probably always stay the same: when he looked at her, he had the ability to demoralize her.

"Ben says there's a frat party this weekend." Lily walked back up the sidewalk with Ben by her side. "We should go."

"No frat party. I went with you last time, and we both saw me the next morning. Lesson learned."

"Uh. And going to The Ville will be different from a frat party, how?" Ben asked.

"Less beer pong. More dancing. I like parties, but they get old if it's every weekend."

The longer Thayer stayed silent behind Ben and Lily, the antsier Severine became. She was still waiting on him to chime in and say something sarcastic. Severine moved her head to the side and looked directly at him. "What about you? Are you going?"

Thayer walked forward and approached slowly. His hands were tucked into his gray Columbia, and his jeans fit his tall frame perfectly. "If I say yes, you won't go. I say no, you will."

Severine asked because she wanted him to go. Her mind was lured at the prospect of seeing him again at a party. Severine shrugged and pretended he didn't affect her. "I didn't say that."

"You were thinking it." He came closer, and Severine smiled. She liked that he drifted closer without even realizing it. When he saw her smile, he froze in place and narrowed his eyes.

"I wasn't. Besides, I just told them I didn't want to go."

He leaned a hip against the chipped railing next to the sidewalk. "You haven't been at the gym lately."

"That's because it was a one time thing. It'll never happen again."

"I was just under the impression you were trying to avoid me."

Severine tsked lightly. "Wrong impression, Thayer. It's a known fact that if given the choice of going to work out or eating a bowl of hair...well, I'd rather eat the hair."

Lily pretended to dry heave in front her.

"God, Severine. Find a better example than that."

"I don't want to hear another one of her examples," Ben said behind Lily.

"But everyone gets the picture—I don't want to party this weekend."

"You're the one who wanted to get out and do something!" Lily pointed a finger in Severine's direction and wiggled her eyebrows.

"Yeah, but I don't want to lay in a pool of my own vomit."

"You have a way with words, Blake." Thayer's voice was deadpan.

When Severine opened her mouth to say something snarky back, she finally noticed the smirk on his face...always another joke to him.

Chapter Eight

Strong hands gripped Severine's shoulders and a voice spoke into her ear. "Are you going to the Ville this weekend?"

Her body was manually turned. Severine smiled up at Macsen. "Probably not."

His eyes bulged. "Seriously?'

"Yeah..." Severine paused and glanced at him as they walked across campus. "Why?"

"For once, I'm going out, and you're not. Something is wrong with that picture."

"I stay at home sometimes," Severine protested lightly.

"Yes," Macsen agreed. His arm went across her shoulders and hugged her tightly to his body. She savored the way her heart kicked up in its rhythm and smelled his cologne. Severine wanted to lick him. "But I want to see you."

Everything with Macsen seemed natural. Spending time with him was something she looked forward to. He brought a smile to her face. "You could always stay back with me. Hey! I know, we can rent some sappy movie and make fun of how everyone cries!"

Macsen peered down at her and his mouth kicked up in a grin. "Your enjoyment over people's tears sometimes scares me, Sev."

Her eyes turned round as she replayed his words. No one called her Sev. She wasn't a nickname type of person, and up until now, she never thought she'd want one. If it was anyone else, she'd be correcting them, but when Sev came out Macsen's mouth she liked the sound of it. "You didn't answer my question."

"I want to. But I told Chris and Thayer I'd go out with them."

Her back went up a notch. Macsen seemed oblivious. "You're actually doing something with your brother?" Severine kept her voice light and played with the zipper of her jacket.

"I know. Hell has officially frozen over," Macsen joked. Severine didn't smile. "He asked me last night. Said there was some new bar in The Ville he wanted to try out."

"Yeah?" Blood was pounding in her ears loudly.

"Someplace called Monty's."

"Sounds good." Keep your voice neutral. He won't notice anything is wrong.

Thayer was doing this to keep Macsen away. He knew she didn't want to go. Everything to him was a game.

"I don't plan on being out long." He glanced down at her once and smiled. "Come with me."

Her laugh came out choked. "Nah. I'll let you go with your brother. You guys need some brotherly bonding time."

"Yeah, that will never happen. Ever."

* * * * *

Come over.

Severine picked up her phone and smirked at the screen. *It's too freakin' late.*

A reply came back instantly. *Just come over. I wanna see you. I miss you.*

It wasn't a love sonnet. But it made Severine feel good. It made her feel wanted. She tapped on her screen to write back, but Macsen texted her again.

The guys are driving me nuts. U'd like to see me. Admit it.

I would. That's why you should've hung out with me tonight.

Wasn't thinkin clearly. Come over.

Keep begging.

Okay. I have no pride when it comes to you.

Severine was sliding her feet onto her shoes and grabbing her keys while she texted back.

I'll be there soon.

*   *   *   *   *

It took her fifteen minutes and many phone calls to Lily for Severine to finally figure out where the Sloan brothers lived. It was a typical apartment off campus. Two stories, tan siding, and a parking lot filled with cars.

Her screen flashed midnight, and she wondered what she was really doing here right now. Wasn't she breaking every rule in her book? She was going; she was visiting. It should be the opposite.

Following Lily's direction, Severine found their apartment on the first floor. The door in front of her was painted a dull brown with a few pieces of paint chipped off. Severine rang the doorbell and heard it ring from inside. No noise was coming from inside, which could only mean one thing: they weren't home.

Severine immediately turned back to her car. She wasn't going to wait for them. She was already generous enough to come see Macsen at this time.

"Hey! Everybody, it's Save-uhhh-reeen," Chris sloppily called out.

With her arms crossed, Severine took in the sight of Chris. Behind him was Macsen, holding up a completely wasted Thayer. He lifted up his head to glance at her and groaned loudly.

Macsen grinned crookedly. "Hey, Sev."

He invited her over for this shit? Severine ground her teeth together and ignored Macsen. If she wanted to watch a group of incoherent drunk people she'd watch *Cops*. There was no reason to stay here.

That was the plan...until she glanced at Thayer. His eyes were as good as dead. As he stared at her with a tortured expression, Macsen dragged them closer to the apartment door. Severine wrapped her arms tight around her torso. She wanted her arms around him.

Sympathy was something she rarely gave out. But right now, she wanted to know the source of his agony.

The truth came out when people were drunk. Dark sides were revealed. Feelings were exposed. And then you pretended not to know what happened the next day. It tortured you, though. Severine wanted to know Thayer's true thoughts. What dragged him down to this point?

Severine looked to the most sober, which unfortunately, happened to be Chris. "What happened to him?" Severine demanded.

"He's El Drunko, Blake."

Severine stomped forward. The smell of alcohol and cigarettes permeated the air around them. They all reeked. "I got that, genius, but I'm just wondering why he's so shit-faced."

Macsen piped in with his two cents. Right now, she wanted to beat him with her purse. "It was his idea to go!"

"Afterafew hours wes figured it was times to stop the drinkfest," Chris slurred out, trying to reach for his keys.

"Here, give them to me." Severine held her hand out. While Chris fumbled around to find his keys, Severine replaced his hold on Thayer.

"Uhh," Severine groaned out. The dude weighed a

ton. Her face was shoved against his pec, on his smoke-filled shirt. It was probably the least sexy position a girl had ever been in with Thayer. She was somehow the lucky girl chosen for this. "I can't hold all his weight," Severine grunted out.

Macsen mumbled something before he quickly moved away. All of Thayer's weight came against her. Their feet became tangled together, and the two of them fumbled backwards in a bush next to the sidewalk.

It could've been much worse. But right now, Severine couldn't think of anything crueler than having Thayer on top of her, especially when he had no clue what was going on.

"I think a twig has gone through my pants and punctured my butt," Severine wheezed out.

Thayer mumbled something incoherent and wrapped himself closer to Severine. Was he aware they were stuck in a bush, and she could quite possibly have some internal bleeding going on?

His knee shifted, and he was one movement away from touching her crotch. Severine's eyes blinked open wide. Punctured wound or not, her skin was starting to feel hot for reasons that it shouldn't.

Severine put her hands between them and tried to push. "Okay bud. You need to get up. My lungs are officially crushed."

"Mmm," Thayer whispered, "I like this position."

Her heart was a coward, it wanted to book it in the opposite direction, out of fear.

"Macsen," Severine rasped out. "Get him off."

"Fuck," Macsen slurred out. His hand latched onto Thayer's arm. Between the two of them, they finally got Thayer off of her.

Her butt was stinging and she probably looked like shit, but she slowly helped Thayer into his apartment. Macsen flipped on the light, and Severine looked around.

Their place wasn't much to brag about, but, then

again, it was an all male apartment. If it was anything different, then it might raise her eyebrows. The walls were a plain, drab white, with nothing decorating them, except the clock hanging across from the table.

A brown suede couch, in surprisingly good shape, was placed against the wall. Across from it was a huge, flat screen TV, spotless of smudges and marks. Severine peered at the clear glass doors of the brown entertainment center and saw a few gaming consoles, with games stacked neatly on the shelves. They couldn't decorate worth a shit, but when it came to electronics, they were on top of it.

Chris walked out of the narrow hallway, shirtless and drinking water. "Uh...he should probably go lay down."

"Gee, Chris, you're good," Severine snorted out.

Her shoulder was becoming numb. And unfortunately, her butt was past stinging and now burning. What did she land on, an arrowhead?

"Thayer's bedroom is the first one on the right!" Chris yelled before belching loudly.

"Make yourself useful and go get a trashcan and washcloth," Severine yelled back.

A lamp was already lit in Thayer's room—a queen-sized bed with messy sheets was in the far corner. Hardly anything was on the walls, save a calendar and thumbtack board. A desk and dresser were the only other furniture in the room.

Thayer lurched toward his dresser and attempted to empty the change from his back pocket. After the fifth try, with him finally leaning on the dresser, he got it.

"Here, why don't you lay down?" Severine stepped forward and helped him to the bed. Thayer said nothing. Everything was too still between the two of them. The silence threw Severine off. Usually, there was an implied arrangement between the two of them. When around each other, darts would be thrown. Seeing Thayer outside of those lines, without any of his quips, scared her.

When he finally dropped down to the bed, he flipped over on his back and glanced at her face with a reverent expression. This wasn't how it was supposed to be with him. Call her a chicken shit. Right now, she couldn't hold on to everything that was happening.

"I'm gonna go. Macsen and Chris are here. I'd like to say they'd help ya out, but they won't. So just aim for the trashcan, K?" Severine positioned the trashcan right next to his bed and rose to her feet.

Thayer wrapped his fingers around her knee, and she froze. If she kept this position long enough, maybe she could just disappear from sight. Her jeans were close to melding into her skin, giving a whole new meaning to the word 'jeggings.'

"Why are you being semi-decent to me?"

"'Cause you look like shit," Severine gently said.

"Here." A wad of clothes flew in the air and landed next to Thayer's waist. Macsen stood in the doorway with a strange expression. He walked out before Severine could say anything.

"Thanks, little brother!" Thayer called out. A hard edge to his words made the smile from Severine's face slowly fade away.

"I need to go," Severine repeated.

Thayer smiled lazily and held his arms out in front of him. "You wanna help, Blake?"

Yes, yes, yes! Instead of saying that, she cocked her head to the side and stared. "You can't take your clothes off by yourself?"

Thayer lifted a brow, shook his head no, and waited.

She was a dummy if she didn't get her fill of what was underneath his shirt. A cheeky smile covered his lips, and Severine swore he knew what she was envisioning.

If she walked away, she'd be doing the right thing, but all of the women around the world would be shouting and cussing at her for not jumping on the bed and helping him.

She gave a brief nod, and the hand wrapped around her knee yanked her to kneel on the bed. What was she hoping to achieve with this? This. Was. Wrong.

Thayer lay in front of her, motioning for her to come closer. She was going to reach forward, even if she regretted it. Her fingers grabbed the hem of his cotton shirt. Thayer shifted forward as Severine lifted his shirt above his head.

Of course, her eyes glanced down. Indents of muscles created ridges on his stomach. Severine wanted to agree with her urges. Her fingers wanted to touch what her eyes saw.

Instead, she kept both hands close to her legs. In the quiet of the room, her breathing seemed amplified. With one quick glance at Thayer, she knew he was trying to keep his wits.

Looking at him made things worse. It wrapped her closer to him and made her want to drag in every breath of air that specifically made him Thayer.

"All right. I think you've got the rest," her voice shook.

She wasn't the type of person that let her nerves take control. When you lost all power, you were far behind.

Thayer remained still. Other than the rustle of sheet, no sound was made from him.

"Are you okay?" Severine asked inaudibly.

Thayer nodded, but his eyes were impaled with pain—pain that didn't come from drinking.

All Severine could do was mimic his nod. Her eyes focused on the black sheets of his bed and toward his waist. This time, it took no effort for her to read Calvin Klein.

How many girls had seen him in this position? Severine had no one to point the finger at for her thoughts—they broke through her shields. She wasn't ready to feel jealous.

Thayer's hand firmly held one of her own. Severine

didn't try to move away. It was time to confront this fear, and perhaps her biggest desire, directly.

He was simply a guy, but the way he was staring at her lips made him so much more than simple.

"Can I tell you something?" Thayer asked quietly.

Severine barely heard him. She nodded her head, and he smiled back lazily. Even drunk, he was gorgeous perfection.

"I saw you first," he rasped out deeply. "Remember that. I saw you first."

Severine, trying to keep the conversation light, smiled weakly. "At the coffee shop?"

His head shifted back and forth, while his eyelids drooped down. Severine was waiting for him to pass out and drift off into a deep sleep. He shifted slightly. "I'd seen you many times before that."

She swallowed loudly. "When?"

"Around campus with your friend, Lily. At a couple of parties." Slowly, his lips rounded into a small smile. Instinctively, Severine held her breath. "You know, you're like no other girl I've ever met. I love that you don't put up with bullshit." His eyes poured out all of his secrets. Her heart was ruined. Without trying, she was falling for him. "You're rare, Severine. Just like your name. It's impossible to forget you."

She blinked rapidly. Severine couldn't reciprocate anything worthwhile. Her brain was mush. It was melting fast.

"Can I tell you something else?"

No, no, no.

Severine sucked in her cheeks tightly and nodded stiffly. "I stole Macsen's phone and texted you tonight."

"So I was talking to you."

"Would you have come over if you knew it was me?"

Swallowing felt painful. "Honestly? No." The truth had never tasted so bitter.

"Then you can't be mad at me for being deceitful."

As she sat there in a state of confusion, Thayer drifted to sleep. Severine shifted away from his bed and reached over to cover him with a blanket.

A deep breath escaped her mouth. Her hand reached out and traced a line from his cheekbone, down to his lips. He didn't react. It was a relief to Severine. She doubted they'd ever have a peaceful moment together like this again. Gentle, harmonious occasions in life were rare. Severine knew that this moment would be permanently captured in her mind.

Severine was a greedy, selfish person. She wanted everything. Right now, sitting here with Thayer, she wanted to keep this moment forever. Nothing gave her the right to desire it so much.

A light cough came from the doorway. Severine glanced up quickly to find Macsen standing there, watching her. He glanced down at his brother, and her fingers shook as she took them away from his face.

She walked toward the door. Her voice a whisper, she said, "I guess I should be going."

Macsen nodded his head miserably. "Sorry about, uh..."

"About getting wasted?" Severine asked as they walked side by side down the hall. "You had fun, Macsen. Something you should probably do more often."

He gave her a brief nod and leaned on the kitchen island.

"Remember to check up on him later," Severine said as she wrapped her scarf around her neck.

"I don't think I'm the person he's hoping will check up on him."

"Are you talking about moi?" Severine tried to joke, but her voice sounded strained, betraying the awkwardness she was feeling.

Macsen picked at the beige carpet with his sock. The silence lingered between them. Finally he spoke. "What were you guys doing in there?"

"Nothing," Severine said stiffly.

He shut his eyes and briefly held them tight before opening them. "I think it would've been more than nothing if I hadn't walked in when I did."

"But you got there just in time, didn't ya?"

The air was thick with tension. Severine stared uncomfortably at Macsen, his expression unreadable.

"Do you like my brother?"

She wanted to tell him that she didn't know. All she could give him was silence.

Sometimes, saying nothing was worse than saying anything. "Maybe you should go to bed too, Macsen," Severine lightly spoke.

He breathed out of his nose and harshly laughed. "Do you think I'm wasted like him? That I don't know what I'm doing?"

That's *exactly* what Severine was thinking. From the way he was acting, she knew he was a little tipsy.

"No. I didn't say that. I'll see you later. All right?"

With the doorknob in her hand, she watched as he nodded and walked down the hall.

Severine knew he wouldn't check on his brother.

Chapter Nine

Remember that. I saw you first.

Was that why Severine was here, because of those words?

She gathered her black pea coat closer to her body and knocked on the door, only louder this time.

Finally, the door creaked open. A mussed up Thayer opened the door. His eyes widened slightly before squinting from the sunlight.

He opened the door as he scratched his bare chest, the same chest she'd gaped openly at last night. A pair of sweatpants hung low on his hips. Even hung-over, he looked amazing.

"Uh...are you here for Mac?"

"No, I'm trying to be friendly." Severine displayed the drinks held between her hands. "Coffee?"

His smirk was grateful as he took the cue and grabbed the container holding the drinks together.

"You really didn't have to."

"Yeah, well, sometimes I get this really weird urge to be considerate." She yanked her gray snowcap from her head and dragged a hand through her messy hair. A strange expression crossed Thayer's face as he watched her.

Severine wanted to keep today's visit on the fence. She wasn't here for Macsen or Thayer. This atypical drop by was for her. When she walked out of the front door, her thoughts of Thayer would be left behind, along with last night.

Severine grabbed a packet of sugar and ripped it open. "I guess today is one of those days. Don't hold your breath for me to *ever* do this again."

While rubbing his temples, he gently sat down on the kitchen barstool. Lily and Severine never had any males at their dorm. So seeing a shirtless and disheveled Thayer, with every muscle displayed, was torture.

Severine shifted her eyes away and repeatedly beat the sugar packet against her palm. "So, was last night barf-fest for you?"

Thayer shook his head and took a drink. "I'm sure you're dying for me to say yes." He placed his drink on the counter and settled his hands on his thighs. "But no, I slept like a rock."

Severine nodded her head. "Good." He'd never know that she slept like shit wondering about him. "You wanna put a shirt on?"

Thayer's lips kicked up into a devious smile. "I was waiting for you to stop drooling."

"I like you better drunk," Severine muttered.

"Hmm?"

Severine leaned back in her chair and smiled sweetly. "I said, I think you wish I was!"

He responded with an expression that said, 'Yeah, right.' When he walked away, Severine examined his back muscles.

Seconds later, he came back out with a basketball shirt on. "Is that your high school team?"

"What?" he glanced down at his shirt. "Oh yeah, as you can see, we were the Cardinals."

"Ah." Severine sipped thoughtfully. "Vicious!"

"Sev? What are you doing here?" Macsen asked. His hair was stuck up in every direction. Instead, of sexy disheveled like his brother, he looked almost innocent.

Severine wanted to walk up to him, push his hair in the right direction and simply hug him.

"I came to check on Thayer." Her eyes drifted toward where he sat. He was already gone. "I figured you would let him sit in his own puke before you remembered."

"And you brought coffee," Macsen stated.

Severine grinned. "I did." He eagerly took the one she held out for him. "Now that I can see you're both alive, I'm gonna go. I have some shopping to do."

"I know that Thayer might not remember, but do you know what happened last night?" Macsen stared down at his drink as he asked the question.

The cowardly part of her was willing to walk away without talking to Macsen about last night. Never mind the fact that his words chipped away at her already exhausted feelings. She wanted Thayer to remember.

But Macsen saw through it. Severine walked around the table and stood across from him.

"Remember what? That your brother drunk-texted me?"

Macsen rubbed his eyes. "I'm not talking about that."

"Get to the point, then," Severine emphasized her words slowly.

"You and my brother. What the fuck was that about?"

Her anger vibrated off her, expanding around the room. If Macsen couldn't feel it, he was choosing to ignore it. "I helped him get to bed. That was it."

"Really?"

"Yeah. Really." Severine buttoned up her coat and walked to the door. Before she opened it, she glanced back at Macsen. She never was good at backing down. "I wanna know. What do you think happened? You seemed pissed at me for reasons I don't really know."

Macsen clenched his lips together. From his red

cheeks, Severine knew he was pissed. "Last night you stared at Thayer like you—"

"I stared at him in no way!" Severine interrupted loudly. Her heart hammered from his words. She didn't want to discover how he would've ended that sentence. "This conversation's going nowhere fast."

"All I want to know is what I saw!"

"What you saw was nothing!" Severine shot back. "Besides, why should it bother you?"

Macsen took a step back as if he had gotten burned. Impossible. Severine would be the one with the scars.

"It doesn't bother me."

Nothing much to say to that. All Severine gave him was a small smile. "Then there you go. You answered your own question."

Her hand reached for the doorknob. She was out of the apartment before Macsen could say anything else to take her spiraling mood to even lower levels.

Walking out into the crisp, fall air only reminded her that the main task for coming here hadn't been achieved. If anything, she was leaving with more thoughts afflicting her mind.

"Hey, wait," Thayer called out.

Severine picked her pace up and dug around for her keys. Why, when she really needed to get away, did her keys magically seem to disappear?

"Are you deaf?" Thayer asked as he caught up to her. His body blocked the path to her car. Severine looked at it longingly. It stood there in the sun, beckoning her to get the hell out of here.

"No," Severine said with frustration. "I just need to get out of here."

Thayer zipped up his jacket and looked around the parking lot. "Why? What's bothering you?"

Everything. Macsen. You. This whole mess we've created.

"I heard you with Macsen."

Severine groaned, "Is there ever a time when you two aren't listening in?"

"From you?" His smile was harsh. "No. We're never too far from you."

"That's a bad idea."

"Never said it was right. We're probably both fucking idiots," Thayer spoke the truth. His words warmed her up just as goosebumps broke across her skin. "Thanks for coming over last night. I think I drunk-texted you?"

Severine narrowed her eyes. He remembered last night. His eyes flicking everywhere but to hers showed he knew every detail. "Did you like me taking your shirt off?" Severine taunted him.

For once, he was shocked. "I'm trying to let you walk away here scot free," Thayer warned.

"Apparently, I'm just like you and your brother. A fucking idiot."

"Look, I'm trying to be decent for once in my life. I'm letting you forget. Unless you want me to go upstairs and tell Macsen how you really looked at me?"

Severine opened her mouth. Thayer's warm hand covered her lips. "You don't always have to retort back with something snarky."

Right now, he was asking her to forget. She wanted to remember. Severine hated herself for desperately wanting to hang onto the feelings from last night. In lieu of everything she wanted, Severine briskly nodded her head. Second choices always had the worst quality.

"You're making me late."

"For?"

Severine stepped to her left and Thayer mirrored her movements. "I'm meeting Lily." He looked bored by her answer. Severine wanted to say something to throw him off his feet. "I want a dress for my date tonight."

He glanced at her for a few seconds. "Really?"

Satisfaction illuminated her face. "Yup."

"Who's the guy?" he immediately asked.

"Will Pratt." Severine moved to the right and left Thayer behind.

Thayer turned. His expression strange, he said, "William Pratt?"

Severine looked up from digging in her purse and saw the large grin on his face. "What?" His smile became wider. "Tell me, Thayer!"

"That guy is the biggest pus-," he rephrased his wording, "the biggest wimp to ever step foot on campus."

Severine shrugged and turned back toward her car. "Ehh, he seemed all right to me."

"Because he's halfway good looking," Thayer said dryly.

"Thayer, he's more than halfway," she said with a saucy grin.

"I'm pretty sure he's on the chess team."

"No, he's not. And do we even have a chess team?"

"I wouldn't know. I have a life. But have fun with Willy."

"It's Will!" Severine snapped back. After digging in her purse for one too many minutes, she groaned. "Where the hell are my keys?"

Thayer reached into his pocket and dangled them in front of her. "Is this what you've been looking for?"

"Gimme."

He held the keys high in the air. Severine was standing next to a dude that was six-foot-nine. Jumping for them would make her look stupid. Grabbing them would be impossible. It'd be like reaching for the sky.

"Give them to me."

"No."

"I'm okay with walking," Severine warned.

Thayer shrugged. "Believe me, I'm okay with watching you walk."

"Quit being a dickchin. Hand them over."

"You're so fucking demanding."

"When you have something I want, yes, yes I am."

"Look, I'll give them to you. All you gotta do is sweetly ask for them back."

"Ask or beg?"

"Both."

One step forward with Thayer could never be that simple. Whenever she was around him, tension seemed to hover. Severine drug her tongue across her teeth and looked around. She never liked saying, 'please' or 'sorry.' It was like she was admitting defeat. Forever and always, it'd be a blow to the self-esteem.

"Please hand me my keys, Thayer," Severine gritted out.

He lowered his hand. "I've been waiting for you to say 'please' to me since the first day I saw you."

Severine snatched her keys from his fingers and quickly opened her car door. "Well, it's the last time you'll ever hear it from me."

"Yeah, right," Thayer mumbled.

She heard his words clearly. With her eyes clenched tightly, she slammed her car door and pulled away.

A block away, she parked in an empty parking lot. Her hands shook as she scrolled through her phone for the number she wanted.

After four rings, a male voice answered anxiously.

"Hey, Severine."

"I changed my mind, Will. I'd love to see you tonight."

Chapter Ten

Tell Severine to do something.

Usually, she ended up doing the opposite. Most of the time, she walked away feeling victorious. That wasn't the case tonight.

She was on round twenty of crossing and re-crossing her legs underneath the table. She had a severe case of restlessness, and it wasn't going to let up anytime too soon.

Everything had started out so great. Will had picked her up, and they talked on the way to the restaurant. Over a plate of breadsticks, Severine realized the truth. Will Pratt had a severe case of momma's boy syndrome.

While she stuffed her face with breadsticks, her date continued to tell her why his mom preferred for him to be called William, and not Will. Will was a child's name. If he was going to someday have a career, who would listen to a Will?

After that, Severine tuned him out. Their food came, and she quickly ate all her pasta. To think she wasted her sexy dress on a dude that couldn't cut the cord.

The highlight of her evening was the sound of her phone ringing. Severine practically banged her head against the table to reach it.

"Hey, Lily." Severine took the phone away from her

ear and briefly mouthed to William, 'It's my friend.'

"So, I have some bad news," Lily said on the other side of the line.

"Oh no," Severine said with shock. "What's wrong?"

"Your mom called me. Apparently, your imaginary brother is gone."

"Is he okay?" Severine whispered. "What happened?"

"He was walking through some unknown city and disappeared."

"That's horrible."

"I am guessing you want me to pick you up?"

"Yes, that would be great. Lily, thank you so much for calling me!" Severine said in mock sadness.

Across the phone, Lily laughed, "No problem. Be there in five minutes."

"Oh no, Will."

"William," he interjected.

Severine ignored him and continued, "I need to go. Apparently my brother is really ill. I need to get there. Now."

"Do you need me to drop you off anywhere?"

"That's so kind, but my friend is picking me up. We're going straight to him." Her hands were through her coat sleeves instantly.

"Well...tonight was fun," William said frowning.

"I know, had a blast. Let's do it again. Adios, Will!" Quickly, she rushed out into the frigid temperature. The air immediately gave her a chill. She could be suffering from hypothermia, and she'd still feel relieved. She now realized Thayer's gleefulness over her date.

The minute she was allowed to date, she created a system with Lily. Call 'em and leave 'em. It was their routine and always ran smoothly. Some may call it cruel. Severine just called it genius thinking. Who wanted to sit through a date that made you lose the William to live?

Her heels clicked loudly on the payment as she made

her way toward Ben's car.

Severine shut the door and relaxed back in her seat. "I should feel bad about interrupting you guys, but...I'm really not."

"You two are going to hell for that stunt," Ben mumbled as he pulled back onto the road.

"Hey!" Lily protested.

"Take it back, Benji. I'll have you know that our stunt has been working for years. Why, I've had cats, baby gerbils, pet wildebeests, and like tonight, imaginary brothers that were in dire straits!" Severine said.

"She's right. Our calls save lives," Lily stated solemnly.

"You guys can drop me off back at the dorms, if you want," Severine offered. She was already exhausted. Adding third wheel to the list of tonight's activities didn't seem fun.

"Nah, it's no big deal." Ben glanced at her in the rearview mirror. "We're just getting some pizza with a few guys."

"Cool." Severine looked down at her dark green sweater dress and knew she was overdressed. It was too cute of an outfit to waste, even if she'd look out of place.

They parked, and Lily waited for Severine to get out. She took in Lily's bomber jacket, paired with a flowery top and jeans.

"You look cute tonight."

Lily rolled her eyes. "Well, I have a hot date...at a pizza place."

"Benji pick this place out tonight?"

"Do you think I'd voluntarily come here?" Lily asked sarcastically.

The minute Ben held open the door, Severine could hear the combined mixture of voices. It was packed with people. Severine followed alongside Ben and Lily as they were guided toward the back. A long row of tables had been placed next to each other. Severine recognized a few faces from around campus.

A loud whistle rang the room. Severine looked at Chris. "What the hell, Save-ah-reen! You've been holding out on me!"

He sat in the back. Severine made her way to the open seat close to him. "Hey, where are Dumb and Dumber?"

Chris answered instantly, "Thayer's coming later. He had a date with this hot freshman. And I think Macsen's playing some game or something."

She wasn't surprised Thayer was out with a girl. Their treaty didn't include sincere. He could go out just like she could.

Things with Macsen didn't end how she wanted—she wanted him here tonight. Parting on a bitter note with him just felt askew.

"I'm surprised Thayer can walk in a straight line after last night."

"Ah dude, it was epic!" Chris rubbed his hands together just from the thought. "I've never seen him that wasted."

"You're such a good influence, Chris," Severine deadpanned.

"Hey!" Chris objected. "I didn't drag him to the bar. He suggested it."

Severine snorted and grabbed a piece of pizza from his plate.

There was a low hum of conversation in the room. It tempted her to text Macsen—she wanted someone to talk to and she wanted to clear the air with him.

Severine grabbed her phone and immediately her hands moved across the screen.

I'm with everyone at Charlie's. Get over here!
I've already eaten. Had Chinese.
I'm choking on all the male testosterone! I repeat, get over here now!

Wimp. Be there soon.

Even though he couldn't see it, she smiled at her screen. He brought a smile to her face. The thought of seeing those chartreuse eyes made her jolt in excitement.

"Ten o'clock." Two hands rounded over her shoulders. They fit perfectly. "You're already finished with your date? I'm shocked," Thayer declared in her ear.

The chair next to her was open, and Thayer's body filled the seat. Severine cut him down with a glare. "We're not talking right now."

"Because?"

The real Thayer was back in the shadows. Severine was now faced with the pretext that he exhibited for the world. He was a chameleon. No one could mask his or her emotions better than him, save Severine.

Severine pretended to go along. That's all she could really do. "You knew he was some puppet momma's boy. They're the worst!"

He pushed up the sleeves of his flannel shirt. "You called him Will?"

"Yeah, that was my first sign he was a freak of nature!"

He laughed silently, but his shoulders shook up and down.

"You could have warned me about the name thing," Severine grumbled.

"You didn't ask if he was still breastfed, so I didn't tell," Thayer corrected.

Severine grunted and crossed her legs. It took one action of movement for his eyes to zero in.

"So how was your date?"

Thayer wiped his hands with a napkin. Funny, his plate was still empty. "Amazing. I'm thinking about taking her to my parents' tomorrow. Maybe picking out china patterns the day after that."

"Your mom will be so happy to know that you've

found love...on a street corner. Like a modern day *Pretty Woman*."

"My parents will go into a coma if I ever bring a girl to see them."

A waitress placed a beer in front of him. Severine frowned. "Weren't you hung-over this morning?"

"Uh, yeah. It's been ten hours, I think I've recovered." He took a deep gulp and flicked his eyes away for only a few seconds. "You wanna sit next to Mac?"

There he went again. Giving her the choice, making her nothing with his questions. Severine would be a shell of what she once was if she talked to him any longer.

Macsen walked around the table with his baseball cap firmly on his head. All his dark hair was covered. Severine was getting used to it; it was part of his signature style. Thayer nudged her arm and raised a brow for an answer.

Severine barely moved her head. It was a gesture no one else around them would notice, but he saw it. Thayer quickly removed himself from her side.

"She's been waiting for you, little brother," Thayer bit out.

It was Severine's turn to wipe her spotless palms. His words were sharp and jabbed into her emotions.

"You seem...dressed up," Macsen remarked and looked around at the people in the room.

"Can't a girl look good?"

Macsen shrugged. "Sure."

"She had a date with William Pratt," Thayer replied from across the table.

Chris busted up laughing. Severine stared at Thayer with a somber expression. He would never make anything easy for her.

"No shit?" Chris said with a big mouth full of pizza. "You had a date with him?"

"I'm glad everyone thinks this is hilarious."

"Oh, it is," Chris said and cracked up again.

"So you didn't have fun?" Mac asked.

His arm was pressed closed to her side as he asked such an innocent question. Severine still kept her eyes glued to Thayer. She could take another emotional step towards Thayer, but that would get her nowhere. At least, nowhere she wanted to be. He would conquer her. Deluge everything she thought a relationship should be.

Severine wanted something apparent. A link that was undemanding and fulfilling all at the same time. When she turned to Macsen, Severine swore on her life that she was making the correct choice. "Mac, you wanna go?"

Macsen paused mid-order. His light green eyes tried to decipher Severine's mood. Finally, he slowly nodded his head. "Uh...yeah sure."

Chapter Eleven

Severine stood up and buttoned her jacket. She kept her gaze focused on the belt of her coat, cinching it securely. Thayer's eyes were centered on her. Her fingers gripped the strap of her purse tightly, her toes curled in her heels as she walked out of the room with Macsen. Thayer's eyes still bore on her, through her, around her. She didn't have to look to know. He looked past the surface of her skin, down to the true marrow of her thoughts.

Macsen led the way. For once, Severine let someone else take the lead. She wanted to turn back and shout out to Thayer to reach for her. But she walked through the door Macsen held open for her. When he let go of the handle and let the door shut behind them, Severine clutched onto the notion that any friendship, future, or hope for her and Thayer was eradicated.

You're making the right choice.

But if she was making the correct selection, why did her heart feel so indignant?

Her mood was obvious. Macsen was silent as he reached for her hand. He held it gently between his own. She could slip away if things became too much, if the walls of her choices came crushing down. Macsen would treat her feelings with easy care. Just what she craved.

Don't break me, please, Severine silently pleaded as they walked closer toward his truck.

She slid into the cab and glanced around at the cloth of the seats. The air around her smelled of cologne, one of her favorites.

Macsen jumped into the driver's seat, and the truck started up loudly. He rubbed his hands together and quickly turned on the heat.

"I never pictured you driving a truck," Severine said.

"Did you picture me in a tiny car? Too compact; I need room."

Severine nodded and glanced at the logo on the steering wheel. "Chevy, no less? My grandpa would approve of you," she joked.

Macsen's lips thinned as he gripped the back of her seat, looked out of the rear window and backed out. "This is Thayer's. He's a getting a ride home from someone else."

Her smiled dissolved. Of course, this truck was his. Even when she tried to get away from him, he still managed to torture her.

"So, do I wanna know why you texted me to come meet you, and we only stayed there for five minutes?"

"I missed you?"

Macsen drummed his hands against the steering wheel, while the red light in front of them cast a faint glow on them. He glanced at her with a confused expression. "What's really bothering you?"

"We left everything so awkward this morning."

"You left this morning," Macsen pointed out.

Severine crossed her arms and angled her body to stare at him. "You were being a dick."

He drove with one hand and moved his head to the side to rub his neck. "Sev, come on. Just tell me what the fuck's wrong."

"I can't understand why you're pissed off!" Severine finally confessed. "Why? Tell me why, because I'm all confused right now."

He pulled up near her dorm and turned the engine off. Finally, Macsen turned his head to look at her. They had never been alone, never given the opportunity. But how he stared at her made her nerves and aggression fade. The two emotions scattered away like leaves in a storm.

Everything happening between them was what she wanted. Severine shifted across the seat, more than drawn. After tonight, she wanted to be close to him. Whether he knew it or not, Severine had made a decision for herself. That choice was looking her in the face with a look of reverence.

His cell phone buzzed, and he glanced down at the screen. Severine followed the action and saw the name Haley flash across the screen.

Severine shifted backwards. Macsen tossed his phone onto the dashboard and grabbed her leg to keep her from moving. She sat perfectly still, not moving, not breathing; just taking in his large hand holding onto her like a lifeline.

Severine released a deep pent-up breath. It sounded like a pant. "You talk to her a lot?"

He shook his head no, his eyes never leaving contact of where their skin touched. "It's not how you're making it sound."

"Macsen, I made it sound like nothing. Just asking."

"You said it in that way. You know it, too." He hesitantly withdrew his hand and leaned against the driver side door, clearly making himself comfortable. "Of course, we talk. But, like I said, not in the way you're thinking."

"What am I thinking?"

His shoulders moved up in defeat. "I don't know. I'd love the chance to figure that out."

Severine didn't want to talk in circles around Macsen. She slid closer, and he watched her movements.

"You have that chance."

"Do I really?" Macsen asked harshly.

Severine took a deep breath. All around her was Thayer. She clenched her eyes shut and placed Macsen's hands in her lap. "Who am I with now?"

Even though he was confused, he pressed closer. "For now, me. I'll give you that. But I want you to only see me."

Afterwards, Severine might regret showing how vulnerable she truly was. Macsen gained the right to view her secluded side. Shoving aside all her fears, Severine pressed closer. Her knees were positioned against his thigh. She unhurriedly guided his hands to her waist. His grasp was gentle. She wasn't a bird; she wouldn't break in his hands. Severine wanted to tell him, but things were hanging on by an already thin string.

"I do only see you, Macsen."

"Can you tell me what's reflected in your eyes isn't the truth?"

Severine nodded but never answered him. Her lips pressed against his. And he was ready for her.

Her hands gradually moved away from his shoulders to his hair. She knocked aside his baseball hat, gripped the strands of his hair, and kissed him deeper.

The consequences of this will come later. The hell with it. All of this felt right. He could collect her. Keep her forever. It might be the greatest capture.

She felt his tongue press against her lips, felt the stubble scattered across his cheeks scrape her skin as he moved his head and deepened the kiss.

Her legs lifted, and she was straddling his lap. His body already seemed accustomed to her. She sank closer to him, just as he moaned into her mouth. All of this was fresh to her. Severine did what felt natural. This moment was a soothing balm to her feelings. She felt sated.

Her fingers drifted down his stomach toward the hem of his shirt. Everything in this moment was running like clockwork.

Until she caught the scent of Thayer.

Severine jerked away. Her back hit the steering wheel with a thud. She had encouraged this moment. Wanted it. Now it was tainted by her thoughts.

Macsen leaned his head against the headrest and stared at her with wide eyes. He swallowed loudly. Severine watched his Adam's apple bob reflexively. She was still wrapped around him, close enough to feel how hard he was.

Inside, her heart was racing. Not from the kiss. It felt natural and easy. Instead, Severine felt as if she had been caught. She glanced around the cab, still paranoid.

Could Macsen feel her worries?

Severine finally moved off Macsen and adjusted her dress. She stared straight ahead, staring at nothing.

"What did we just do?" Macsen's question came out with a slight shake. She wanted to take his nerves away. She had enough for the two of them. Her conscience urged to kiss him again, to snatch back the moment that was taken away from them.

She didn't play upon her actions. Her heart warned her not to get any closer. "Are you worried?"

When he turned to look at her, Severine could see his honesty, even in the dark. "I'm worried about nothing." For a second, he paused and raked a hand through his hair. "Where are we now?"

I have no fucking clue...

Even as her mind yelled out those words, Severine wanted to hold on tightly to Macsen. Everything about him was right. He was absolute in himself. Right now she needed him. People like Severine, the ones that were too strong, too prideful, needed someone to keep them grounded. Maybe all this time, she had been waiting for someone like him.

With each thought that tumbled through her mind, she mentally shifted back. Severine was too ahead of the game. It was just a kiss. But it represented everything she could have, if she just plunged from the ledge of her fear and simply trusted.

Her smile was sweet as she nudged him, but her stomach was in complete knots. "I don't know? The same place we were before we kissed?"

Those green eyes of his, that were normally so cheerful, bore straight at her with determination. "And what just happened...it meant nothing?"

This time, Severine veered away. He clutched her arm tightly from moving any closer to the door. Severine clenched her teeth together and frowned at his hand. She snatched her arm away. "No. Not nothing. Haven't you ever just kissed anyone without anything happening afterwards?"

"Someone like you?" Macsen shook his head and slammed his baseball cap onto his head. "No. No one like you."

"Me neither."

"Tell me. Why the hell aren't we together?" Severine gave him a bare expression. He pushed closer, his voice hushed. "You didn't enjoy that? You haven't been waiting weeks to do that?"

Severine was slow to respond, but when she did her words came out firmly. "I've been thinking about it."

"Then what's wrong?"

I'm sitting with you, in your brother's truck. His presence is painted everywhere. "Nothing is wrong."

"I know that's bullshit."

"It's not bullshit!" Severine snapped back quickly. "You think that kiss hasn't already changed everything?" Her mouth opened up to say more, and on second thought, she meshed her lips tightly together to keep any more words from escaping.

"Go ahead, say the rest. What are you thinking?" Macsen said in a rush.

"I'm really thinking nothing except that maybe,

maybe if I hadn't kissed you, you wouldn't be saying this stuff right now!" Her finger blindly reached behind her for the door handle. The air hit her lungs with a contentment she had never experienced. Thayer's essence couldn't smother her now.

She forced the door to close with her hand. It never slammed shut.

Macsen scrambled out behind her and ate her footsteps in seconds. Severine whirled around. Only inches separated them from crashing together.

"That was going to happen in the long run."

Her mouth opened before she could think her words through. "By your watch, it would have been later."

Severine wanted to regret it. But when he wrapped both of his hands lightly around her neck and kissed her aggressively, it was hard to feel anything but a strong amount of satisfaction. His lips moved over hers persuasively. Everything about this kiss made her positive she would be agonized by it later. Who would ever really want to pull away from this? Severine's arms wrapped her arms tightly around Macsen's waist. This time, she was the one to moan out her approval.

He was the first to pull away. With their noses touching, he rasped out, "What's there to really think about?"

Chapter Twelve

Everything could change in a minute.

Sometimes, it took longer than sixty seconds. Sometimes, it took a day, a week, and even months...

For Severine, everything was altered after her kiss with Macsen. It was only a few weeks ago. Five, if she was being truthful. Their relationship was an existence that, up until a few weeks ago, she doubted could be possible for her. Because, let's face it, Macsen had passed her record relationship by four weeks.

Anything consequential always came with a sacrifice, though, and for Severine, it was something she had never had in the first place.

Things might have been strained before with Thayer, but there had always been a certain amount of understanding. All that understanding was wiped clean. If Severine entered a room, Thayer found a reason to leave.

He was doing her a favor. Severine would repeat that over and over. Everything about him was slowly ebbed out of her world. Macsen made it all easy. He adjusted the transition with a quality that made Severine have a permanent grin on her face.

She wrapped her dark brown hair around her shoulder and quickly twined the separated strands together. She smirked at Macsen in the mirror. "What?"

He leaned against the bathroom door and smiled at her. "Nothing. I'm just watching you."

"Yeah? I don't work well under pressure," Severine teased back.

"You realize it's the pool, right?"

"You realize that my hair without serum looks like I visited the Magic House, right?" Severine tightened the band around her hair and nodded at her handiwork. "Believe me, I'm doing everyone a favor."

"Everyone?" Macsen came up behind her and ran his hand down the long braid her hair created. "It's kinda cool."

"Tell me I'm not the first girl you've ever seen with a French braid."

He looked back at her in the mirror. It was beginning to be their form of communication. "Yes, Sev. But I've never seen it done. My mom always had someone come over to do her hair."

"Plus with a brother, I doubt there was much curling and braiding going on."

His hand pulled away and settled down by his swim trunks, "Mmm."

"Can you get out of here? I gotta pee."

"Consider me gone," Macsen laughed as he backed out of the crammed space.

Muffled voices sunk through the cracks of the door and into the bathroom. Severine quickly finished and leaned her ear against the wood.

She was snooping. There was nothing else to it. It was Thayer's low-pitched voice that ensnared her attention.

"What the fuck. I thought you guys left?"

"Obviously, we haven't...we'll be leaving soon. So chill."

Their voices became hushed as they stepped away from the door.

If she didn't realize before how fucked up the Sloan brothers were, she knew it now.

Did all siblings have such hostility toward each other? Was there a whole microcosm for siblings? Something she'd never understand?

She had never witnessed the two of them getting along or even having a friendly conversation with each other. What problems ran through their family that made it impossible for them to forget? Severine wasn't one to go asking away over someone's family. Hers had enough drama and strain to create its own soap opera.

She walked out of the hallway and down the hall. Thayer's door was closed.

"Ready?" Macsen asked from the living room.

Her gaze rested a second longer on the barrier restraining the two of them from connecting. Severine turned to smile at Macsen. "Yeah, let's go."

* * * * *

"Get in."

Severine carefully walked around the edge of the pool. She sat and dipped only her legs into the clear water. "Are we going to prison for this?"

Macsen ducked underneath the water and swam where her legs kicked. When his head reappeared, he slicked back his hair. Droplets covered his face, including his inky black lashes. His eyes stood out even more. Severine felt like she was watching an ad for new cologne. Whatever Macsen was luring her to buy, she'd willingly purchase.

"What's with you and prison?"

His palms moved up and down her thighs. The water felt like ice against her dry skin. "I'm afraid one of you Sloan brothers is going to get me in trouble."

He shifted closer and placed his body in between her legs. "I hope I'm the only Sloan brother you get in trouble with."

"You are."

Macsen eyed her baggy t-shirt. "Are you really gonna swim in that?"

"No." If she watched him carefully, Severine could see crimson stain his cheeks. "Macsen, am I making you nervous?" she crooned softly.

"I'm hardly nervous right now," he said deadpan. His eyes kept staring at her t-shirt with such concentration. It was like he was hoping to make it disappear if he glared at it long enough.

Severine gripped the hem of her shirt in her hands and lifted it above her head. Her yellow halter two piece, with black ties on her bikini top and bottoms stole all of Macsen's attention. His response was exactly what she wanted.

She collected swimsuits like a regular hoarder. It was a healthy addiction. Because of her obsession, she was able to see Macsen enchanted. His eyes stayed focused on her chest.

Quickly, she took the plunge and submerged her whole body in the water. Even though the pool was heated, the water still felt cold to her skin. It was a rush to her body. Her head reached the top, and she took a deep breath. Macsen waited with a grin on his face. "Glad I brought us here?"

Severine waded toward the deep end and floated above the water. "Mayyybe."

"I used to swim in high school," Macsen admitted.

This was the first memory he was sharing with her. They'd been together over a month, but she was getting to know him slowly and effortlessly. Severine loved the pace they were keeping. She switched her position and moved closer to him. "So you're a lover of water?"

"In high school it was my only obsession."

"Were you nerdy?" Severine asked jokingly.

Macsen snatched her around the waist. "As nerdy as

I am now."

"Clearly, I should've been scoping out the library in school," Severine whispered.

He looked at her with an expression filled with craving. For the two of them, it was the same—they were each other's propensity.

"You're trying to kill me with this suit, aren't you?" His fingers traced the edges of material covering her breast, drifting from the middle of her chest and back toward her straps, repeatedly.

Her skin became covered in goosebumps, and Severine tightened her grip on his forearms. "That's exactly my goal." Her voice was confident. It completely covered up the crazy feelings pounding inside her, making her heart rate escalate.

Her feet could touch the bottom. Wrapping her legs and arms around Macsen was what her body chose. Immediately, she settled her cheek next to his neck. "So you swam in high school." Severine glided her hand across the still water around them. "I wanna know more about you."

His fingers linked around her thighs, keeping her firmly to him. "Germany, New York, Virginia."

Severine raised an eyebrow. "You've been everywhere."

"Can't stay in one place too long."

"And your brother..." his muscles tensed underneath her cheek. "He probably loved it all."

His shoulder moved upward. "Didn't affect him in the least."

"Tell me more."

"Everyone in my family is tall," Macsen answered instantly.

Severine dropped her feet to the bottom, and she looked up at him. "Come on," she prodded.

With fingers dripping wet, he brushed a few strands sticking to her neck, back into her braid. "I wanna just focus on you. There's no other reason than that."

"Too complicated?" Severine asked.

"They're just memories." His head ducked down, to her lips. "I like the path I'm on now."

"The one with me?"

"The only one."

Chapter Thirteen

"I love this look on you," Lily admitted happily.

"Stress? Blood shot eyes?"

Classes were kicking Severine's ass. Hard. She was keeping up as best she could, and from her haggard appearance, it was her body that was taking the toll. Thanksgiving break was coming up, less than a week away. She kept repeating those words in her head. A break from school was what she needed so much right now.

Lily hip-checked her and adjusted her bag slung around her shoulder. "No, you in a relationship. You've been so quiet and content."

"It's something new for me, that's for sure." Severine looked down at the ground. She needed a break from all the books. And if she read one more note card, she was going to flip out.

Ben walked toward them and kissed the top of Lily's head. "Hey, baby."

Thayer was with him. He looked close to bolting. Severine wanted him to stay.

"So have you decided if we're going tonight?" Ben asked excitedly.

Lily smiled back at him. "Not yet."

Now Severine's curiosity was piqued. She walked

back in step with everyone. "Where?"

Ben's head peeked around Lily. "I want to try a new bar out near The Ville. Lily was supposed to ask you to come."

"I'm getting ready to ask, psychopath. You just snuck up on me like a ninja." Lily flashed Severine a small smile. "You up for going?"

Severine was opening her mouth to say no. Thayer laughed lightly. It was acerbic, filled with bitterness.

Looping around Lily and Ben, Severine walked in step with Thayer. For a quick second, her body brushed against Thayer's. He clenched his lips tightly and kept his gaze forward. "What, Thayer? Enlighten us with your words."

"Macsen? Going to a bar willingly?"

"Who said I was taking him?" Severine sniped out. She was still talking to his profile.

It was theatrical of her, but he seemed different in her eyes. A sharper edge was laced within his words and expressions. Maybe Severine was really seeing how it was to be hated by him.

"I assumed since you're attached at the hip he'd tag along like a puppy dog."

"You realize that's your brother, right?"

Thayer barely looked interested in their conversation. "Severine," he sighed out, "that means nothing in our family."

"What does that mean?" Severine pounced on his words with eager determination.

When he kept walking without answering her question, Severine reached out and grabbed his arm. It got his attention immediately.

"Tell me," Severine demanded. "What makes you two so hateful with each other?"

His hand grabbed each of her fingers, one by one, extracting them away from his arm. He stared at her the whole time. At the end, her hand was cradled inside of his own. Severine felt paralyzed. "Am I with you?"

Thayer's words made her feel empty. Instead of responding, Severine stayed silent, keeping her hand enclosed in his.

"You just answered your own question," he said as he broke their contact. His fingers brushed her skin as he retreated back. "Ask the one you chose."

He walked away, and Severine watched him. She was a coward for saying nothing back, but her pride stopped her from admitting he was right. Everything he said was the truth.

Her phone vibrated in her pocket. Severine jumped and answered it without looking at the screen.

"Hello?" Her voice sounded raw and unused.

"What's wrong?" Macsen asked on the other end.

Severine stared at Thayer's back as he extended the distance between them further and further. "Hey, let's go out tonight." It wasn't a question, but a demand. She wanted to prove to Thayer that she and Macsen could mix their two worlds together, and that he didn't know his brother as well as she did.

"Ah..." Macsen said slowly. "What are you thinking?"

"Ben and Lily are going to a new bar that's just opened."

"That seems fun to you?" Macsen teased.

She wasn't smiling. "Yes."

"That's not really me, Sev."

Severine leaned against a tree and glanced up at the bare limbs. "I saw you at that frat party, and you got drunk with Thayer and Chris a while ago," she pointed out.

"I think I've only been to about four parties in my entire college life."

"So that's a no?"

"You can still go," Macsen offered. "I'd rather see you, though."

"I'm not studying. My brain is about to explode,"

Severine warned.

Macsen laughed. "We won't study. I promise."

"Where are you?"

"Walking," Macsen said evasively.

"Walking where?"

"Toward you."

A big hand pushed her into a body. Macsen. "Yuck! My face is in your armpit!" Severine's anger slowly disappeared as she looked up at Macsen.

"Then it's probably bad I forgot deodorant?"

Severine made a face as she dropped her phone into her coat pocket and peered back at him.

Macsen looked almost anxious as he smiled at her. "Come over instead. I'll let you watch some stupid reality show or whatever you want to do."

"Why are you in such a chipper mood?"

"It's almost break. I know we're both ready to leave this fucking campus."

Severine mussed up his windblown hair. "You sound so torn up over being apart from me."

His arm wrapped around her shoulder. This time, he kissed her head. "That will be the only shitty part about break. I'm hoping you'll send me lots of sexy texts."

"Sexting? Yeah. That's not gonna happen."

"Video chat?"

Severine bent her arm back to link their fingers together. "Maybe. Between turkey day and listening to my mom, grandma, and Aunt Rachel bicker about things, it might be hard to squeeze you in."

"Then I should probably make the most of my time with you now?"

"Uh, you should always do that. Every day you should be kissing the ground I walk on," Severine teased.

"I should just quit studying and follow you around everywhere?"

Severine reached up and nudged the bill of his cap. Sunlight shone brightly in his eyes, and he squinted at the light and immediately lowered it back down. "I'd love for you to follow me everywhere. You can sit behind me in class and give me all the answers to my test. I won't have to study so freakin' much."

"I can't do that. But I *can* take you somewhere tonight."

"Where?"

"Do you always need to know what I have planned?"

"Yes, all the time."

Macsen rolled his eyes and wrapped a hand around her waist. "It's a fun place. Trust me, you'll enjoy yourself."

Chapter Fourteen

Everything was quiet on this side of town. What did Macsen consider fun?

"Come on, let's go." Macsen held his hand out. Severine anxiously took it and slammed the door behind her.

"Where the hell are we?" Severine asked him with an antsy tone. Her eyes flicked around the streets. The buildings they passed were boarded up and closed. Most of the neglected spaces had their windows broken out and expletives spray painted on the sides. "I don't want to die, Macsen. I happen to like my life."

Macsen gripped her hand tighter and smirked at her. "You're not gonna die."

"Then why are we practically running?"

"You're not gonna die out here. But I definitely don't suggest that you shuffle across the street with what you've got on."

"What's wrong with what I'm wearing?"

He lifted a black brow and gave her a once over. She could count on the fact that his cheeks were probably tinged red. They had been together for weeks, and he still acted nervous around her. But for Severine it meant that she had authority over him. It felt good. Any more power and she'd become drunk off of it.

"It's a lot of skin." Macsen motioned to her sweater.

Severine didn't have to look down. Her coat was buttoned up practically to her neck. She was tempted to unbutton it. Just to tick him off. "Are you secretly taking me to meet your parents? Are they Amish and will shun you when they see me?" Severine teased.

Macsen chuckled and shook his head. "No. But I think even if I introduced you to my parents, they'd shun me for my thoughts."

"I've shown more in my bathing suit," Severine pointed out.

"Yeah. But that was just in front of me. Right now, it's torturing me."

"Yeah?"

He loosened their fingers and wrapped his arm around her shoulder. His mouth moved to her ear right as his hand crept past her shoulder and past the edge of the collar on her coat. "Like right here." His index finger touched the edge of her breast. The feel of it zinged through Severine. It burned past her shirt and bra. "I know there is a mole there, and it's driving me crazy that I can't see it."

Her heart slowed, and her steps followed suit as his finger drifted closer to her nipple. When he was a second away from making her collapse in the middle of the sidewalk, he moved his hand back to her shoulder. "I swear," he whispered, "my fingertips could sink right into you."

The resistance she had painstakingly constructed to ward off foreign emotions swayed around her. It wasn't as solid as she thought. Severine wasn't used to feeling unprepared.

Macsen hummed a tune as they walked down the street. He seemed lost in his own world, unaware that she was proclaiming to herself repeatedly that she had the jurisdiction to control her life. A part of her wondered if she'd ever be able to unclench the ropes holding her back.

"Here we are." Macsen's hand found hers. He pulled her to a bar slammed in between two brick buildings that had both seen better years. The sign above the door flashed on and off. After a few tries, Severine finally made out the name—Kasser.

"You're taking me to a bar?" Severine let out a dramatic sigh and pretended to fan her face. "If you keep spoiling me, I don't think I'll be able to resist you tonight!"

Macsen picked up on her sarcasm and let out a deep breath. He smiled widely as he opened the door for her. "You'll get why I brought you here," he explained as he walked closely behind her into the bar.

For a weekday, it was busy. It wasn't packed body to body, but many of the seats were filled with people talking. No one looked up as they walked down the open space in between the bar and stage.

They picked a seat close to the stage. Severine noticed the instruments and people testing out the three microphones placed around the stage. Macsen's face beamed with contentment.

Severine smiled at his happiness. He was close to bouncing around like a young child. "Why are we here, Mr. Sloan?"

His palm positioned itself to its most favorite place: the back of his neck. He rubbed it a few times and nervously moved his feet up and down. "A buddy of mine found Kasser a few months back. I try to come when a certain band plays."

Severine turned in her chair and glanced at the stage. "What's their name?"

Straight, white teeth came into view, and Severine discovered the small dimple on his left cheek. "Skinned Knees."

His grin was contagious and made Severine's lips turn up into a wide smile of her own. "Skinned Knees.

That sounds rocky. Are they going to be screaming out all their songs? Should I have brought some earplugs?"

"Easy with the questions. No—to the earplugs. And a massive *hell no* to the screaming."

"Will I like them?"

Macsen leaned back in his chair and crossed his arms in front of his chest. With a thin gray t-shirt paired on top of a black long sleeve thermal, his style was comfortable, but hot. Severine looked down at his arms. The fine dark hair that coated his arms shone against the bright lights of the stage.His arms shifted to rest on his stomach. Severine lifted an eyebrow at the sinew of muscle that became easy to see. *Thank you, bright lights.*

"Wait to hear them, will ya?"

All the lights in the room turned off. Severine couldn't see her own hand in front of her. "Oh God. Did this place lose electricity? Are we going to get slaughtered by the village idiot?"

"Relax. The band is coming out."

"And they need complete darkness? Because I have to say, that kind of gives me the creeps."

"Just wait," Macsen whispered.

A second later a spotlight came on and illuminated the stage, and nothing else. A guitar started to strum, and the drums picked up soon after. In total, there were four guys on the stage. The attention was directed on the lead singer. He grabbed the mic and held it between his hands as he started singing a song unknown to Severine.

The tune was catchy, and soon Severine's foot moved up and down to the beat. She leaned over to Macsen and cupped a hand to her lips, "They're a lot like OneRepublic."

He nodded his head and focused back at the stage. "They're great, right?"

For two hours they listened to Skinned Knees, and Macsen's smile never left his face. Severine could've stared at him the whole night.

When they left the crappy bar, Severine sighed and looked up at Macsen's profile. "I didn't know you had this side to you."

"What side?"

"A love for music. Do you play any instruments?" Severine asked.

"Ha. Fuck, no. My mom pushed me into piano lessons as a kid. It's definitely not my niche. I'm better off being a spectator."

"What other part of you have I yet to discover?" Severine teased.

He shrugged, trying to appear shy. When his arms reached out, he snatched her up easily and dangled her in the air. Macsen made her feel as light as a ballerina. Severine yelped and let out a laugh.

He kept walking, and her elbows lightly rested on his shoulders as he slowly walked them further from the bar. "I'm thinking about taking you in between one of these buildings," Macsen admitted.

Many factors should stop her from smiling at his declaration. They were in a dangerous part of town ranked up there as number one. But she could think of nothing else. Her one good reason escaped her mind as Macsen turned to the left and guided them into the dark alley, away from the streetlights.

Her feet touched the ground, and she felt the uneven concrete beneath her feet. She felt as broken as it looked. Macsen matched her steps until she felt the side of the brick against her back. "Scared?"

He moved closer, until her body was covered from the world. Severine shook her head. "No."

Macsen nodded and reached out to loosen her scarf. The red piece dangled around her neck like an unknotted tie. Cold air tickled her skin. Severine kept her mouth shut to prevent the gasp from escaping. Goosebumps broke across her skin, and she knew he saw it. He saw everything.

Two calloused hands settled at the base of her. Macsen turned his body to the side. Her throat contracted against his palm. "Sometimes I think you should be scared of me."

Severine flashed her eyes up to his face. His fingers methodically rubbed her skin, and she prayed her eyes wouldn't close from his touch. "Why..." Severine licked her lips and tried to speak firmly. "Why should I be scared of you?"

"You give me control, when I don't know what do with it. I can barely dominate you, how could I ever have authority over us?"

"Don't ask. Just take what's in front of you," Severine urged. And if he didn't, she gladly would.

Before she could finish her thoughts, he firmly kissed her. His lips and tongue went to a limit and pushed the boundaries of any other kiss before this one. Her arms became bands around his neck, and she stood on her tiptoes to return everything he was giving her.

She could feel how hard he was. He pressed himself against her leg, and Severine moaned. He pressed her against the wall until a gasp escaped her lips. The buttons of her coat became unbuttoned, and his hands shaped her body with frantic touches. His hands grasped her breast and teased her until she couldn't remember her own name.

Severine. I'm Severine.

She jolted back and panted out heavily. "See." Her smile was weak. "That wasn't so hard."

He pressed against her and laughed out in between breaths. "I think I have to disagree with you on that."

When they moved away and walked back to his truck, Severine demanded her heart to slow down. But it didn't.

She sketched this moment into her mind, because nothing could be so perfect. Nothing could stay right, and last.

Chapter Fifteen

Given the chance, her heart could start a tune with its erratic beating. Severine wanted this high to stay forever. And as long as Macsen remained by her side, that feeling would never leave. When she glanced across the couch at Macsen, she smirked.

"Stop staring."

"Why?"

"You're distracting me," Macsen replied with his eyes glued to his laptop.

For the past hour, the two of them had studied. Severine's brain was fried. Macsen's obviously hadn't shorted out. His fingers flew across his keyboard. Occasionally, he would glance at his notes before bringing his concentration back to the words on the screen. He looked rushed and typed furiously.

Severine smiled. "You're going to break your keyboard, Macsen."

"I'm trying to finish so we can really spend some time together."

Severine sighed in response and settled her legs into his lap. Macsen barely seemed to notice, and leaned forward only a little. She felt his stomach and wiggled her feet. He only smirked and typed away. She watched his hands type faster until he pressed the period button, turned to her, and placed a hand firmly on her knee.

"Yes?" he said while he smiled.

"I think we need to go out this weekend." Severine gave him her most charming smile.

He watched her thoughtfully and smirked. "Really? We need to?"

"Lily invited us to go to a new club. I said yes."

He scratched the top of his head and frowned slightly. "Wasn't there a bar they all went to only a few days ago?"

Severine moved close enough that her legs dangled off his thigh and spoke quickly, "Yeah. But it's Friday. The weekend!"

Macsen stared at her with a blank look.

"We need to do something, or I'm gonna lose my mind! I know it's not your scene, but, come on!"

"I'm not what you'd consider the slickest dancer."

"So what? No one will notice. You can dance with me. Closely," Severine emphasized slowly. He stared at her, and she drifted her foot up his thigh. "I'll be wearing a really short dress," Severine threw in for good measure.

Macsen groaned and leaned back. "I don't know."

"It will be fun, Macsen. I promise," Severine pleaded lightly.

"I'm sorry, Sev. You should still go."

"What? And dance by myself?" Severine jokingly asked as she inched her foot upward.

He grabbed it from going any further. "You'll dance with someone and have fun."

"And that doesn't make you jealous?"

"Yes," he growled and tackled her to the couch. "That's why I won't think about it."

His lips moved to her neck and kissed everywhere. She could feel how hard he was becoming and tried a cruel tactic. Her hips moved against his thighs. His groan sounded tortured.

"You won't have to think about it if you come with me," Severine said in a seductive voice; one that usually gave her everything.

She watched as his eyes glazed over as he stared at her. He broke eye contact and placed his forehead on her neck. "It's not my thing, Sev."

"Macsen, it's fine, don't worry." Severine paused to wrap her arms around his waist. "I'll go with Lily and Benji. It will be great. I'll be that annoying third wheel and barge in on all their conversations."

His expression was sweet. The stubble he always forgot to shave gave him an edge. But with him right now, Severine saw how gentle he truly was. "Are you going to lose control like you did near Kasser's?" Severine whispered.

Macsen pulled back and narrowed his eyes. "Are you questioning or wanting?"

He'd probably never push the boundaries too far with them. Severine sometimes wanted that other side of him to come out. She wanted him to be confident and sure. She was his; there wasn't any other way around it. Her hand dragged the zipper of his hoodie down, and Macsen sat up quickly.

His cheeks turned red, as he took off the piece of clothing. He raised an inquiring eyebrow in Severine's direction. She nodded her head and grabbed the hem of his dark green t-shirt. "I want, Macsen."

Next his shirt came off. Severine's eyebrows immediately jumped up in approval. He was lean, but more muscle was hidden underneath his shirt. His hands rested on his knees, and Severine noticed his abs flex at the movement. When he shifted closer, Severine wrapped her arms around his neck and grabbed onto the dark strands that were always covered with his trademark baseball cap. He suspended his body above hers. "What do you want me to do with you, Severine?"

Her full name never came out of his mouth. When it did, it captured her attention immediately. Her body reacted to the deep, soothing sound of his voice. "I'd like anything you could give me."

"I don't know if it'd be enough for you," Macsen admitted quietly.

Severine pulled him closer. Her lips grazed against his slowly. He still hovered above her, but his warmth started to push closer and closer to her until their bodies touched fully, completely.

Soon, his lips and his tongue skimmed across the seam of her lips. Her arms pressed against his back with force. Macsen's hands drifted down her stomach towards her jeans; his hands were insistent as he undid the button and lowered the zipper.

Through his pants, she could feel him. Severine shifted her hips, and Macsen's hands moved across her stomach toward her hips to hike them around his waist. His belt buckle dug into her skin. Even with the discomfort, Severine didn't want to pull away. All of this felt too good. She didn't want to ruin this.

The door crashed loudly against the wall. The wall rattled, and Severine's body completely froze up. She didn't have to look up to know who was home.

Macsen shifted slightly to discreetly move the waistband of her jeans together. All his action did was rub his dick against her thigh.

His eyes fluttered shut, and Severine smiled. "Bonjour," she whispered in his ear.

"It's not funny."

"Given our situation, and the fact that my pants are close to falling off, there's nothing left to do but laugh."

He went to respond. Chris's loud voice boomed across the room. "Fuck, dude. You're going to break the door off the hinges!" Chris exclaimed.

Thayer was hidden in the kitchen while Chris noisily dropped his things and kicked off his shoes.

"How are you two love birds?" Chris asked with a cheesy wink. He openly stared at the two of them entwined on the couch.

"Well, I'm effectively finished for the night," Macsen mumbled against her neck. He pulled away and discreetly zipped up Severine's pants. "We were doing great until you guys came barging inside."

Chris held his hands in the air. "Hey. Don't give me that shit. I didn't slam the door like a maniac!"

Things slammed around in the kitchen. Severine cringed over the action. She knew what was in store next: Thayer being pissed off at everyone, glaring in Severine's direction and avoiding any room that had her in it. All she wanted to do was leave. Thayer braced his arms on the kitchen island and practically snarled at Severine. "Don't you have a fucking home?"

Severine wanted to choke him. "No, Daddy Warbucks, I don't. Are you offering? Do you guys want a fourth roommate?"

Macsen laughed next to her and grabbed her around the waist. "God, I'd love that. You could be my roommate. I'd have no problem sharing my bed with you."

Thayer slammed his mouth shut. For a minute, it look liked he was going to say something else. Nothing came out of his mouth. The muscles corded up his arm clenched tightly, and he pulled away from the counter, disappearing toward the refrigerator.

Severine grabbed Macsen's hand and squeezed. "I should go."

He shook his head no, and Chris laughed and dropped himself into the lazy boy. "Are you sure? Your make-out session was so hot."

Severine gave him a dull stare. Chris only laughed harder.

Macsen cringed and nodded his head. "Yeah. You should go."

"Aww. You're leaving so soon?" Thayer crooned from the kitchen entrance. He stood with his arms crossed. Sweat dampened his shirt around the collar and sides.

Severine looked away quickly and mumbled a quick good-bye to Chris. There was no point in saying anything to Thayer. Every day things became more and more tense between them. One of them was going to snap soon, and it'd be an ugly battle of wills.

"I'll see ya later." Macsen said as he hugged Severine tightly and kissed the top of her head.

"Yep." She wanted to ask him, hell, plead with him to come with her tonight. She kept her lips pressed together and quickly whispered in his ear, "I'll stop by later, okay?"

Macsen nodded his head but looked confused.

Severine waited until she was halfway to her car to take a deep breath. How long could the tension keep going before it became impossible to take?

Chapter Sixteen

"Slow it down! It's cutting off my circulation," Severine choked out.

Lily smacked her hard on the butt. "This is what you get for wanting to be all smexy. Spanx are a bitch, but trust me, you'll be thanking me later. You don't want your cooch hanging out for all the world to see."

Severine shifted in the mirror and took in her figure as Lily helped her with the sleeves of her dress. It clung to her body and stopped mid-thigh. Around her waist, the material was ruched, making her hips and waist look even tinier.

The color choice tonight: a dark red. Pretty much Severine's entire wardrobe consisted of dark colors. It just wasn't her to flounce around in bright pinks and oranges. The selections she chose were a reflection of her—daring and edgy.

A few rollers were still scattered in her hair. Severine plucked them out and dropped them onto the floor. With some hairspray—and a few spritzes of perfume, Severine was done.

Lily made a cat call. "Lookin' good, babay!"

"At what point does breathing become easier?" Severine questioned as she searched for a pair of heels. Bending was impossible. Instead, she sprawled down stomach first to search around in her closet.

"By the time we get to the club, you'll be used to the discomfort," Lily stated confidently. "But I must say, you look killer in that dress."

"I hope the ER doctor says that as he cuts me out of it, trying to save me as I slowly suffocate." Severine found the shoes she wanted and held her hands out. "Help me."

Lily rolled her eyes and hefted her up. "You'll be thanking me later."

Severine chose not to answer her. With both heels on, Severine checked out Lily.

"Too much?" Lily asked nervously.

"Nah." Severine grinned. "I like it! Printed dress with a skinny belt...completely you," Severine stated.

"I know!" Lily squealed out happily. If her parents saw her, they'd probably shit a brick and kidnap her from ever seeing the light of day again.

In a passing glance, anyone on the outside would judge Lily's incredibly strict family life. With parents that believed women needed to be covered, and males took care of everything, Severine had been around them to know that those things aside, they loved all four of their kids so much—almost to a suffocating point. They'd never see it, but Lily had more light in her eyes away from them.

Severine gathered her hair to one side and slipped her arms into her black, ruffled coat. The way it flared out at the ends made it the perfect coat for tonight. "I can't believe I'm actually ready before you!" Severine called out. "I think we're trading places."

"Noo..." Lily drew out. "I would've been ready before you. I had to help you mold your body into your dress!" Severine threw a coat, and Lily snatched it mid-air. "See, I'm ready now."

"Then let's go!"

"My, you're in a rush," Lily stated calmly.

"I need this night. This week has been rough."

Lily gave her a side-glance and nodded her head. "So is Macsen coming?"

"No. It's not his thing."

They made it to the car, and Lily stopped at the driver's seat. "And you're going without him?"

Severine settled her arms on the car roof. "I'm still my own person, Lily." Doubt still etched her friend's face. "I'm not going to change myself for him."

"Sure. I understand." There was so much more to her words. Lily was agreeing to agree, just to make Severine calm.

Severine gritted her teeth together and slid into the passenger seat. "I wanna stop by and say hey to him."

Lily snorted. "He's going to crap himself when he sees you."

"That's the reaction I was aiming for—to see my boyfriend poop his briefs."

"He wears briefs?" Lily gave her a funny look and turned back to the road.

The harmony between them was back. It caused a smile to spread across Severine's face. "I don't know! I was just using that as an example."

"I bet he does. He seems like a brief dude."

"Well, when we go in there you should ask, since it's clearly important."

"Wait...shouldn't you know that? You're the one dating him."

Severine adjusted the sleeves of her jacket. She knew what Thayer wore. A flash of the night on his bed came into her mind. She slammed her eyes shut before looking up at Lily. "We haven't gotten to that point."

"Oh, stop." Lily put her hand up. "That sounds so middle school."

"That I haven't slept with him?"

"Uhh...hell yeah!"

"My bad. I'll change that tonight. Just to make you happy."

"You don't get it," Lily groaned dramatically.

"No, I really don't."

"When I just asked you if you had done anything with him, you shrugged your shoulders, and acted like I told you I was getting a bone marrow transplant."

Please stop talking about this. "It's been a rough week. Okay?"

"I'm just saying that passion needs to be there," Lily stated firmly.

"I know that." Severine didn't need to be told. Their moments together should ignite the room. But they weren't there. Macsen and Severine were so close to reaching that high. "It's kinda nice not doing anything yet."

"You are shitting me!" Lily sputtered out. She pressed her foot against the brake. Severine was close to making best friends with the dashboard.

"Chill out about it. It's not a big deal."

Lily grinned sheepishly. "Sorry. I just can't believe it."

They were coming up to Macsen's apartment. Severine was starting to feel antsy. It showed in the way she tapped her foot repeatedly. Her conversation with Lily made her want to reaffirm her relationship. Severine wanted to see him to know she was making all the right choices. Was there an empty space between them?

Lily parked, and the two of them practically ran to the door. Severine didn't bother at knocking. Her presence was a common thing around here. The heat blasted Severine as she entered the door.

Chris peeked his head around the kitchen island. He took in Lily and Severine's appearance and whistled loudly. "Mac! Hey! Some girl who's out of your league is here for you!"

With a sub in hand, he walked out of the kitchen and winked at the two of them before walking down the hall.

Macsen was walking down the hall before Severine

could settle into a stool. She stepped forward and took in his blue jeans and gray hoodie; some t-shirt of a band she didn't know showed underneath.

Slowly, Severine turned and let Macsen inspect her.

"You look hot," Macsen said thoughtfully. His hand wrapped around her waist as he pulled her close to whisper in her ear. "Why can't you wear that to class?"

What do you feel with him? Her conscience prickled.

Severine laughed and quickly kissed the corner of his lips. When she looked at Lily, she saw her friend staring at Macsen ruthlessly. No words were coming out of her mouth, but as she tapped her heel against her bar stool, Severine knew she was taking stock.

Macsen let her go and walked toward the kitchen. "Hey, Lily."

"Mac," Lily said with a nod.

Severine kicked the chair Lily sat on. When she got her attention, Severine mouthed, "What the hell?"

Lily played dumb and turned away. "So Mac, you still have time to get ready if you wanna go." Her offer was sweet, but it was all a test.

He was completely unaware and leaned on the cluttered kitchen island. The cap of his Gatorade was in his fingers. He spun it repeatedly. "Nah. I'm good staying here."

"I gotta pee," Severine announced awkwardly.

Lily raised her head. "Cool."

She had to get out of there.

The bathroom door was shut. Severine knocked and tried to open the door.

"Uh, someone's in here," Thayer shouted out gruffly. It broke through the door and reached her ears and blasted her heart enough to make it stagger with uneven beats.

"I have to go pee, Thayer!" Severine called out.

An awkward pause passed between them. "Tough! They have bathrooms at the dorms, right?"

"Thayer! I'll release my fluids right here."

"That's fucking nasty, Blake," Thayer shot back.

Chris popped his door open and peeked out, shirtless. "Please don't! It's my turn to vacuum this shit hole."

"Chris, I would never do that to you. I'll just go into Thayer's room." Chris laughed and shut his door, just as Thayer ripped open the door.

His eyes moved over her, up and down. It completely overpowered her. "The bathroom awaits you."

Severine nodded but didn't move. He was dressed to go somewhere. Pieces of his hair were styled to give the appearance of bed head. It was the kind of hair that a girl would yank during sex. Severine wanted to reach up and tug him close to her.

Severine was reminded why the two of them in close proximity was always an epic fail. She felt about as thick as tissue paper. All Thayer had to do was tap her on the shoulder, and she'd cave into him. Behind her, she leaned a hand against the wall. "You took forever."

"Yeah, well it's my fucking home. Maybe Macsen needs to buy you a bag of Depends."

"Oh!" Severine crooned. "Straight to the heart!" Her body was solid again. Leave it to a good bout of sarcasm to toughen her skin. Severine stepped forward and motioned for Thayer to scoot. "You wanna move out of the way?"

"You wanna ask nicely?"

His cologne wafted toward her. Severine inhaled greedily.

Her soul was tar black. She was going to hell for enjoying being near him. It was hard to care how tarnished her thoughts were. Thayer brought a dangerous stream of urgency through her body. She was back on that rollercoaster ride. There was no way she wanted to be absent from what she was feeling.

Her arms were laced behind her back, firmly kept to

herself. At times, hands-off was more threatening than a simple touch. That time was now.

Severine clenched her hands tightly together. "Thayer, let's be honest, do either one of us know what the word *nice* means?"

The conflicted male from weeks before was gone. Thayer used his height and stepped closer to tower over her. Severine inched her shoulders back, her posture straighter than ever. "You want me to sing hymns in your honor?" Severine couldn't tell if he was serious. That's how solid his poker face was. His fingers reached to her shoulders and lifted a lock of her hair away from her neck, to join the rest of the strands hanging down her back.

Macsen's touch was merciful. Every move was thoughtful. Thayer's vitality was barely contained. Severine glanced back up at his sharp features. She saw the truth. He wanted to do so much more.

"Wouldn't that signify that you know me?" Thayer asked as he took one step closer. "How much of me do you know, Severine?"

"Never mind. I don't have to go that bad." Severine turned on her heels, away from the conversation she had initiated.

Thayer was close on her heels.

When she came back into the light of the living room, Lily still sat chatting with Macsen and Chris as they ate.

"Oh, yeah!" Lily rushed out happily. "You're here." Macsen stared at her and then behind her. Severine watched the rush of emotions pass across his face. Lily kept speaking. "Why are we wasting time? It's ten. Let's gooo!"

Macsen stood close as Severine gathered her clutch and re-buttoned her coat. "Maybe you should stay here." His eyes drifted down to her heels, back to her face, and back down again.

Severine patted his stomach, and he grabbed onto her hand tightly. "It will be okay, Macsen. I promise to not dance up on some other guy."

Chris popped his head around the corner. "Uh...I don't know if Macsen told you yet, but he gives you full permission to dance up on me."

Macsen flipped Chris off and spoke quietly to Severine, "Okay, you're not going."

With a firm kiss to his lips, Severine tried to show him that everything would be okay. She was with him. One night wouldn't change that. By the time they broke away, Macsen was dazed and red in the face.

The moment was seconds away from leading to his bedroom, until Thayer dropped an arm across Macsen's shoulder, effectively breaking her contact from him.

Thayer's gaze at Severine was a challenge. "You shouldn't worry, little brother, Chris and I will take care of her." He closed his words with a smirk, and Severine's stomach dropped. The ride was over.

"Wait...you're going?"

"Does that bother you?" Thayer immediately asked.

Both brothers gazed at her. Both brothers waited for her response. Severine wasn't a squirmer, but she was close to shifting her feet and gazing down at the floor.

"No." Severine held tight to her clutch. "I just figured there was a nearby Déjà Vu Strip club that was calling your name."

Chris slapped Thayer's arm. "Dude, is there really?"

He was the perfect buffer for the strain framing its way around the three of them.

"Okay. Seriously, I'm going to leave everybody if they don't start hauling ass!" Lily griped.

Severine turned to Macsen, giving him the tightest hug her strength could remit. There wasn't enough time to hug her worries away. "I'll call you later. Okay?"

Macsen's smile was abrupt. He nodded, looking more unconvinced by the second.

Between Thayer and Chris, she walked out of the apartment with Lily impatiently honking her horn.

"Are you thinking of ways to get out?" Thayer questioned innocently.

He was in the mood to taunt her every action. Severine was in the mood to fake a cough and call it a night.

"Nope." *You need to leave, Severine.* "I'm looking forward to tonight."

Chapter Seventeen

Why did Severine torture herself with heels?

They had only been there for an hour and her feet were practically howling at her to chuck the damn black heels across the room and never let them see the light of day again. None of her bitching would change her mind. Severine would keep complaining, and she'd keep buying them just for fashion's sake. Having piles of shoes that she hardly wore made her nonexistent bank account weep and then caused her to spew out every cuss word her grandma hated.

But it channeled her inner Carrie Bradshaw to lust after every Jimmy Choo and Christian Louboutin available. She got lured into the vicious cycle the minute she stepped into them. She felt lithe and in complete control of her body. It doesn't hurt to know that when anyone is clad in a pair, everyone stares. They just demand attention.

With one last sip of her drink, Severine pushed it aside, stood on her already blistered feet and walked back to the dance floor. The energy was toxic. Everyone fed off each other as they danced on the floor. She scooted around people before spotting Lily and Ben close together.

Chris stood by them with a girl wrapped around him.

He caught her coming in their direction. "You going to dance with me, Save-ah-reeen?" Her name came out slurred. Chris was officially shit-faced.

"Ask me in an hour."

"You told me that an hour ago!" Chris shouted over the music. For being drunk, he had a freakishly good memory.

"I'm feeling generous." She held out her hand and he took it, brushing off the girl on him like a piece of lint. It didn't piss her off—the random chick blended in with everybody else. "I'm gonna warn you once. If your hands go below the waist, I'm giving you a swift kick to the baby maker. And then the world will never be repopulated with tiny Chrises."

"Follow me, Save-uh-reen!" He held her hand in the air, led her to the floor, and shouted loudly, "Move aside, bitches!"

His actions were hyper. It was a cross between someone doing a jig to get the spider over his or her shoulders, and a person trying to stop, drop, and roll.

By the time they were walking toward Lily and Ben, Severine was exhausted. "You dance like you're choking!" Severine shouted in his ear.

"It's the only way to go. It attracts the ladies!"

"To do the Heimlich on you?"

Chris wiggled his eyebrows. "Does that involve her tongue in my mouth?"

The smile on her face faded. Thayer was back at their table with a girl. Everything about her was the opposite of Severine. Short in stature, a bob cut curved around her chin, and from where Severine was sitting, she could see her eyes were dark.

She wanted to snarl her upper lip in disgust, but it was hard to hate someone when they were unaware of the havoc they were creating. The small girl turned and spoke with Thayer. He nodded to her, but focused on Severine.

It was provocative; taunting her to say something. Severine wanted to—there was nothing to lose. Alcohol swam in her veins, making her words come out quicker than normal.

Thayer wanted a response. He was waiting to bite.

The longer she remained silent, the more apparent the frown covering his brow became. Finally, he turned away. His back became hunched as he leaned down and talked to the girl. The picture they made was all wrong.

"Are you having fun?" Lily shouted across the table.

"Of course!"

"Do you miss Mac?" Chris asked and mimicked tears coming down his cheeks.

Both the midget and Thayer turned back to the conversation. Severine subtly shifted her shoulder, blocking them from her sight. "It'd be great if he was here."

"Dancing has never been his thing," Chris confessed. "You think I'm bad? Watch Mac dance. He'd make me look like Usher."

"A drunk Usher," Ben shouted out.

"Come dance with me, Usher. I want to see your spaztastic moves again." Severine dragged him away from the table. Away from Thayer.

She stayed there till two in the morning.

"My feet are going to fall off," Chris moaned. "Unless you're putting out tonight, I'm going to sit down."

Severine held on tight and tugged on Chris's hand. "Come on. One more dance."

Chris bounced back on his heels and examined Severine. "Dude. Is this about Thayer?"

"Dude, no."

"I'm not blind."

"But aren't you drunk?"

"Correction. I was drunk, and then you challenged me to a dance off for the past hour. Buzz is long gone."

Severine saw the clarity in his eyes. "To answer you,

no, nothing about Thayer. It's just weird to be the third wheel." Severine glanced over where everyone stood. "Weirder than I thought."

"You no longer have to worry about that. Now that I'm going home with no pussy, you can tag along with me."

With more people leaving the building, Severine was able to listen in on Thayer and the tag along. Her name was Vanessa. Vanessa shared a class with Thayer. Vanessa just loved this club. Vanessa was having a great time. Severine walked to the bar and sat down at one of the open barstools.

Impatiently, she drummed her fingers against the counter. The bartender raised an eyebrow in her direction. "I need a shot!"

"Of?"

"Anything."

He absently nodded his head and handed it over as if she was already gone to the world. Unfortunately, she was not. Severine still had eyes that could see clear as day.

Quickly, she gulped down the liquid and chased it down with Coke. It burned. But after a second, the taste wore off, and it wasn't too bad at all.

Maybe it was fifteen minutes later...maybe an hour. Chris firmly held her elbow. "Easy, killer. We're gonna leave."

"Where's Lily?" Severine shouted.

"I'm here," Lily calmly replied. She linked arms with Severine, and the two of them walked out the door.

Severine eyes stayed glued to Thayer and Vanessa. They walked in front of her, almost taunting her to say something. Jealousy was a dark, ugly color. It was ironic that it was finding its way into Severine's heart. She was finding out a lot about herself tonight. Her only hope was that she'd remember none of it tomorrow.

A girlish laugh sounded in front of them. Lily

tightened her grip on Severine. "I shouldn't have brought you here tonight."

Liquid courage could work in peoples' favor. For Severine, it was a bad, bad thing. "That girl." Her finger could barely stay straight as she pointed in front of them. "I've never met her."

"I know," Lily agreed.

"She's a bitch."

Thayer heard every word. Severine wanted to hate him. But it was hard to when it was a move she would've done herself.

With her hands tucked deep into her coat pockets, she walked past the couple. Her steps were careful, and she made sure to walk far from where he stood.

"When we get back," Lily murmured, "take a shower and go to bed. Tomorrow you'll feel better," she promised.

No amount of promises could kick the fear that had taken up in her conscience. It was rooted deep and refused to leave. She had something with Macsen she needed. Doubts could snatch her thoughts from where she wanted to go, but the facts were clear. Severine's armor was slowly being ripped away. One more cut, and she wouldn't know what she wanted anymore.

Chapter Eighteen

"Lily! Answer your phone," Severine shouted out.

"It's not my phone, genius." Lily moved across her bed, grabbed Severine's phone, and chucked it at Severine's head.

"I hate you so much right now." Severine picked up her phone, trying to stop the annoying ringing. "Yeah?" she finally groaned.

"You're still asleep?" Macsen asked.

"We got home really, really late."

"I can tell."

Severine could barely hear him over the sound of wind hitting against his phone. "Where are you?"

"I'm getting ready to pick you up and take you to get some coffee."

"I look like shit," Severine warned. As she stated the truth, she shuffled like an old woman across the room to grab some clothes and her toothbrush.

"Sev, I don't care. I wanna see you. Did I mention coffee?"

"You know the way to my heart," Severine grumbled.

Macsen laughed. "See you soon."

"Sounds good." Severine moved around as quickly as she could to get ready. Her normal routine was out the window, and she hurriedly put the bare minimum of makeup on, brushed her teeth, and yanked on a pair of black leggings and a loose white tunic. The girl that looked back in the mirror didn't look half bad.

By the time she dropped her stuff off at the room, Lily was passed out and snoring. Loudly.

Severine still nudged her. "Hey. I'm getting some coffee with Macsen. Do you want some?"

Lily made a face and rubbed at the eye crust near her eye. "Yeah." She waved her hand in the air. "How are you not still out of it?"

Severine slid her arms into her purple, pleated coat, the only one in her closet that didn't smell of smoke. She covered her messy hair with a black snowcap. "I have no idea."

Still huddled underneath her sheets, Lily peered at Severine. "You doing okay, though?"

"Why wouldn't I be? Just had too much last night."

"I'm not asking about that."

"About me acting like an idiot? Yeah, let's just forget about that."

"Ten-four."

"No truck driver talk, please. Too early for that," Severine called out from across the room, escaping the conversation before Lily became any noisier.

Macsen waited for her outside. She hurriedly walked over and got into the truck.

"Did you really just wake up?"

"Yeah. I just set a world record for getting ready."

Sitting across from her with a sweet smile was what Severine needed to see. She leaned over to kiss him innocently and pulled back.

"Hey. You can't do that and move away," Macsen said with a grin.

Severine stayed in place, wanting him to kiss her again. When he did, his fingers wrapped around her neck as his tongue entered slowly. Everything about it teased her. Severine clutched at his arm and pushed him closer.

His body willingly gave way. He moved the armrest up and clutched her hips tightly in his large hands.

Now wasn't the best time for a kiss like this. Severine stopped caring the minute his hands lifted her sweater up and spanned her waist. The contact made Severine grab his face and move her tongue into his mouth hurriedly.

Macsen choked out a laugh and slightly pulled back. His green eyes focused on her face, and Severine let out a gasp as his hands crept towards the edge of her bra. For nine in the morning, it could easily become the hottest kiss.

"Hi," Macsen pronounced leisurely. His fingers drifted across the lace of her bra. When it seemed like he was going to touch her further, he went back to teases.

"Did you really want to get coffee?"

"That was the intention." He pulled his hands away. They left a lingering touch on Severine's skin.

Severine pulled her sweater down and turned to buckle up. She needed that kiss. It was an affirmation that everything she was arranging in life should have Macsen included.

His hand reached across the seat and fastened their hands together. "So, did you have a good time last night?"

It was impossible to tell if his question was innocent. Severine answered anyway, "Yeah, it was great. I danced with Chris till my blisters had blisters."

"That's what he told me."

What else did he tell you? Severine nodded and scanned through his iPod. All the titles were unrecognizable to her. She pressed play anyway. The song wasn't half bad. It filled the silence building in between the two of them. "Chris was an idiot," Severine replied casually.

"So, no dancing with Thayer?"

Severine frowned over at him. "No, he was with

some girl."

"If Vanessa wasn't there, would you have, though?"

Her grip on his hand tightened. "No."

Have you known her long? How do you know her name?

As he turned into the parking lot of the coffee shop, those questions demanded her full attention. She'd never get the answers because those questions weren't hers to ask.

The truck idled and then became silent. Macsen stared straight ahead. Severine shifted her eyes around, trying to figure out what was going on between them. It could be something small, something so insignificant that you'd never look twice at the issue, but for Severine and Macsen, it was an ugly mess.

"What are you mad about?"

Macsen swung his head in her direction. All his insecurities were exposed and laid out in front of them for her to see. It was dirty; an expression Severine never wanted to see on his face again. "Am I everything you want?"

Her eyebrows rose, and she instantly responded, "Of course."

Disappointment showed in his eyes. She'd answered too quickly. "Answer me honestly. Not with the first thing that comes to your mind."

"What do you want me to say? I gave you the truth. You're making this a harder question than it needs to be."

"Am I?"

Her patience was wearing thin, along with her guilt. All her fears about who she might be were so close to cutting through the facade she had worked so hard to create.

"Yes!" She shouted out.

"Are you sure that Thayer did nothing?"

"I think you're freaking yourself out." Severine faced

the door handle. Macsen locked it.

"Don't," his demand came out gently. Even when he tried to be firm, he was kind. Severine would, sooner than later, run over him.

"Don't be an ass," Severine paused and glanced at his tense body. "Where is this even coming from? Why are you freaking out over nothing?"

Macsen's anger blasted out of him, and he punched his steering wheel. It was only a smash. It was enough. "My brother worries me!" His breath came out harshly. "I catch every look he gives you. He went last night because of you."

"Is this about last night? You could've come! I wanted you to come!" Severine shouted out. If Macsen wanted anger, she could give him just that. "I can't control what he does!"

"I think you control more of him than you'll ever fucking know!" Macsen shot back.

Severine didn't need to hear that. Her hands wanted to reach up and cover her ears. There were no take backs. It would all replay later when she was alone. "I'm not doing this with you. You can stay bitter about this. But I'm leaving in a few days for break. I'll leave whether you're over it or not."

When she glanced at those chartreuse eyes, the ones she always loved, they looked crushed. "You'd leave knowing that you could potentially be the fire in my life? The same fire Thayer needs—even though he has no fucking right to it?"

"No," Severine grounded out. "I'm leaving with it on my shoulders. I ignited it all."

He unlocked the doors, and Severine practically clawed her way out. She was leaving early for break. There was no way she was staying on campus any longer than necessary. Her mind needed clarity from everything that belonged to the word Sloan.

Chapter Nineteen

"Are you sure you want to leave so early?"

"Yes." Severine slammed her trunk louder than necessary. "You don't have to leave campus if you don't want to."

Lily shrugged and tossed a duffel bag into the backseat. "Nah. I kinda miss my siblings."

"Kinda?"

"Give it a few days, and then I'll be begging for you or Ben to come pick me up."

Severine stretched out her legs and started up her car. "Let's get out of here."

"Don't you want to say good-bye to anybody important?" Lily asked.

"Nope. Macsen and I already talked this morning."

That was a lie. But Severine wasn't going to tell Lily the truth. After coffee yesterday, Severine decided to pack up earlier than planned. Her exams were done. Lily was finished. Why stay and do nothing when they could hit the road?

Severine was ready to escape.

*   *   *   *   *

Blue Mound, Illinois was just the same. Nothing about her small hometown had changed. Most of the time, that was a bad thing—it was the reason she had applied to schools out of state. But as she drove down the main street, she realized it was the security she wanted the most right now.

Her back ached, and she needed to pee about four hours worth of chugging on a Big Gulp. Behind her a CASEY'S sign flashed, but she wanted to be home. She wasn't getting out of this car until her mom's driveway came into view.

Her heart tugged with relief as she parked in front of her childhood home. Her mom stood tall on the porch and waved wildly like a happy person...like a mom who had missed her child.

Would Macsen be missing her?

She wasn't going to waste any energy on him. They were better off with a few days of no communication.

"You're waving like you're happy to see me!" Severine shouted out as she leaned against her car door.

Dressed in a sweatshirt and jeans, Clacy walked down the pathway. Her thick, dark brown hair fell down to her shoulders. With the sun shining brightly, she shielded her eyes with her hand and squinted at Severine. "It's been a while, kiddo."

"I know," Severine grunted out. *God, did she know.* She grabbed her book bag and hooked her arms through the straps. If she kept herself busy, she wouldn't latch onto her mom and never let go.

"Do you have anything in the trunk?"

"Yeah, just a couple of things." Severine moved her seat forward and started piling her bags out of the car.

"Severine Joi!"

Severine wrapped a bag around one shoulder and grabbed another before she looked at her mom. "Yes?"

Clacy stared down at the trunk. When she looked at Severine, her light blue eyes were sharp. It didn't take long for her to get back into Mom mode. "This isn't, 'a couple of things.' This is trash bags FULL of things."

"Okay. Let me rephrase that then." Severine trudged toward her mom. Her shoulders were already aching from the weight of her bags. "I ran out of suitcases, so I packed some items in trash bags. I honestly don't see what the big deal is."

"Are you taking all this back ?"

"No. I'm gonna keep some crap here."

"More things for me to store away?" her mom asked with false enthusiasm. "My day is complete."

"You know you missed me."

Clacy carried the bags with her and wrapped her arm around Severine. She smelled like cookies. She was her mom, and she was the same. Severine blinked back the wetness in her eyes and returned the hug.

Chapter Twenty

It was eight in the morning, and she was already up.

Severine stared at the pattern on her ceiling and listened to the sound of the TV playing downstairs. Her mom had always gotten up freakishly early in the morning. Even though it was Thanksgiving, her routine would stay the same—it would just also include a crap load of food to make.

Lying on top of her nightstand was her phone. She swiped a finger across the screen. There were no missed calls. Severine wasn't surprised. She and Macsen hadn't parted on good terms. A large part of her was tempted to call him, to ask how his day was going. The truth was she didn't want to fight with Macsen, and she didn't want him to worry about Thayer. But she couldn't make him see the truth. Severine could tell him until she was blue in the face. But he'd have to be the one to realize it.

She stretched slowly, her muscles sighing in relief, and went downstairs to the kitchen. "Morning," Severine scratched out.

"I didn't think you'd be up at a decent time. How'd you sleep?"

"Good. I forgot how comfy my bed was."

"Your dorm bed that uncomfortable?"

"It's like sleeping on box springs," Severine

grumbled and poured some coffee. "So what's the plan for today?"

Her mom stopped frantically mixing the ingredients in front of her to blow the dark brown strands away from her forehead. She was already getting stressed out. "Grandma's coming over soon. She's bringing a few pies and seven-layer salad."

Severine's mind may have been shaken, but the mention of food perked her up. "Ah! Sounds yummy. She makes the best pies." She grabbed the cinnamon creamer from the fridge and poured too much into her cup for it to be called coffee. "Who all is coming this year?"

"Your aunt and uncle, a few of your cousins, two of Grandma's sisters..."

"Not too many."

"I'm still gonna be on a warpath to clean this house," Clacy grumbled.

"Then I'm going to go change." Severine carried her coffee mug with her up the stairs and listened to her mom shout.

"Get down here after you're done!"

Her room looked like it had vomited up her clothes. All the trash bags were emptied. Things she wanted to leave here or take with her back to the dorm were mixed together. Severine walked over to the piles and her suitcase. You never dressed to impress on Thanksgiving. It was an unwritten rule for all women. Or, at least for Severine it was.

Thanksgiving was National 'Eat Until Your Top Button Pops Open Day.' She grabbed a loose v-neck sweater and a pair of blue jeans, before ratting her hair up into a low ponytail.

Her phone was still sitting where she had left it last. If Macsen was waiting for her to call, he might as well give up now. Severine was the one domino no one could push down. Macsen wouldn't be the first one to try. But she did want him to be the last to fail.

The front door slammed, and she heard the bustle of her grandma. Severine smirked and walked back down. A smile was on her face by the time she whirled into the kitchen, just in time to hear her grandma bossing her mom around.

"Grandma!" Severine announced loudly.

Her grandma stopped talking to look in Severine's direction. When she saw her granddaughter standing there, she lit up.

Severine may have a few physical attributes from her grandma: her dark hair, green eyes, and light complexion. The similarities ended there. Her grandma was a petite woman. Severine outgrew her by the time she hit fifth grade. She was someone you'd never want to underestimate, though. Severine had watched her lecture grown men at church and leave them with tears in their eyes.

She moved around the kitchen island, and Severine took in her blue-jean skirt that ended at her ankles and a sweater that was buttoned up modestly. Severine could see her reflection in her grandma's glasses, but it wasn't hard to look past that and see her grandma's narrowed eyes. Her mind was still set in a time where women should always remain covered up. They'd never see eye-to-eye on styles of clothing. It didn't change the one thing that stood up against all their opinions and differences. She loved Severine fiercely. It'd be the biggest thing they'd always have in common.

"Severine! I didn't know you'd be here today."

Clacy turned and frowned. "I told you yesterday, Mom."

"Lily and I decided to come home a little earlier than planned," Severine explained before she squeezed her grandma in a tight hug. She was starting to realize that there would hardly be any more moments in her life where she would feel one hundred percent protected.

"Now who's Lily?" her grandma asked confused.

It was getting worse with her. Sevcrine kept a smile on her face, "My friend, Grandma."

"Oh right, right. That pastor's child." She smiled as if she knew the answer the whole time. "Just look at you— you're stunning, Severine!"

"Thanks." She held Severine's face in her hands, and her eyes misted up slightly. Severine grasped her grandma's shoulders and hugged her tiny frame to her tall one.

"Let's bake!" Severine stated enthusiastically.

"Alright, Severine, I need you to get all the ingredients out. Clacy, can you gather them utensils from my car?"

Severine made eye contact with her mom as her grandma called off directions. She may be confused more often, but you bring her to the kitchen and she was back to her old confident self.

Severine enjoyed the moment and gathered everything that her grandma called out. "So how's school going, dear?"

"Pretty good. I have a couple of easy classes and, of course, a few hard ones that keep me busy studying."

"Good, good. You need that. Keeps you away from those boys," her grandma called out as she washed her hands and dried them.

"You're against me dating?"

"Well, does he go to church?" Severine looked thoughtfully at the table. They had never had that conversation. Macsen was too busy letting jealousy eat at him. "Probably, Grandma."

"Probably is no good, Severine. He needs to go." Her voice was no-nonsense. In her grandma's eyes, Macsen was as good as gone.

"I'm lacking in attendance since I started college too, Grandma." In fact, she had lacked attendance in the last few years.

Her grandma looked up at her sharply. "Well, you

need to change that, don't you, dear?"

Severine needed to change a lot about her life.

Chapter Twenty-one

"Severine! It's nine thirty! Lily just got here!"

"Shit, shit, shit," Severine groaned out. She threw a stack of clothes back into her suitcase and tossed it toward the bags that were steadily building near her door.

One glance around her room, and it was just as she left it. She was going back to school, with a mind that had been wiped clean. There were prints all over her. She'd have to deal with that when she got back to campus. She didn't want to deal with it any earlier. But every head was turned in her direction. Severine would have to make a move soon.

She gripped the two nearest suitcases and dragged them behind her. They thunked loudly on the carpeted stairs.

Clacy frowned as she waited for Severine on the first floor. "I once had a beautiful pink suitcase," her words filled with sarcasm.

"Hey! You told me I could have it!"

"That's true. Suddenly, I've forgotten why."

Severine rolled her eyes and wheeled her suitcase toward the open back door. Lily stood on the deck and smiled. "Well, the princess has arrived. I though the plan was to leave by nine?"

"Yeah, well, I had more crap than I thought."

"More stuff upstairs?" Lily asked.

"Yup."

Lily's bags were sitting on the driveway. The fun part was always trying to figure out how to cram everything back in. Severine started piling her bags into the trunk. After thirty minutes of cursing and arguing where to put what, Lily, her mom, and Severine were finally able to fit everything.

"You guys should be going. I don't want you on the road too long after dark." Clacy gave Severine a firm hug and kissed her cheek. She pushed back and stared at Severine for a long moment. She was dressed nice, making it clear she had somewhere to go. Makeup only illuminated her European features. She discreetly wiped underneath her eyes and gave Severine one last hug. "Love you."

Severine clenched her eyes tightly together and kept a smile on her face. "Love you, too."

In the entire world, the two of them were the worst at saying good-bye. It was awkward, and most times, filled with tears. It was better to say, 'See ya later!' It seemed less final.

"Call me when you get back to the dorms."

"I will," Severine confirmed as Lily quickly hugged Clacy.

Severine took a deep breath and pulled away. She was driving to a shit storm of problems.

Lily sifted through her iPod and Katie Costello's voice came through the speakers.

"When we get back, I need to talk to you about something." Her face was alight with a contentment that never went hand-in-hand after leaving her parents.

"Just tell me now."

"Or," Lily dragged out, "I can wait and tell you when we get there."

"Is it good?"

"I'm not telling," Lily sang mysteriously.

"Anything to do with Ben?" This game could be fun on the long trip back to campus.

"Maybe." Lily tapped her fingers on her thigh and watched the road fly by.

Severine pulled out her sunglasses and smoothly put them on. "Tell me, Lily, have you ever wondered what it'd feel like to be a hitchhiker?"

"What kind of question is that?"

"It's a viable question. I'm so close to kicking you out of my car if you don't tell me your big news."

"No! I'm proud that I even went this far without saying anything!" Lily wailed.

"I'll call your parents right now and tell them that you're pregnant and don't know the baby daddy. But that you do know you're having a boy, and you're naming it Glenn."

"That came out way too quickly to be from the top of your head."

"Just get it over with and tell me. I'm already dreading going back."

"Why?" Lily's face contorted into concern. Their joking was pushed aside. Severine was ready to disclose some of the chaos in her world.

"Things are just tense with Macsen." Severine kept her gaze focused on the road as she spoke. It was easier that way. "Everything goes back to his brother."

"Thayer?"

"No, his evil twin, Michael," Severine stated dryly.

Lily barely glanced at Severine. "What's the problem with Thayer again?"

"Macsen thinks there's something more." Severine squirmed in her seat awkwardly.

"Well, duh." Lily put her sunglasses on. They barely stayed put on her pert nose. She twisted her blonde hair into a knot and reclined her chair. She was relaxed, completely at ease. Severine was ready to bust apart at any minute. "That dude wants to have you all to himself," Lily finally added.

Severine finally glanced at her friend, and when she did, her mouth was agape. Her heart was racing with paranoia. How much could Lily see?

"From your facial expression, I can tell that's exactly what you wanted to hear. My work here is done," Lily announced.

"I didn't need that, Lily."

"What? The truth? I know you know. And I know your thoughts are along the same line as his," Lily paused. "Well, that might not be true. He looks like he has some naughty thoughts."

"Do you see why this is so messed up?"

"Yeah. But it's just so hard to care. When a problem looks that good, what's the issue?"

"Hitchhiker!" Severine reminded.

"BUT, since you're my friend, and I love you dearly, I will remind you that even though your *problem* makes a cut off look like an Armani suit, you do have one good thing that looks equally gorgeous."

This complication would always wring her tightly and drop her harshly to the ground. "I know that."

"Do you really?" Lily asked quietly. "You don't have to know anything. It's okay to be mixed up!"

Severine came out with the truth. "When you're mixed up over two brothers, it's not okay. Especially when one of those brothers is your boyfriend."

"So...who do you want?"

"I need Macsen." Severine's words were firm and unwavering. "He's stable—someone I can depend on."

"Yeah," Lily nodded in agreement, "but I didn't ask what you needed, I asked what you wanted."

* * * * *

By ten o'clock that night, her car was emptied out.

Severine's luggage sat at the edge of her bed. The bed that she normally hated now looked like the snuggle bear on the Downy container. Severine just wanted to cuddle tightly with it.

Across from her, Ben and Lily stood, looking ready to pounce on each other at any minute. On a normal night, Severine gave a shit what they did. But all she dreamed of doing was having a sweet, sweet sleep affair with her bed.

Her body dropped to the bed, and her arm covered her eyes. After a few minutes of listening to Ben and Lily murmur quietly, Severine propped open an eye. "What's up, guys?"

Lily jumped, looking ready to rocket toward the sky. Her smile was way too perky. "You know that exciting news that I refused to tell you about in the car, and you threatened to kick me out of the car, but then it was all right because we moved onto another subject?"

"I remember," Severine affirmed with a slow nod.

"Well, I wanna tell you now!" Lily eagerly chanted. Her small hand reached out for Ben's. He beamed at her with tenderness. Severine knew before Lily declared the truth. "I'm moving in with Ben!"

"You're moving in together," Severine repeated back.

Severine couldn't help it. Her eyes drifted back and forth between the two of them slowly. This was a big step, something she had never expected Lily to do. They had planned on sticking out their college life together. This was an issue Severine had never thought about because...Lily was Lily. Moving in with a guy for her, even thinking about it, seemed like light years away.

"Are you pissed at me?" Lily inquired.

"No, not angry. Just really, really shocked. I had no idea that you two were that close."

Benjamin stepped forward. "Severine, I live ten minutes away. I expect that you'll always be there hanging out with us."

"Come on," Severine laughed, "I'm not going to barge in like that!"

"That's what I'm afraid of!" Lily protested. "I want you to come over anytime. I mean it! We won't be living together, but I'm still your best friend."

Any other guy and Severine would be pissed. This was Benji. She was more than okay with him taking over her spot in Lily's life. Her friend was happy; she was moving forward.

Severine *wanted* Lily to be happy with everything in her life and if living with Ben created that, then she'd put on a bright smile.

But it was hard to imagine not sharing a dorm room with Lily and not seeing her all the time.

Severine stood. "I'm happy for you, I really am!"

"Ah! I'm so relieved!"

Severine smiled. "So I'm guessing you're not staying here tonight."

Lily nodded, her eyes gauging Severine's actions. "You promise you're okay with this?"

No, she wasn't okay with this. But her head was already nodding. "I swear."

Chapter Twenty-two

Severine was sticking her neck out. There was no Lily to talk to. Her room felt too quiet.

Her hand paused briefly. Its hesitance told her she shouldn't be here. Severine ignored that warning and knocked loudly.

Thayer answered the door before her hand had even pulled away. Before her was Severine's problem, the source to Macsen's insecurities and Severine's conflict.

"Oh," he stated, "hey."

"Hey," Severine mumbled back. "Is Macsen around?"

His eyes narrowed for a second before leaning against the doorframe. "No. He's out."

Severine shifted on her feet. Thayer seemed to enjoy her discomfort. "Well, I just came over to talk to him."

"You can wait for him if you want to."

Not with you here, Thayer. You scare the shit out of me. "Sure." Severine might regret her choice later.

The entire apartment was quiet. The TV played an episode of Shameless. Thayer went back to sitting in the lazy boy. He looked uninterested in whatever she decided to do.

"This is a great show," Severine announced awkwardly as she sat down on the couch.

Thayer moved his arm above his head in a relaxed position. His arm became more pronounced with muscle. Nothing for Severine was relaxed.

"You're a complexity, Blake," Thayer expressed deeply.

"Because my DVR isn't filled with the Kardashians like the bitches you bring home?"

"What bitches am I bringing home?" Thayer challenged.

Severine ignored his question and asked one of her own. "So, where's Macsen?"

"I don't know. I'm not his fucking nanny," Thayer paused. "Is there trouble on Lover's Lane?"

"No trouble," Severine lied. "I just wanted his help on something."

"On what?"

"My Mac."

"Why?"

"Because it broke," Severine uttered slowly.

"I got that," Thayer snapped out. "But how?"

Severine casually shrugged a shoulder and took off her winter hat. "I sorta tossed it."

Thayer sat straight in his chair. Talking about computers was the one thing she never expected to garner his attention. "What?"

Severine flipped her hand through the air. "It kinda got plucked from my hands, and the next thing I know it was sitting next to the wall."

"So, are you saying that someone took it out of your hands and threw it? Or that you chucked your computer—a Mac, no less—at the wall?"

"You know, I don't appreciate the word 'chucked.' It sounds so hostile."

Thayer stared at her with bulging eyes, like he couldn't believe what was coming out of her mouth.

"Quit looking at me like that!"

"I'm sorry. I guess this is a normal thing for you?"

"No, it's not normal. I just lost my temper. All right?"

"Okay...psychopath."

"You're gonna see me go all Linda Blair on your ass if you don't help!"

"Oh, now I'm convinced," Thayer responded dryly.

Severine looked at him with a dull expression. "Come on, help me out!"

Thayer leaned back in his chair and flipped the channel. "What if I'm just as lost as you when it comes to computers?"

"Are you?"

He flicked his gaze toward her face. "No."

"Okay..." Severine grumbled out. "Let me rephrase my question. Can you help me figure out what's wrong with it?"

"Yup, you threw it."

"Just check it!" Severine snapped.

He shrugged in a 'sure, whatever' way, and Severine quickly unzipped her messenger bag and fished out her precious MacBook. Yes, it wasn't the wisest thing to do: throwing her Mac. But, to say her patience was frazzled to nonexistence was an understatement. It seemed like her computer had decided to stall and slow down to the point that none of her programs were working. Everything shut down without saving any of her progress on her paper. That's what led Severine to give a frustrated scream as she picked up her laptop and threw it.

And here she was, watching Thayer, the last person she pictured messing around with her baby. "So...how long have you had this?" Thayer asked with his eyes glued to the screen as he clicked away on different pages and programs.

"I don't know. I think maybe a year and a half?"

He looked up at her quickly. "And has it always looked like it's been dragged behind a school bus?"

"Look, today is the only time I've caused it physical harm!"

"You're in complete denial," Thayer laughed out and turned her laptop toward her. "See here, Blake?" He pointed at the sides of the computer where pieces of white chips were missing. "I'm beginning to think you really live in the wilderness and trek through some majestic mountains to get to campus each day."

Severine rolled her eyes but smirked at Thayer. "I didn't know you were such a nerd."

"You don't know much about me then."

Severine was beginning to think she knew nothing about the Sloan brothers. "You're probably right," she admitted.

Thayer stared at her sharply for a long moment before turning back to her laptop. His eyebrows practically touched as he focused on whatever he was doing.

Sitting in front of her was a side of Thayer that he never showed anyone. Severine finally noticed his nerdish behavior. There seemed to be so many layers to him. The quiet, content Thayer fit him so much better.

If she stayed around long enough, what else would she discover about the one person she thought she had all figured out?

The silence around them was compliant. As he worked on her laptop, she stole the remote and watched a show on the Style Network.

Silence needed to be filled with noise. She made sure it was never around her long enough, because dead air made someone think. But between Severine and Thayer, the peace pushed away the loneliness that she was starting to feel, the loneliness that Macsen was supposed to never give her.

She kept tabs on Thayer. He seemed to know what he was doing and almost seemed to be enjoying figuring out what was wrong. He looked up and captured her stare. His eyes were questioning. Even when it was something innocent between them, it always crossed a few lines.

The doorknob turned nosily, and Severine whipped her head toward the door. Macsen walked in. He looked the same, with his usual baseball cap on and winter jacket. His cheeks were flushed from the bitter weather. When he saw Severine, he froze. "Hey."

"Hi."

"What are you doing here?" He dropped his book bag on the floor, flipped off his hat and tossed it at the kitchen table. His steps were anxious. Maybe he was as starved as she was. Severine wanted everything back to normal between them.

"I wanted to see you. You weren't here, though."

He seemed unsure where to sit and finally sat down close to her. The outdoors clung to his clothes. It made Severine want to inhale him. "I was working on a project at the library." His eyes did a beeline to Thayer. The color slowly seeped away from his cheeks.

"What are you and Thayer doing?"

Thayer raised his eyebrows at his brother but said nothing. This one was on Severine. "He's helping me fix my laptop."

Macsen nodded his head, accepting her answer. It wasn't believable, not when he was still frowning at his brother.

"What's funnier than you being a serial laptop killer is the fact that you thought Macsen would be able to fix it," Thayer said dryly.

"Screw you," Macsen grumbled and leaned into Severine, glaring at his brother. Severine looked at Macsen curiously. "I thought you liked the whole computer thing?"

"Xbox, Blake. He plays Xbox."

"I can fucking talk, you know," Macsen said with a glare, his eyes clouded with anger. He didn't look like himself.

"Macsen, calm down," Severine laughed.

"Severine's right," Thayer taunted from his seat. Her name sounded favored coming out of Thayer's mouth. "You should really calm down."

Macsen hopped up from the couch like it was burning his skin. "Sev-"

Thayer shut her laptop. The noise interrupted Macsen. It was planned perfectly. "It still works."

"Ahh! Thank you, thank you!" Severine gushed out gratefully. She ignored Macsen's scowl.

"But..."

"But? Don't ruin this victory for me, Thayer!" Severine pleaded.

"But," he continued, "you broke your disc drive."

"How much is that going to cost?"

"If you get it replaced, a shit load."

Severine groaned.

"BUT, and this but is good, if you get a portable drive it's around eighty bucks."

"I can handle eighty dollars." Severine grinned as she placed her laptop back in her bag. She couldn't help her smile. She thought she had destroyed her only laptop. "Thanks so much, Thayer!"

He smiled back. His entire face transformed. Their eyes engaged. And for a few seconds, Severine saw the Thayer before Macsen had walked in. That beautiful smile dimmed out, and he looked at his brother. Everything was washed away as he stood up to his full height. "I need to go to the gym."

"Thanks again!"

He didn't respond and walked out of the room. It was stupid, but the blow off made Severine feel cast down.

Macsen raked a hand through his hair before he slowly turned to look at Severine. "Well, that was cozy of you two."

"Him helping me with my computer? Nothing cozy about it. If you call that cozy then I've been cozy with the Geek Squad at Best Buy for the last two years."

"Sev, you know what I mean." He wiped a hand over his upper lip, looking stressed.

"I really, really don't." Everything between them smelled like rain. A big downpour was coming their way. "I'm not here to fight."

By the slow nod, Severine knew he saw the merit in her words.

Macsen held out his hand. Severine immediately took it. "Let's go talk."

When the door to his bedroom shut, Macsen took a deep breath. Everything seemed different with him. Or maybe all these characteristics were ones that Severine had always skipped over when it came to him.

Macsen moved closer and pulled her to his chest. His face became buried in her hair. He breathed deeply. "I fucking missed you."

Severine moved her head. "I missed you too." Her words were the truth.

When he pulled away, his hands possessed her face. His kiss was eager. It veered on the edge of desperate. His lips licked the seam of her lips. He wanted an entrance. Severine was still catching up to him. She was trying to decipher how she had missed this intensity from Macsen.

Another layer of a Sloan brother was thrown to the ground.

Her mouth opened. Macsen groaned blatantly and guided her to the bed. Severine held her ground. His touch felt like a brand. When she left his room, everyone would see to whom she belonged.

Severine didn't want to be in this role if she wasn't seeing Macsen for who he really was.

"God, I need you. You know that, right?"

"I know." Severine pulled away and walked toward

the opposite end of the room. "Are we going to ignore the fact that we haven't talked this whole break?"

"I thought I was giving you the space you needed."

"No..." Severine drew out. "We left for break with a lot of issues between us."

Macsen snorted and flopped onto his bed. "And that's my fault?"

"No. It's both of ours for letting it get that bad in the first place!" He sat up and stared at her sharply, and Severine sat next to him on the bed. "A kiss doesn't make everything okay."

"This break has been hell, because I thought backing off is what you wanted," Macsen explained.

"All I want is for us to get along... and for you to not let your brother create distance between us. The fact is that I chose you, and I'm with you. I don't want everything that we have to be destroyed," Severine's voice broke. The weeks of letting everything fester came to the surface.

He did a double take at her expression and quickly wrapped an arm around her. "Fuck," Macsen muttered. "You wanna know what I did all break?"

Severine stared at the stubble across his chin and nodded. "Tell me."

"I studied, I sat around, and I thought about you." He moved closer, into her space. Severine let his arms wrap around her. "I've been a fucking dick. I know that. But I don't want what I've said to push you further from me."

The urge to kiss him, to seal away all the regrets, took over her mind. Severine sealed her lips firmly over his and hugged him as tight as she could.

Severine believed his words. This was Macsen. The person she thought she might be falling in love with.

"I wanna know how your break went." Macsen linked his fingers together with Severine's. "Let's get out of here and just have some coffee."

His grin was relaxed and happy, but Severine picked up on the hidden truth even if he couldn't.

Her chest ached with questions. A secret was wedged in between the two of them.

Macsen angled his body close. He bent his head lower so their faces were inches away. "Maybe me and you together is too much."

They stared at each other for what seemed like hours, until Macsen swallowed loudly. "But I think that maybe...maybe together, we could blow everything else away."

Severine did the one thing that really made sense. She grabbed Macsen's head and kissed him to show that she still needed him. No matter how fucked up everything was with his brother.

Immediately, her mouth opened up to him. Severine was aware of every action, every touch. She heard her own moan, she felt Macsen's arms wrap around her waist tightly before he pulled away.

"Severine," Macsen mumbled her name into her hair. "Are you still doubtful of anything else?"

Chapter Twenty-three

Everything was bare: the ground, the trees, everything. They were officially in winter.

School had started back up a week ago.

The one thing she required was back. Slowly, the tension with Macsen dissolved. He'd tell her everything she wanted to hear, and she'd believe every word. She didn't want to take what they were working on and fracture it all.

Severine stabbed her fork at the salad in front of her. Lily sat across from her. A table down was Thayer. It never failed—he was never a great distance away from her. Only now, there was a separation between them that Severine made sure was never breached.

"I'm thinking we need to do something fun," Lily declared. She swirled her fry in ketchup and stabbed it in Severine's direction. "Let's go see an incredibly stupid movie and make fun of it the whole time."

Severine smiled. "I could do that."

"Good. Because I saw that there was-"

Beside her, her phone rang. The screen flashed 'Mom.' Her mom never called her, especially during school. That feeling that formed in your gut when something was wrong festered inside Severine. She didn't want to answer.

"Hello?"

"Severine." Her mom said her name painfully. It declared more than Severine wanted to know. Her instinct was right. Something was more than wrong.

"What's wrong?" Severine asked slowly. Her eyes connected with Lily's concerned gaze. Her hand reached out, and Lily squeezed tightly.

"Honey, I'm sorry. Grandma passed away this morning."

Everyone knows that at one point death will strike in his or her life. Some are struck by it more than once. This was Severine's first time colliding with something so black. Her heart ached. "What?"

She doubted her mom. Doubted that she was telling the truth. Severine stared away from Lily's gaze. Thayer paused eating. His eyes bore into hers with questions.

Severine pulled her head down and rested her forehead against her palm. Her eyes were pooling with tears. She wasn't going to break down with everyone around her. It felt wrong for people she barely knew to see her pain.

She grabbed her bag and hurried to the exit as her mom kept speaking. "It happened this morning. Her nurse went to check up on her, as usual, and she had already...."

"From what?" Severine asked sadly.

"They think it was a heart attack, Severine," her mom replied gently.

Her mind was reeling, but she knew one thing. There was no way she was staying here. Severine took a shuddering breath. "I'll be home tonight."

"Are you sure?" her mom asked brokenly.

"I'm not staying here. I'll be home tonight," Severine repeated.

"I love you, Severine."

"Love you, too." Severine put her phone away and tucked her hands into her shirt.

A coat was placed around her shoulders. Lily came up beside her and smiled sadly. "Is everything okay?"

"My grandma died," Severine whispered.

"Severine, I'm so sorry." Lily wrapped an arm around Severine. "I know how close you were to her."

Severine nodded, trying to absorb her friend's warmth and strength. Lily continued, "Are you going back home?"

"I'm leaving immediately."

Lily nodded her head without any questions. "Do you need anything?"

"Ah no, I'm good." That phrase seemed like the worst thing to say. She wasn't okay. Severine now understood what pain to the heart really felt like. Problems with Macsen, stress of school, none of that mattered. She had lost someone who had been there her whole life.

Sometimes, she still felt like a young child of eight. She'd spend the summer break with her grandma and grandpa on their farm. The whole day was spent outside riding bikes from her mom's childhood and playing dress up with her grandma's heels.

Later on, when the sun was setting, they'd pick tomatoes. She'd help her grandma find the best ones. To her grandma, every one she picked out was the best. They'd gather them all, wash them off and sit at the kitchen table to talk. Her grandma would cut them apart and always share her half. She'd convince Severine to sprinkle salt on her half, telling her that it made it taste better.

She was right.

Severine discovered as she grew up, that Grandma was right about so much.

Those moments seemed small and probably little to most. When those memories were written down, when they created pages upon pages, it started to define part of Severine and who she was.

It became so much more than a simple loss.

Lily accepted Severine's short answer and stepped away. "Call me later, my friend."

Severine smiled sadly. "I will."

The wind was bitter against Severine's tear-stained cheeks. She slipped the coat on and stared down at her shadow on the ground. She felt alone. No one would be accepted into her tiny world right now.

A tall shadow took residence beside hers. Severine stared hard at the shoulders on the ground. Her tears trailed down her cheeks and dropped, landing on her jacket. Thayer stood tall beside her. He was alive and breathing.

She wanted to walk back inside and worry about things that were never really that important to begin with. Her feelings weighed her down. She wanted to collapse to the ground. Severine wasn't ready to accept this news.

Thayer held his hand out between them. Severine stared at the shadow his hand made on the ground. She followed the path her own hand made as it gripped Thayer's warmth. His lips were set in a firm line as he stood close to her, blocking her from the view of the doors and the wind. She felt protected from everything. Severine wanted to stay there, close to him.

"I heard you talk to Lily." His voice was gruff as he spoke. "I'm really sorry, Severine."

His words were spoken carefully. It made the progression of her tears speed up. She was done watching his shadow and turned into him. Severine looked at him fully. His face demanded that she didn't hide her pain.

Thayer reached out to wipe one of her tears away. His touch felt supportive, and she stopped herself from leaning into his hands. On a rush, he pushed her to his chest. Severine crashed into him gratefully. His arms were solidly wrapped around her as she cried.

The one person in the world she never thought to console her was now holding her, trying to take away her pain. When she stopped, she looked up. His face wasn't too far from her.

His mouth quirked up in a sad smile, "I can get Macsen for you, if you want."

It seemed like the right thing to do. Severine nodded and leaned into Thayer.

His arm wrapped around her shoulders as they walked across campus toward Macsen. "Lily said you were close?"

Severine let go of a shaky sigh. "I've always been close to her. Mom and I spent a lot of time with her and Grandpa. She was always a part of my life."

"I enjoyed my grandpa," Thayer disclosed.

"Yeah?" Severine asked. He was trying. His efforts caused her heart to become pliable.

He looked down at her and smirked. "Yeah. He was tall and huge. But he was a complete softie around kids. I would always ride with him in the combine."

"He farmed?" Severine asked.

"Blake, I grew up in Missouri. What else did you think he did?"

Severine smiled as they made their way closer to Macsen's class.

"How long has he been gone?"

His arm tightened around her. "About eight years."

"Oh."

"I'm not trying to depress you. All I'm trying to say to you is that I know you're sad. But you'll be okay, Severine." He shifted closer. Severine could see her reflection in his eyes. "Everything will be okay."

"Thank you, Thayer," Severine whispered. He nodded into her hair and inhaled deeply. If Severine let him, he'd probably hold her forever. Gradually, Thayer was making it impossible to stay away.

He moved away and wiped away the wetness from

her cheeks. "I'm gonna leave you with Mac... you're good, right?"

"I'm good," Severine repeated back.

When he walked away, Severine wanted to follow after him. He made her feel better; he made her forget.

Severine made her way into the brick building in front of her and easily found Macsen. He sat in the front, as usual. It didn't take long to capture his attention. He glanced at her once and did a double take. She motioned for him to come out, and he briskly nodded his head.

"Is everything okay?"

"I gotta go home for a few days."

"What's wrong?"

"My grandma died. I have to be with my mom."

"Sev, I'm sorry. I wish there was something I could do." He pulled her into a hug.

There was nothing he really could do.

His body shifted back. "I'll call you later, okay?"

"You're going back into class?"

"Do you want me to go back with you to your dorm?"

"No." Severine backed away slowly. "I'll see you soon. All right?"

"Severine!" Macsen called out her name. Severine looked behind her shoulder. "I'm sorry about all of this. I'm sorry."

Severine had to wonder if he was sorry for reasons entirely different from her grandma.

Chapter Twenty-four

Cloudy days should be meant for funerals. Who wants a sunny sky when you've lost a loved one?

Behind them was her grandma's resting place, in front of her was the limo. Severine held her mom and Aunt Rachel's hands tightly.

She's in a better place. That phrase had been said to them more times than she could count. It was a small merit; no one really knew what to say to convey their condolences, but it wouldn't ease the pain.

Her dress brushed against her knees as she slid in after her mom.

When the car started moving, her mom took a deep breath. "I wonder if we could skip the potluck."

Severine assessed Clacy as she stared up at the roof. Bags that were never there before were now underneath her eyes. It made Severine nervous to go back to school. Her Aunt Rachel reached out and held Clacy's hand. If her mom didn't have Severine, she had Aunt Rachel. She'd be okay.

"It will only be for a few hours," Severine offered weakly.

"I just want to spend some time with you before you leave."

Severine nodded in agreement, "But I'll be back for

Christmas break."

"I know, baby," her mom said thoughtfully and stared at Severine.

"What?" Severine asked self-consciously.

"How are you and Macsen?"

Severine kept her face neutral. "We're good."

"Severine, don't lie," her mom said sternly.

"Mom, I can't give you much. We're still a fairly new couple."

"I know. That's why I am asking. You seemed down and anxious during Thanksgiving."

Severine gave her a helpless shrug when all she wanted to do was cry. That's all she seemed to be doing lately.

"Let's just talk about something else," her aunt announced.

"I just want my daughter to be happy." Her mom's chin was held high. "The new relationship phase is never supposed to end this quickly."

Severine didn't know. She couldn't nod in understanding. All she wanted to know was what exactly went wrong.

*   *   *   *   *

Severine was still in her dress from earlier. People had slowly filtered out of her house until it was just Rachel, her mom and her. The silence in the house drove her crazy. In the dining room a grandfather clock ticked back and forth. If she heard the noise one more time, she was going to go insane.

Her foot pushed against the floor of the porch and the swing gained more momentum. Outside, the peace was a given. It wasn't unexpected or strange. The minute she sat down on the porch swing and stared around at the dark night, Severine felt more at peace.

This was her home. And no matter how many times

she'd wanted to escape this place, it still held memories for her. She turned her head and glanced across the street. It was the same elementary school she had attended. Across from the clean building, there were three lines of houses all taken care of; all picture perfect. Life went on around her. People slept in their beds. Maybe a few were leaving work, going out for the night—they'd be smiling and happy with their friends. As they talked about what the night held, Severine wondered how people could move forward from a death.

It scared her—terrified her—to know that a person that held so much significance in her life was gone in a blink. Her grandma deserved more than a second.

"How you doing, kid?" Her Aunt Rachel stepped out onto the porch and slipped her arms into her black wool coat. She leaned her body against the porch railing and crossed her legs at the ankles. She was still dressed in her funeral clothes. But with Rachel, it looked normal. Dresses and heels were something she could pull off.

Severine leaned her head against the swing and sighed. "Well, I'm home...but only for a funeral. I've had better days."

Rachel nodded and buried her hands in her coat. "When are you going back to campus?"

"I'll probably leave in a few days." Severine glanced at the window next to her. A lamp was lit, but with the shades drawn, it was impossible for the world to see inside. "When are you leaving?"

"In a week." The happy, upbeat aunt that she was used to was gone. Rachel looked worn and tired. Everyone was after today. "I think I'm gonna stay and be here for your mom. You don't have to worry about her."

"What is she doing anyway?"

"I think she's curled up with a bottle of wine and sobbing to Steel Magnolias."

Severine groaned and pushed off her black headband. Behind her ears, the skin throbbed from the pressure. It was inevitable that she was going to get a headache, and with her mom drinking, that meant they were in for a long night. "Why is she watching that?"

"Your dad called, and he's coming through town tomorrow."

Severine sat up straighter and froze at the mention of her dad. She wasn't used to the word. It felt foreign to her, like a word from a different language. "Why?"

Rachel rubbed her face and sighed. "He heard about the death in our family."

"You just told me not to worry about her."

"And you won't. Your mom can take care of herself. It's Christian I'm worried for."

Her feet landed on the ground, and Severine stared at Rachel. "You know what's weird? I'm more used to his name than him actually being called Dad."

The look in Rachel's eyes was sympathetic and heartbreaking. "Look, I know he's never been around. Every kid deserves to have both parents in their life. But sometimes it doesn't work out that way...I'm convinced that bad things happen early on in life to prepare us for the real world. It's harsh out there," her voice raised in conviction. Rachel slammed her mouth shut and cleared her throat before continuing. "People won't care about your life story. We're all trying to survive out there. But I know that if anyone could survive, it's you. After all, you were raised by a freakishly strong woman."

Severine nodded, knowing that her aunt was right. Strength was embedded in her blood. It was all she had seen growing up. But if her mom had one weakness, it was her dad. Severine could count the amount of times Christian had visited them here in this small town. But when he did, it was always a short visit. It always left her mom quiet and with bloodshot eyes.

"Why visit now?" Severine asked. Rachel looked at her blankly. "I haven't seen the guy in probably two years," she explained. "And he wants to have a quick visit?"

"It'll be short...you know your dad."

"Not really," Severine replied quietly.

Rachel moved away from the railing and sat next to Severine. The swing creaked slightly as Rachel moved her legs. "If he wants to stop by and give his condolences, then let him. He'll leave, and we can all go on with our lives."

"But can Mom?"

Rachel raised a brow. She asserted her words strongly. "Of course she can!"

Severine didn't mean it to be bad. Her mom was incredibly strong. Growing up, each chance her mom got, she tried to remind Severine to only rely on herself. And part of the reason was because of her dad and what he did to her mom. "I don't think I can be like that," Severine admitted.

Her aunt's head slowly turned in her direction. "Like what?"

"Like my mom," Severine declared. "I don't want to hand over my heart so willingly."

"Then you can never love. Once you do, you're gone. If you've given yourself to someone else then you've already taken that risk of being crushed."

Severine stared at Rachel sharply. She thought about Macsen and what he made her feel. She didn't know what she felt some moments. But the thought of giving him her heart...it didn't seem so terrifying. "So you think she's brave?"

"Isn't anyone who has ever been in love?" Rachel asked back.

"So why aren't you with someone?"

Rachel gave her a sad smile. "Because I'm not as strong as your mom. My thoughts were like yours...it scared the shit out of me. And look at me, I'm alone and travel everywhere. Livin' the dream..." She shifted her body toward Severine and added, "Which one would you rather be? Your mom who's experienced love or your stubborn aunt who can't tell you what the word love truly means?"

*   *   *   *   *

Severine watched her mom run around the house, wiping down already clean counters and re-folding the blanket spread out behind the couch. She was putting more effort into this one afternoon than any past holiday.

The doorbell rang, and Clacy stared at both Rachel and Severine.

"Do you want me to yell 'come in?'" Severine asked cheekily.

"No, it's your father," Clacy hissed out. On her way to the door, she whacked Severine's thigh. "Get up, you're gonna at least say *hi* to him."

Her time spent at home wasn't supposed to involve seeing her dad. When he came around, she just felt awkward. Those seconds when the door would open and neither one knew if they should hug or shake hands was just unnecessary discomfort. Most times, they both just mumbled out *hello*. If Severine was lucky enough, he'd ask her about school or her hobbies. When he left to go his own way, she honestly doubted he'd remember.

"Just go," Rachel admonished on the recliner.

Severine rolled off the couch and walked through the dining room and into the open kitchen. Her steps were cautious as she leaned her body against the fridge. She was acting like a Jehovah's Witness was at the front door.

And that's all it came down to—she knew nothing about her dad. You could lock an unwanted visitor or solicitor out of your house. But in this case, it wasn't an option.

Voices drifted from the front room towards Severine. By the time she stood in the front entryway, she realized her dad wasn't alone.

He brought her stepbrother, Rennick, along with him.

"Severine," her dad called out. Her attention immediately went to him. "It's good to see you."

For a moment, all Severine did was stare at him. His smile was wide, but at the corner of his lips, she could see the strain. She looked his features over, trying to note if anything had changed in the past two years. His coal black hair was still cut short, his face was clean and shaven. When she looked him directly in the eye, he flinched. She couldn't read anything in his dark brown irises because she wasn't around him enough to know his reactions...to anything.

A hand reached out and nudged her in the side. Her mom pointedly looked at her. Everyone was waiting for her to say something back. "Good to see you, too," Severine said cordially.

Feet shifted awkwardly, and Severine looked away from him and to the one person that was semi-fun to be around.

"What are you doing here?" Severine asked Rennick with a friendly smile.

He returned the smile. It looked mischievous. "I talked to Christian." He paused to look over at their dad and smirked darkly at the obvious tension. His dig was on purpose. "He said he was driving here to see you and Clacy...I figured I might as well bother you."

"Are you coming in?" Rennick hesitated and Severine quickly spoke, "Or, we can freeze our asses off outside."

"Severine," Clacy warned. She said nothing else, but the message was loud and clear. She wanted Severine to stay and talk to her dad.

For her mom, she'd suffer through it and for that sole reason alone. She looked over at her dad, and he moved away from the door. "If you wanna see your brother, it's fine."

It took her two seconds to nod her head and grab a pair of shoes and her coat hanging on the coat rack.

Rennick waited on the porch with his hands in his front pockets. He looked too much like their dad—all dark hair and dark eyes. Only his hair was wild; the strands reached ear level. With Rennick everything was half-paced or nothing at all. His life had been filled with more disappointments than Severine's, so she didn't blame him for being cautious.

"I had no idea you were gonna be here."

He shrugged a shoulder and looked at the houses around them. "I'm back in the states and I wanted to visit my mom's grave...and I figured I might as well visit Christian."

"Ah..." Severine drew out, "gotcha." She nodded her head and looked down at the chipped paint on the railing.

When she was young, she never understood where Rennick came from. He'd show up with their dad and leave with their dad. When Severine was nine, her mom finally told her that Rennick's mom, Tara, died when he was only a month old. She didn't know how until she was old enough to Google the term 'brain aneurysm.'

He was only five years older than her, but there might as well be ten years of life separating them. While she had her mom, he had the friends he made in boarding school in Switzerland.

He got into so much trouble that Severine started to lose count. Those mistakes made him the black sheep of the Blake family. But the two of them understood each other in a way that no one else would; neither one knew what it was like to receive any love from their dad.

"I'm sorry to hear about your grandma," Rennick finally blurted out. His voice was deep and stilted, like he wasn't used to speaking that much. Usually, when he did talk, only sarcasm came out.

She warmed her hands up and rubbed them together

before she nodded. "Thanks."

He sighed and his breath came out into the cold air. "She was nice," he admitted, "although I'm pretty sure she hated me."

"No, she didn't," Severine protested.

"Yeah, she did." His dark eyes sparkled and he gave a small smile. "To quote her: *He's a complete heathen.*"

"It's only 'cause you didn't go to church with her. I'm sure there were times she called me a heathen too."

Even though it was freezing out, Severine didn't want to go back inside. When they did, she'd have to keep up a conversation with her dad, when neither of them wanted to be there.

"You wanna take a walk?" she offered.

Maybe his thoughts were going down the same path because he nodded his head in agreement. "Sure."

The two of them started down the sidewalk. Severine looked up at the tall trees around them. In the summer, the leaves shaded the sun, feeling like a warm blanket. But in the winter, they offered nothing but an idle prop—they gave nothing.

"Have you seen Christian lately?" Rennick asked.

"This will be the first time in two years."

"He must love you, I'm on three."

Severine stepped over a gap of concrete and turned her attention to Rennick. "Why is he really here? Why did he bring you with him?"

"Well, I only came along because I hadn't seen you in a long time. He came because he's..." He struggled for the right word and pushed his black hair from his face before he stared solemnly at Severine. "Because he's Christian, and I think he wants to try and be there for us."

"You're twenty-five, and I'll be twenty next August. I find it hard to believe that he'd magically wake up and decide, 'Oh shit. I have those two kids...you know, I think I want to get to know them.'"

"So you don't buy his bullshit?"

"I'm not saying I believe it, or expect him to fall back on his word. I'm neutral on the whole thing. It wasn't like I had him for a few years. He's been in and out of our lives since day one."

"I guess we'll see what happens."

Maybe Rennick wanted to have some form of a relationship with their dad, but she didn't. The whole conversation about Christian made Severine's hands sweat. Partially, because if she did think about it, she'd start to think how it'd be to have a dad and know what it actually meant. "Can we talk about something else now?"

"Sure." He gave her a brief look and zipped up his brown leather jacket. "Where's that friend of yours?"

He had only met one 'friend' of hers. He knew exactly what her name was. Severine turned around to go back to the house. They were only a block away, but the cold air made it feel like a mile.

"Who, Lily?"

For a quick second he bent down to grab at a warped tree branch. He banged it repeatedly against his leg. "Yeah."

"She's back at campus."

Rennick tossed the warped stick in the air. It landed near the side of the road. "She still scared shitless of me?"

"The first time she met you, you threw up in her mom's rose bush...you weren't exactly charming," Severine pointed out.

"But I'm a changed man. When I'm drunk, I aim toward the toilet now."

"Other than aiming at a white bowl...what else are you doing with your life?"

He stared up at the sky, and Severine admired the sharp profile of his face. She didn't know what his mom looked like, but he must have gotten his sharp cheekbones and exotic features from her. "I'm getting my Masters in literature. When I get bored of school, I think

I'll teach."

"You make it seem like I just asked you if you wanted McDonald's. You're way too relaxed about your future."

"Think about it...who do I have to worry about other than myself?"

"What am I, chopped liver?"

Rennick gave her a funny expression. "Should I be worrying about you?"

"No, I'm good. I have a boyfriend, and he's super dreamy," Severine said dramatically. "I rely on him for everything."

"Yeah...I don't know how to respond to that."

The large white house came into sight. Severine knew that once they went inside, Rennick would become ruthless and cold to everyone, her mom would be half the person she was before her dad arrived, and Severine would be counting down the minutes until her dad left. Just an average Blake family reunion. "Thanks for coming to visit. This trip was depressing enough for me, but you made it...less depressing."

"Anytime...actually, not really. This place is a fucking shit hole."

"I'll give you that, but there's a bar west of here...about fifteen minutes away."

"And that's where I'll be."

They walked up the pathway just as her dad and mom were walking out onto the porch. A flush was on her mom's cheeks that hadn't been there before. The closer Severine came closer, she saw the brilliant smile on her mom's face. "Severine!" She called out cheerfully. "Your dad and I were thinking of taking the family out...the four of us. What do you think?"

"Where's Aunt Rachel?"

"She had to go do a few errands in town."

Lucky bitch.

"Come on! It'll be great for us to all catch up."

Severine turned to Rennick and he shrugged. "As

long as there's alcohol."

"This is great!"

Rennick followed her mom, and Severine was left with her dad. He stepped forward uncomfortably and gave her a small smile. "How are you, Severine?"

When he said her name, it came out formally and with a slight accent. She could only imagine that's how it'd be pronounced in France. A part of her wanted to shake him back and forth and yell into his ear that he was from Kentucky, therefore, he had no foreign accent.

"I'm okay. School is going great, and it's almost Christmas break, so after finals I'll be even better."

His expression was anxious as he nodded his head and listened. "Your mom told me you're with someone?"

Severine nodded her head and looked away. "Mmhmm...he's a really nice guy."

"Well...it's good to hear that you're happy." He shifted on his feet. The two of them were pulling away from Awkward Street and were now veering right into Painfully Quiet Boulevard.

Time tended to do that. Severine had no idea where to begin with her dad. There were no right words for her to say.

"I'm glad you're doing well." He opened his mouth to say more and slammed it shut. When he finally talked, his voice was gruff. "You've turned into a beautiful girl, Severine."

He turned toward his black SUV before she could respond. It was the closest to a compliment from him that she had ever been given.

Rennick looked over at her and gave her a smile that was grim. He pretended to hold a grenade in his hands and pulled the safety pin out. He threw it and made the sound of an explosion.

Once their dad left again, everything would be in ruins.

Chapter Twenty-five

Severine was only gone for five days. It felt like five weeks.

The hurt was still raw, but what made her mad more than anything was the fact that her dad's visit overshadowed the true reason for her visit.

She tried to focus on homework. The open laptop beckoned her to finish her report. She couldn't focus on anything because she kept replaying the dinner spent with her mom and dad. They talked like everything was okay—like they were the closest of friends. When he left that night, true to form, her mom was more of a basket case than before he arrived. The silence inside her dorm room was killing her. Severine grabbed her phone and quickly texted Lily.

Meet me at the coffee shop. Overwhelmed.

Lily's reply was instant. *K chica. See you soon.*

Severine could call Macsen and meet him. There was a chance that he wouldn't answer. There was an even higher percentage that he would be distant if he did meet up with her. He was treading lightly around her, acting afraid to say anything wrong.

Severine just wanted things to be normal between them. Everything else in her life was already turned upside down. She didn't need for him to change. Right now, she needed him the most. She needed his shoulder to lean on and for someone to open up to.

In a rush, Severine grabbed her jacket off the back of her chair and hurriedly put it over her tan sweater. She didn't give her car time to warm up, rather, she pulled out the minute it started and sped to the coffee shop.

There was so much on her mind. Lily was the only one she could trust with her feelings. She wasn't a journal type of girl. Most times, she harbored everything. Right now, she had to have her friend.

She saw Lily already sitting at a couch facing the windows. Her coffee sat on the coffee table and next to it stood a frappe. Severine hurried inside and sat down next to her. This was the exact same spot she had discovered the Sloan brothers; the same spot Thayer had challenged her with one glare, and Macsen had snatched her curiosity. It seemed like a fitting place to be.

"Please tell me that drink is for me."

Lily glanced up at her magazine and pointed. "Spiced chai frappe, with extra whipped cream. It seems like an extra whipped cream kind of night."

"Are you psychic? This is exactly what I needed."

"What's up? Why did ya wanna meet so late?" Lily still flipped through the magazine. She was giving Severine time to say what was really bothering her.

Her hands held the plastic cup tightly. Straight to the bone, her fingers felt numb—just like her feelings. "I saw my dad while at my mom's."

Beside her, the pages stopped turning. "Are you serious?" Lily asked quietly, for their ears only.

Severine clenched her eyes tightly and turned her body towards Lily. "He came with Rennick and only stayed for a few hours. But it just ticked me off."

"Maybe he wants to reconnect."

Severine shrugged. "He's had nineteen and a half years to do that."

"So do you think he has an angle?"

Severine snorted and leaned back against the decorative pillow. "I have no freakin' clue. It's just weird." Lily nodded her head, but she was already flipping through her magazine. "Rennick was with him though."

Lily's eyebrows rose high in shock. "Really? Now that's interesting."

"I know, I haven't seen him in so long."

"So how's that piece of hot man meat doing?"

"Blech, Lily, stop."

"He is..." Lily stared off. Severine cringed, knowing Lily was thinking about him. "God...what I'd give for one night with that dude."

"You're with Ben," Severine mentioned.

Lily wiped the goofy smile off her face and was back in the real world. "I know that. I'm just saying, if I had a chance at that..."

If Severine mentioned anything about him asking about her, their conversation would quickly turn into an episode of 90210. Lily had a teenage crush on him that Severine had assumed she was over. Clearly, they were harder to forget than she thought.

"If we're done with girl talk of the century, I need to pick out a book real quick and finish up some homework."

Severine gave Lily an amused smile. "If? You were the one gushing over Rennick like a middle schooler."

The two of them stood. "I'll always go all middle schooler on that dude. He is-"

Lily paused mid-grab for her magazine. She stared at the window in horror.

"Lily, come on. You're in the wa-"

Lily snatched Severine tightly by the wrist, dragged her to the back of the couch and yanked her toward the ground. She crouched there with flushed cheeks and eyes as wide as saucers.

"What the hell are we doing?" Severine hissed out.

Lily ignored her and peeked over the couch. She lowered her head back and banged her head against the back of the couch.

Around them, a few customers gaped at them like they were idiots. Severine turned her face away from them, toward the couch. This was bordering on psychotic.

"I think you need to call Macsen and ask him where he is."

Severine had seen that look. She had given that look to so many girls throughout the years. It was a look of pity when they'd been steamrolled by a guy. Her heart slowed. She wanted to look over the couch to see what Lily was talking about, but there was no need, she already knew.

Mutely, Severine nodded and found his name immediately. When she called his phone, he answered after the fourth ring.

"Hey, Sev."

"Hey..." she paused and glanced over at Lily's frantic face, before continuing. "I think I'm gonna come over and hang out. I really want to see you."

She strained to hear anything as he breathed across the phone. Nothing seemed out of the ordinary.

Lily peeked her head over the couch once more and quickly moved back down. "Still there," Lily mouthed.

Severine closed her eyes tight. *Please don't lie to me. Please don't lie to me...*

Her stomach was already dropping before he spoke, "Really? Okay, that's fine. I'm not home yet though."

"I'm just going to stop by Java. Do you want me to get you anything?" she gritted out through her teeth.

He paused on the phone. It felt like minutes. Severine glanced back at her spy, and found her looking over the edge of the couch. Lily reported back instantly and pointed her index finger at Severine, whispering. "Looking around for you!"

"You don't have to," Macsen said back. "But that's really sweet of you."

Severine mouthed to Lily, "Girl?"

Lily's gaze was painful. But she nodded her head up and down. She confirmed it all.

Anger made her voice sure. It fueled her to speak. "You know what? Let's forget coffee. I'll see you in a few minutes."

She hung up before he could respond, stood to her full height, and walked with determination to the clear glass door.

Lily trailed behind her. "Severine, you need to wait."

If he turned, he'd be able to see Severine looking at him. If he turned, he might be able to prepare himself for the shit Severine was about to unload on him. But that would give him a heads up. It was something he had never given her. Severine wasn't going to extend him any favors.

He bent his head down to whisper in the girl's ear. Severine could hear the laughter clearly. "I'm gonna kill him."

"Shit," Lily muttered. "I could be wrong. That could be his niece or cousin visiting for the holidays! Maybe his family is super close."

Severine gave Lily a look and rammed her back into the door and walked outside, toward Macsen.

Chapter Twenty-six

Dark strands blew around her face wildly as Severine ran across the road to Macsen and the unknown girl. The sky was black, and the stars twinkled beautifully. A storm was coming up on them. The tree branches waved back and forth in the air and a slight drizzle of rain coated the asphalt. In an hour, it would turn into ice and everyone on the road would be more alert and careful. Severine was kicking herself for not applying that same theory to her life.

Behind her, she could hear Lily's mumbling, "Shit, shit, shit. Double shit. Shit on a spatula, this is bad."

Severine wasn't stopping. Her eyes were glued to Macsen's back. The closer she got to him...them, the more her hands shook. She considered herself to be a very pessimistic person, but the one thing she had predicted to bring her joy was now blowing her hopes into smithereens. And it hurt so fucking bad.

"Hey you," Severine called out in a playful voice, if playful was the new vicious.

He turned around and those green eyes that had consumed her before looked at her with horror. If she weren't the one getting crushed, Severine would've thought Macsen's face to be priceless. Confusion mixed with fear. "Sev! I didn't know you were here," he uttered in a raspy voice. He sounded completely taken aback.

"I know you didn't," Severine snapped out. She looked behind him and saw the petite blonde that had been laughing earlier. She was the size of a Polly Pocket. With her bright blue eyes and pouty mouth, she could technically be labeled as pretty. Everything about her was unlike Severine.

Her lips wanted to quiver so badly. Instead, Severine bit down on the inside of her cheek to keep the action from happening. She didn't want to give either one of them the satisfaction of seeing her pain.

Macsen was still in front of her—still frozen. Repeatedly, he blinked. His eyes never left her, and it was like he was unable to believe she was standing right in front of him. Like he couldn't believe he had been caught.

She didn't want to catch him on anything. He was hers. He was supposed to give her happiness and laughter. All of this felt like a joke. Severine was waiting for a bunch of people to run from the side of her car and yell out that she had just gotten *Punk'd*. Anything. Anything, but this.

"What are you doing?" It was his one chance to rectify the entire situation. This was Macsen's one chance to step up and say that everything was a complete misunderstanding—that this blonde girl was a friend, a distant cousin, a random stranger...anything except what Severine's mind was telling her it really was.

"I-I was just..."

The longer he stuttered, the more Severine's pulse quickened.

"Who's behind you?" Severine asked quietly.

He shook his head back and forth. He didn't open his mouth up once, but the look in his eyes implied everything...everything he refused to admit. Severine took a shuddering breath and stared down at the asphalt.

"Mac, what's going on?" the blue-eyed blonde behind him asked.

Severine's heart was breaking. It was clenched tightly in Macsen's hand, and the pieces of everything she trusted him with slipped in between his fingers.

Lily ran up to the three of them and stopped short when she saw the expression on Severine's face. "Oh shit..."

With Lily by her side, Severine stepped away from Macsen and moved toward the blonde. Lily latched onto her forearm and followed. "What's your name?"

There was nothing vindictive about this small girl. She looked just as lost as Severine. Right then Severine knew she wasn't to blame. She had no idea Macsen belonged to somebody else. Even as Severine was running through her thoughts, this girl probably thought he was only exclusive with her. When she finally spoke up, her voice was meek—very timid. "Verity."

Lily tsked lightly and glared darkly at Macsen who was watching the conversation unfold like it was a horror story. "Well, Verity," Lily uttered with disgust, "from the shocked expression on your face, I'm gonna go out on a limb here and say that McSleazy over here didn't tell you he had a girlfriend?"

Severine could see the insecurities playing across the blonde's face, as she shook her head no.

"Sev-" Macsen pronounced slowly with his hands in the air. He appeared innocent, but Severine knew he was treading lightly. Soon he'd try to reason with her.

Verity stared between the two of them with wide eyes. Severine was humiliated. Macsen was the reason for this pain.

Lily held Severine's wrist to hold her back, but she moved closer to Verity. "You know, you look nice and I'm sure this isn't your fault, but if you don't leave, you'll more than likely be walking away with pieces of your Jessica Simpson clip-on extensions in your hands."

Verity shifted nervously before she abruptly turned back to the coffee shop. "Mac, I'm gonna head out."

"Yeah. I think that's best," Lily remarked coldly. With one squeeze on the shoulder, Lily moved away from Macsen and Severine. Her phone was glued to her ear, and she talked at a rapid pace.

She could've been talking to Ben, her mom, placing an order into Dominos...Severine would never know. Her eyes stared unblinkingly at Macsen, trying to figure out what he could possibly say to make any of this better. Her trust was solidly placed in him, and he had destroyed it all.

"Have you known Verity long?"

Macsen's eyes filled with pain. "No, only a month."

It didn't take long to do the math and figure out when the betrayal had first started. "During Thanksgiving break?" she whispered. He nodded his head. "And when my grandma died, you were with her?" she asked with a crack in her voice.

"Severine, I'm sorry." He didn't know about her dad or brother. He didn't know the pain that came along with seeing Christian. When his voice broke, Severine wanted to pound her fist all over him for doing this to them—to her.

Controlling her anger had never been her strong suit. Tonight, her rage was boiling. It broke free from her emotions and guided her actions. When she stepped forward, she went at Macsen with everything she had. She had never thrown a punch before, but it came naturally. Maybe when a person went into self-preservation mode their body took over and controlled all movements. Her fist extended back and met him square in the jaw.

Her hand throbbed and hurt like hell. But it was worth the pain—worth seeing Macsen grab his jaw and rub.

Severine was ready for round two. She wanted to connect more punches to his face. She heard Lily's yelp, but it came out muffled in her ears. Her anger made everything hazy.

A pair of large hands banded around her body and kept her immobile. "Down, girl," Thayer muttered into her ear.

It was the irony of Thayer holding her back from Macsen made her laugh out crazily. She didn't know which way was up, which way to go. Severine leaned her head back against his chest and clenched her eyes shut for a quick minute before she looked at Macsen.

"He's a liar!" Severine screamed out. When she tried to jerk out of Thayer's hold, he pressed her closer. It made her fight back more to get away. "He was fucking another girl! Shy, sweet Mac!"

"Severine, don't," Thayer remarked firmly.

She stopped fighting, long enough to pant out her words. Ben and Lily stood next to Severine's car with identical expressions of shock. "I assume that I was one of those stupid girls and everyone knew but me?" Severine yelled out. She didn't care who answered, she just wanted a response.

"Severine...it was just once," Macsen disclosed quickly. "I promise you, I-"

"Silly me. Just once, why, that makes it all okay! Cheating on me is a completely normal thing to do."

"Fuck," Thayer muttered behind her.

"I...care for you so much, Sev," Macsen declared his words with so much pain, Severine was surprised it didn't bleed out of him.

Sleet picked up around them, and Severine could feel it coating her hair. It plastered around her cheeks, making her cold. But his words were more frigid than what the sky produced. It was just doing its job. Macsen had gone out of his way to bring her pain—whether he knew it or not.

He had never loved her and had at no time declared it. Severine had thought she was close to feeling that way with him. It hurt more than she wanted to admit, that she knew nothing about the word *love*. All it showed her was that cruel four-letter word was the color of onyx.

"But you 'cared' for her more. Clearly. I mean, you screwed a random girl but not your girlfriend."

"Severine..." Thayer said gently in her ear. "I'm asking you to stop."

Severine turned in his grasp and stared at him fiercely. "Yes, he did!" She made no sense. All she wanted was to get everything off her chest. "We never went far. He never did anything. That should have been my first clue!"

Thayer cringed and tucked her tightly underneath his arm. "Have Lily take you home."

She didn't want to leave—not when she was just getting started. Severine never had the opportunity to reply.

"You wanna step in now?" Macsen shouted at his brother. His rage came out as he clenched his fist. "You're gonna sweep in and take her?"

"You can't take what's not yours, Macsen!" Severine screamed out.

Macsen didn't back down like she expected. He pushed forward. Maybe he knew it was all coming to a close. He tried to touch her, but Severine recoiled away. It led her back to Thayer.

With his baseball cap in his hands, he held the bill with a knuckle white grip. "So you're done then? You're gonna walk away?"

Severine leaned toward his face. Her pain showed clearly. "With you? Yes. I'd rather walk alone!"

Thayer held both shoulders back, but she kept going. She was on autopilot and couldn't stop if she wanted to. "I was stupid enough to believe that I could trust you!" Severine yelled out. Macsen recoiled back from her, and she quickly spoke before her voice became hoarse. "So go back to Haley, Verity...I bet one of them will still be waiting for you."

"Let Lily take you home," Thayer repeated again. His words broke through her anger, and she nodded as she stared at Macsen with a dead expression. Fitting, because that's what he was to her.

Lily stepped forward to hold her hand tightly. Severine gave one look at Macsen, and his mouth was wide open like he couldn't believe she was truly walking away. She couldn't believe it herself.

"You're a quitter, Sev! You're running away!" Macsen's harsh words felt like a whip had been cracked across her face.

"Just get the fuck out of here!" Thayer shouted. "You're making this worse than it has to be!"

Macsen laughed darkly and gave his brother the finger. Severine didn't know the person in front of her. "Fuck you, dude. You just want her for yourself."

Severine shoved her face close to Macsen. "Stop it," she hissed out. "You messed up. I'm not running away from anything! I'm leaving. Leaving because YOU," her finger jabbed forcefully at his chest, "fucked up! You ruined everything!"

Both of his hands reached out to cup her face. Severine pushed away, but he held on. "I'm completely crazy about you, Severine! I made one fucking mistake! Just one!"

Ben yanked him away, and Lily slipped a comforting arm around her shoulder. "Let's go."

They walked across the pavement to Severine's car. Behind her, Thayer talked to Macsen. She wanted to know what he was saying.

Severine finally had both Sloan brothers out of her life. And God, it hurt.

"Severine. Wait till we get home. Wait. Let loose then."

They were close to her car when Ben looked back, "Ah, shit."

He ran back, and Severine watched just as Thayer

tackled Macsen to the black asphalt. It was a perfect place for him to be. His heart was as black as tar.

It didn't hurt to watch Thayer throw punches onto his brother's face. It also didn't feel good. She was watching a relationship diffuse in front of her.

*   *   *   *   *

"I'm pathetic," Severine's voice hiccuped as she slammed her elbows on the kitchen table. All of this felt humiliating. What hurt the most was how she had trusted him.

"You're not pathetic," Lily said firmly. She rubbed Severine's back and leaned down next to her chair. "He's pathetic. He did this. No one made him."

Severine moved her face away from her hands and glanced at her friend miserably. "I never thought he would do this. I gave him a chance."

Lily nodded in understanding and wrapped a solid arm around her. "I know, honey."

A pounding sounded in Ben's house. Severine whipped her head toward the door.

"Ben," Lily warned, "don't you dare let him in!"

Ben was caught in the middle. He stared at Lily, and the door opened up behind him. Macsen walked across the room.

"Are you kidding me? Always lock the door behind you, Ben!"

"Sev, you and I need to talk about this," Macsen pleaded as he walked closer.

Severine stood from the seat. It crashed to the floor behind her. Lily stood next to her and pointed a finger at Ben. "If you can't lock a door, at least get him out of here!"

"Come on, bud." Ben placed a hand on Macsen's shoulder. "Let's cool off outside."

Macsen shook him off and walked in the kitchen.

"We need to talk alone."

"You'd love that, wouldn't you?" Lily bit out.

Macsen flicked an annoyed glance in her direction. "None of this even affects you. Back off, Lily!"

"You cheated on her. I encouraged her to date you, to trust you!" Lily shouted out.

"Just let me talk to him for a minute."

Lily shook her head no. "You don't have to talk to him. You don't have to do anything you don't want to do."

"I want to do this." *When this is done, maybe he'll leave me alone.*

The need for some explanation made Severine want to talk to him, nothing else. All she wanted to know was why.

Why, why, why.

"Okay." Lily leaned down and whispered into Severine's ear, "I'll leave, but I'm gonna camp out in the hall. The minute you want him gone, he'll be outta here." She turned away and settled her wrath on Macsen. "And you. Say anything out of line, and you'll regret it. I'm short, but I gotta lot of anger I wanna get out. And you're my target!"

"Come on, let's go." Ben rubbed her shoulders, but Lily kept talking. "Ben has a shovel somewhere! Believe me when I say no one would miss you!"

"Easy, Cujo," Ben gently said.

They walked away, and Macsen ventured closer. The light revealed his swollen eye and lip. Severine felt nothing for his damaged face. It was all fair. Maybe he'd feel half the pain she was experiencing.

"Just talk. Get this over with." Severine leaned against the kitchen counter.

"God, Severine, you have to know this was not planned. I fucked up once. I know that." He was wise and stood on the opposite side of the room. His eyes still touched her even with the steps in between them. "I'm sorry. I can't take this back. If I could, I would."

"This changes everything."

"It doesn't have to," Macsen pleaded. "It'll take a while, but you could trust me again."

"Maybe you're confused. There's no *again*!" Tears fell down her cheek as she spoke, "Being with that girl made it permanent. There's never an 'us' again."

Macsen nodded his head. Maybe he had come into the room expecting her to say that. It didn't matter whether he had been careless one time. Severine was the one to have everything stolen from her.

"I can't walk away from you."

Severine's mind was made up. Her words still came out on a choked whisper. "You have to."

"I can't." Macsen's face crumbled. His shoulders were pressed against the kitchen wall. With his fingers linked behind his neck, he stared up at the ceiling. "I'm too fucking selfish to walk away."

Finally, something the two of them could agree on.

"I think there's no way back to us. I think that path's been destroyed."

"I'll give you time."

"I don't need time. If I thought for a minute that I could believe you, I'd ask you to stay." Severine couldn't breathe. Her lungs burned, and her head felt like it was being shoved underwater. Too many emotions. Too many feelings for one month. "I think you need to go."

"Sev-"

Lily turned the corner and loudly clapped her hands to break the moment. "You heard her, bucko. Out ya go!"

Ben followed behind her, although he had the decency to look apologetic.

Macsen didn't look toward the interruption. He concentrated on Severine. Months ago, she was convinced she had him pegged. Someone that kind and thoughtful couldn't hurt her. Severine had set herself up to be crushed by him.

"Severine," Macsen implored.

Another request from him—Severine had given him enough of herself.

"Nope. She gave you more than a minute." Lily crossed her arms, "Leave, Macsen."

Ben settled his hand on Macsen's shoulder. "Come on. I called Thayer to get you."

The door opened just as Ben finished talking. Severine slanted her eyes in the direction and saw Thayer. He placed himself next to the door, crossed his arms, and silently stared at the scene in front of him.

When he rubbed his lip, Severine saw blood that clung to his fingers. She was close enough to see it all and far enough away to keep herself from reaching out to touch him. The tables were turned. Thayer defended her. Severine's alliance went to him.

Macsen walked side by side with Ben out the door. Thayer looked back her way and mouthed the words, 'I'm sorry.'

Severine gathered more from his apology than she ever would from Macsen's.

Chapter Twenty-seven

"It says to leave those on for five to ten minutes," Lily dutifully announced.

"I've hit ten minutes," Severine answered awkwardly as Lily shifted the tea bags to cover more of her eyelids.

"Dude, it's been two minutes," Anne said dryly.

If Severine could see, she'd chuck something at her. The day after seeing Macsen with someone else was, so far, a bitch.

Lily stayed with her last night. And when Severine finally went to sleep it was well into the morning. The minute she opened her eyes back up, Anne and Lily talked quietly on Lily's old bed.

On the nightstand, in between the beds, stood a hot coffee waiting for Severine. She would've cried, if her tear ducts hadn't shut down from overuse.

Her swollen, puffy eyes were a disaster. That's what led Severine to lie awkwardly on her bed like a patient talking to their shrink, with tea bags covering her eyes.

The remedy might be ridiculous, but Severine had hope that it'd work. She'd rather wrap a noose around her neck than walk into class looking like shit in front of Macsen.

"Okay. It's been five minutes. Let me take these off. My lids are freezing."

Lily sighed. "Take them off."

Severine snatched the tea bags off her face and blinked her eyes repeatedly. "Any better?"

"You look like you have pink eye," Anne remarked solemnly.

Lily's hand made solid contact on Anne's arm. "Shut up. It's gonna look worse before it gets better." She smiled at Severine like she was a child who had just received a shot. "It helped. It's just a little reddish."

The sides of Severine's lips were starting to turn up—until she heard her phone ring.

A new ring tone rang throughout the room. Justin Timberlake's, "Cry Me A River" sounded from her phone.

"Do you like your new ringtone?" Lily wiggled her eyebrows as she snatched Severine's phone and pressed ignore.

Severine sat speechless and watched Lily turn to speak to Anne. "That was ten!"

Anne frowned and grabbed a notebook from Severine's desk. "Oh shit, you're right. I thought it was call number eight."

"You guys are keeping track of his calls?"

"What are friends for if they can't screen your calls after a bad breakup?" Lily huffed out impatiently.

"You changed his ringtone to a Justin Timberlake song?" Severine reached for her phone, but Lily dangled it out of reach and went back to messing with it. Her concentration was unwavering.

"No, I changed it to a cheating song."

Anne looked up from the notebook. "I wanted to pick "Unfaithful" by Rihanna. Lily thought it was too obvious."

"Of course," Severine remarked dryly.

Her phone rang again. Only this time, Carrie Underwood's voice belted out a chorus of, "Before He Cheats."

Lily winked at Severine and tossed the phone to her

bed.

"I told you," Anne gritted out, "no Carrie Underwood songs! You know how I feel about country music."

"Can we stop with the ringtone game?" Severine rubbed the side of her temples. A massive headache was starting to build behind her temples.

"But there are so many good ones!" Lily said desperately.

"How is this helping with my depression?"

"Just try to think of a song," Lily suggested happily.

Severine took a short sip of her drink. "I can't."

"You didn't even try. Believe me, purging out all that anger will help. Remember Nate from high school?"

Severine nodded her head.

"What did I do after our breakup? I started a bon fire and burned the shit out of his stuff! It's completely therapeutic!"

"Lily, it made you look like a pyromaniac."

"Just try it."

"Puddle of Mudd, "She Hates Me"..."

"Boom! That's a good one! But it would be a song he used for your ringtone."

Lily snapped her finger, and jumped off of her bed. "I have the perfect one! "I Hate Everything About You" by Three Days Grace!"

"And Bingo was his name O!" Anne shouted out.

It helped for a minute. But when Anne and Lily stopped talking, the memories from last night came back.

Everything just hurt. And the worst part was the embarrassment.

How many people knew what was going on? Was she the only one that was left in the dark?

Severine could keep asking herself those impossible questions all day. She'd never get a sound answer.

Her bed shifted, and Lily sympathetically smiled at Severine. "How are you doing?"

"Do you think everyone knew but me?" Severine

blurted out.

"No." Lily smoothed her hand over Severine's comforter as she talked. "I was just as shocked as you."

"It's killing me that this happened underneath my nose. He's made me feel stupid and I hate that," Severine explained.

"He's a total ass face," Anne said as she tossed a piece of candy in her mouth.

For Anne, it was about as close as she'd get to a heart-to-heart.

Lily glared at Anne before turning back to Severine. "What Anne is really trying to say is, that he's an idiot and that no one knew about this. You saw what happened last night—Thayer beat the shit out of him."

"Whoa." Anne's feet dropped to the ground. "How did you miss that detail, Lily?"

"Oh, it was great, Anne." Lily stretched her body on the opposite side of the bed. "Macsen had a black eye and swollen lip. The only thing I regret is that I didn't get a punch in."

Severine shook her head and sipped her coffee. "For a good church girl, you're really aggressive."

"Severine, I have a Christian heart, but I still sometimes wanna cut a bitch...well, in this case, it's cut a dick."

"Pastor Partlow would be so proud."

"My dad was the one who taught me to protect myself and everyone close to me. I know my self-worth, and I know yours too. You didn't deserve what happened to you."

Severine clenched her teeth. She felt the tears building up. Lily had nothing but concern for Severine. Her words only amplified how pure her crazy, aggressive heart truly was. Kneeling on her bed, Severine gave Lily a grateful hug. "Thanks for being here."

Anne threw a Tootsie Roll at the two of them. "I'm not deaf, you know."

Severine pulled away from Lily. "Thanks to you too, Anne!"

"You wanna go get something to eat?"

"No."

"Too much pain?"

Severine nodded. "Yes."

"No, you're not," Anne said solemnly.

All Severine could do was raise her eyebrow. Girl Code was being broken. You sat back, you consoled, and you watched every chick flick out there. But you never, ever told your friend she wasn't in pain.

Both Lily and Severine gawked at her. Anne rolled her eyes and moved toward the empty bed across from Severine's.

"I've seen you in pain. And right now, you're ticked off, but you're still there. When you're broken, when the life is wiped from your eyes, then you can say you're in pain."

*   *   *   *   *

After Anne's comment, Severine agreed to go out with them. Right after she took the world's longest nap.

The three of them piled into Lily's car and did what girls do during a nasty breakup. They ate junk food.

Severine tucked her feet underneath her thighs and stared at Anne and Lily, both attacking their food. They had stuck by her the whole day.

"Why do we always go after the girl?"

Lily lowered her burrito and glanced over at Anne. "Who?"

Severine looked around the empty Taco Bell. She was on her fourth taco. "When a guy cheats, why do we always go after the girl?"

Anne snorted and took a long sip of her drink. "Because it's easier. It's first instinct to point the finger at the female than to blame the male."

Severine had to agree. She nodded her head, stared down at the taco wrapper smoothed out in front of her. "I don't blame her."

"Who? Verity?" Lily blurted out.

Severine still cringed, but she nodded. "You saw how she looked. She was just as confused as me. That wasn't a girl who was aware of what was going on. That was a girl who was hurt."

"Can I still hate them both?" Anne asked with a full mouth.

"I'm not saying that I'm gonna become best friends with the girl. This whole thing has me wondering..."

"Well, don't," Lily interjected. She tore off a piece of her soft taco shell and tossed it onto the plastic tray beside Severine. "If you start thinking about it again you're gonna start crying, and when you start crying, we have to get out the emergency stash of Oreo cake. I'm pretty sure all local grocery stores are out of the dessert."

Severine couldn't shut her brain off. She couldn't stop replaying the scene over in her head. Her eyes focused on her plastic fork and repeatedly she stabbed the leftovers of her soft taco. She wished it was Macsen's head in front of her. "Were there other girls?" Both Anne and Lily looked at each other and said nothing. Severine continued, "I mean, he conned two girls into thinking he was this great guy. How many other girls were under the impression that he was this shy, sweet guy that would never harm anyone?"

"Maybe you didn't know him as well as you thought?" Lily offered gently.

"I know what I felt."

Lily reached across the table and patted Severine's hand. "But there's a chance that you didn't know as much as you thought you did. I know he didn't appear to be the kind of guy that would do this. I'm just as shocked as you."

Just then, the door opened. A fast food restaurant

wasn't exactly the hot spot to be at 11:32 p.m. It was part of the perks of having girl talk so late at night. But it always left the chance that Severine would run into someone she didn't want to see. Someone that would just give her a headache.

Haley walked in with a friend.

Severine looked away and immediately made eye contact with Anne. "Oh God. Not here."Severine groaned.

"Why is that girl looking at you?" Anne asked loudly. This was now the golden moment for Anne to keep her mouth shut and her thoughts to herself.

"That's Macsen's 'girl pal'," Severine muttered.

"Realllyyy now." Anne plopped her elbow on the table and placed her chin in her palm. She lifted her hand into the air and moved her fingers back and forth. "Wow, she's really into staring at your back, Sev. And why does it look like a group of first graders ganged up on her and used her face as a canvas for Art time?" She said out of the corner of her mouth.

"You need to get a muzzle on your mouth," Lily whined. "Thanks to you, she's coming over here. I used all my snark on Macsen. I'm too pretty to go to jail. I'll end up being someone's bitch."

"Hey girl!" Anne squealed out and ignored Lily's protest. Haley stood at the front of their table, and Severine kept her gaze on Anne. Just as she smiled brightly and said, "Oh my gosh, it's so great to see you!"

"Enough bullshit." Haley placed her palms on the table and looked down at Severine. Severine looked back at her boldly. She didn't want to deal with this girl right now, but it didn't mean that she was going to back away and crumble in a corner. She faced the fake brunette full on. Haley's brown eyes gleamed back with hatred. "I heard of this one girl. She dated a guy for a short while. Behind her back he was seeing this freshman that he met from the library."

Severine smirked. Before she spoke, she gave Anne a

subtle shake of the head—enough to let her know that she had this. "Really? 'Cause I once knew of this girl that trailed after him like a dog looking for scraps." Severine widened her eyes in mock shock. "Shit. You're right here in front of me."

Haley's back straightened, and she cut a Severine a glare that normally had every other person ducking for cover. "Cute."

"Don't waste my time and I won't waste yours. Blah, blah, blah. You hate me. Blah, blah, blah...just say what you have to say, before I slam your face into my nacho cheese dip."

Haley was tenacious. She wouldn't stop until she got the last word and dig in. She leaned down and the gesture looked private, as if the two of them where having their own personal conversation. Severine knew better. "I've known Macsen a long time. He's never done this." Severine held her breath and waited for Haley to continue. "Shouldn't that show you how he really felt about you? He didn't care enough about you to tell you the truth."

It seemed wrong to Severine that another girl would go so out of her way to cut her down. All over a guy. Severine leaned back in the booth. Her smirk was dark as she took in Haley. "Okay, now I'm pissed off. Bitch mode is officially on." Haley looked weary. "You know what's really shady? The possibility that you knew and didn't say anything to me. If you sat back and let the dominos fall, knowing perfectly well that I was the target, then fuck you, Haley."

"I'm just try-"

"You're trying nothing," Severine interjected quickly. "All you've tried and succeeded at is being a bitch. If you want to be with him, go ahead. Go be his rebound, and then when he does the same thing to you we can braid each other's hair and talk about our fond memories with him."

Haley blinked, and Severine saw the hurt displayed in her eyes. In a brief second, she saw that Haley saw the truth and merit in her words. She'd probably walk away and do the opposite of what her gut told her to do. Severine had no doubt that Haley would go to Macsen and try to console him.She left with her friend minutes later without any food. It confirmed that all she was out for was to put Severine down.

"So that theory must be true," Anne stated cryptically.

Lily slid her phone onto the table and stared at Anne. "What theory?"

"The theory that you're always seven people away from a dumb whore."

Lily looked at Severine and smiled widely. A laugh ripped from Severine's throat and burst out of her mouth. Given the choice, Severine would always pick laughter. It was way better than sobbing her eyes out any day.

"Thank God I have you guys," Severine finally said after the laughter had faded.

"And you always will," Anne stated firmly. "No matter how many dumb idiots come and go."

Chapter Twenty-eight

You need to remember, Severine, that a lonely heart is better than a heart left in pieces...

Severine cringed at the advice her mom had given her as a teenager. She couldn't be more right.

It had been seven days, only seven crappy days. Her emotional wounds were fading, but the humiliation was still there. Severine wondered if that would ever go away. It wasn't enough to make any classes with Macsen okay. In fact, Severine weaseled her way to another seat in the back. It was on purpose that she picked the seat furthest from Macsen's.

Sometimes, she was optimistic that she'd get over it all. And then she'd see Macsen walk into class or around campus, and anger like she had never felt before would kick in. For now, her hatred for Macsen was a constant. Or maybe that was the only way she knew to protect herself.

"So are you sitting here the rest of the semester?"

Severine cut a look at the girl she had been sitting next to for the past week. Her name was Tosha. She didn't say much, but when she did, it instantly held Severine's attention. "Yes. It's permanent."

Tosha rolled her eyes. "I don't believe that." She

stopped typing and pointed a finger at Macsen. "Tall, dark, and brooding makes eyes at you during class."

Severine adjusted her laptop screen and stared at it blankly. "Good for him."

"Did he fuck up?"

Severine gaped at Tosha. This was the only class they had together, and usually, Tosha sat by herself. It wasn't a statement or a cry for help. Everything about her was too much. If there was anything scarier than a beautiful girl, it was a girl that had brains to go with it.

She intimidated Severine like no one else could. But sitting next to Tosha made Severine feel protected. No one would come over here and say something to her. Not even Macsen. "Yeah. He did."

"Sorry." Tosha shrugged her shoulders, but she didn't look sorry. "People sometimes aren't ready for my word vomit."

"I wouldn't be sorry. I'd rather have someone blurt out the truth than hide it."

"Ah! So you're a lover scorned." Tosha smiled like she had Severine's biography figured out.

But there were always two sides. What would Macsen's story be?

"Lover scorned? How many historical romances have you read?"

Tosha turned her head and focused all her attention on Severine. "I don't read that mush, unless I'm bored at my mom's and it's the only thing to read. Then yes, if I have to deal with reading how a Duchess's bosom heaved, okay. One book is better than nothing."

The lecture went on in front of them. Tosha reached into her book bag and slid a book in her direction. "I read her."

"Noelle Rae? Who's that?"

"God." Tosha rubbed her forehead repeatedly. "Are you kidding me? I want to punch you in the face for not knowing who she is." Slowly, she slid her copy towards

Severine. "Read my copy; although, if you lose it, I will find you and kill you. It's my signed copy."

"Why-"

"Oh, and if I see any pages have been dog-eared, I will make you buy ten hardback copies. Ever bought a hardback?"

This girl was a psycho. Severine slowly shook her head. "No."

"Yeah, trust me. It isn't cheap."

"If this is your beloved signed copy, why are you carrying it around? And why are letting me borrow it?"

Tosha smiled. It was a smile that altered her face completely. An iota of content peace consumed her smile. The rest was monopolized by hidden discomfort. Everyone had a story. Tosha just hid hers better than others.

"I'm letting you borrow it because you need it. And Noelle Rae's writing is complete genius. It will take you away from your problems, even if only for a little while."

Severine slid the book back. "Since you look like you're ready to have a stroke, I think I'll pass." Tosha's face fell slightly. Severine spoke quickly, "I'll just buy my own copy."

"Is that one of those, 'Oh, I'll buy my own copy' just to get you off my case, or 'Oh! I'll buy my own copy' because I need to smell the pages and carry it wherever I go?"

Severine smiled. "Like you?"

"If you carry it around like me, you're a fucking genius."

"Why does this story mean so much to you anyway?"

Tosha shifted in her seat and held her copy in her hands. "It's a story—one that I'll never forget. The characters have changed my life. They made me cry, they made me feel pain, but now I feel grateful for my own life." Tosha glanced at Severine sadly. "Whatever you're going through, I can promise you that someone out there is feeling something worse."

Severine nodded her head. Not because it seemed like the right thing to do, but because Tosha was right. "What are you, a shrink?" Severine whispered.

"Nah." Tosha shrugged her shoulders and smirked. "I should be, though. I tried to get my friend Emilia to read it, but she refuses to."

"Too much for her?"

"Everything is too much for her."

"She go to school here?" Severine asked.

"No. She's transferring next year, though."

Professor Bannister ended class for the day. Severine had no idea what was said. She really wanted to care, but Tosha had her attention.

"She's touring the campus today."

"Not much to see," Severine mumbled as she shut her laptop and slid it into her bag.

Tosha stopped in the middle of the aisle and moved her head to the side to stare at Severine. "You should meet her. You two have a lot in common."

Severine didn't know whether to take that as a compliment or insult. "Yeah?"

"Oh yeah," Tosha smiled cryptically and slung her bag over her shoulder. She scooted over so Severine could walk down the wide steps next to her and continued talking. "She'll like you. I can just tell."

Severine smiled anxiously. It would be nice to meet someone who didn't know she had been screwed over by Macsen Sloan. Her slate was clean with someone new. A smile came to her face at the thought.

They walked out the doors, and the freezing air met them brutally. Severine wrapped her scarf tightly around her neck and followed Tosha.

"Oh," she nudged Severine in the side. "She's over there."

"Emilia!

Severine scrunched her eyes and saw a girl with light

caramel hair sitting on one of the tables scattered across the frozen grass. She inclined her head in greeting and stared at Severine. "Why is she sitting outdoors...willingly?"

"She's a people watcher."

"A what?"

"You know...someone who watches other people."

Severine talked as she dug through her pockets to find her pair of gloves. "That seems kind of creepy."

"It sounds creepy. But believe me, people are oblivious when they're talking, fighting, gossiping. You can find out so much when you're in the shadows."

Severine squinted to look closer at the girl sitting statue still. She wasn't pretty. That was too simple of a word.

Her face was lovely. One glance wouldn't be enough. With every new glimpse, you'd find something special about her.

But the intensity in her gaze made Severine want to back away and run the opposite way. She smiled in their direction. Severine felt like it was only directed at Tosha.

"Severine, wait!"

Her eyes slammed shut before she turned to have another confrontation with Macsen. Emilia would get her people watching in for the day. Even if this conversation went nowhere with Macsen, someone would get something out of it. All Severine would possess afterwards was more confusion and a whole lot of anger.

"I'll leave you alone," Tosha recited quickly. "Emilia and I will be waiting at the table."

Macsen jogged to where she stood. His dark locks were covered with a baseball cap, as usual. The strands that peeked around the cap showed he hadn't cut his hair in a while. It gave him a boyish charm. It made him look sincere. Severine knew what was really behind his sweet smile and captivating eyes. She wanted to warn every girl to ever cross his path again.

"You actually waited for me."

"Are you dying?"

Macsen frowned. "No."

"If you're not dying or bleeding from the eyes, let's not talk." *Because it hurts too fucking much.*

"Shit." He adjusted his bag. His hold on the brown strap made his knuckles turn white. "You won't make this easy for me."

Severine glanced down at the ground before looking back up. One look away could refuel her determination to stay firm. "Everything could've been easy between us. Someone couldn't keep it in their pants."

"I told you I fucked up!" Macsen's voice rose slightly. They were now being people watched by everyone. He moved his face closer and lowered his voice for only her ears. "Do I need to grovel on the ground for you?"

Before everything crumbled around them he didn't have to do anything. He already had her. When Severine spoke, her words came out choked. "I'm not asking you to do anything."

Macsen held his hands in the air. The gesture showed how he was just as lost in this situation as she was. Severine wanted to link her hands with his. He took that want away from her with his mistakes. "I'll leave then."

"Wait," Severine gritted out. She regretted it the minute it came out of her mouth.

Macsen was barely a few steps away. He was by her side in a second. "Yeah?"

"I want you to answer something for me."

"Anything."

"I need this for myself. Not you." Snowflakes fell from sky and landed all around them. One of them touched Severine's lips. She brushed it off impatiently. Macsen stared at her fixedly. When he gazed at her like that, Severine doubted everything. How could the person in front of her screw up?

"I just wanna know why. Tell me why you did this to us?"

His shoulders tensed, and he stepped away. "I made a huge mistake."

"I get that." Severine put her hands up to air quote, "'Mistake' is your new favorite word. There was a reason behind it. Just tell me."

Severine wanted an acknowledgement to her question. Mistake and fucked up, could only get you so far. She wanted the truth.

Macsen adjusted his hat and nodded his head back and forth. "I can't give that to you."

"Because you don't know?"

"Because it'd break you, and you'd never want to see me again."

"I'm already broken," Severine admitted. "Just give me the truth."

For a brief second, it looked like he was going to. "I'm not doing that to you."

There was no response to that. And even if she wanted to say anything, she couldn't, because he walked away. Severine stared at the place he'd stood with anger building up in her body. She asked for his help and even that hurt.

None of this could be let go. The image of him with another girl reared up angrily in her head. It was a record stuck on repeat. One minute it was gone, but the image would reappear to replay again.

Over, and over, and over.

Severine made her way to Tosha and Emilia and sat down on the frozen seat across from them.

"That seemed intense," Tosha mentioned lightly. She was dying to hear the details.

Severine nodded at the two of them. "Not much to say about it. Macsen's a dick."

Emilia placed her elbow on the table in front of them and propped her chin on her fist. Her dainty body was encased in a dark red coat. The collar was popped up, not for fashion, but to keep the wind at bay. It caused her fish tail braid to wrap around her shoulder and hang in all its caramel glory.

Emilia was her own unique brand. She was a vintage chic. It made Severine envious to see a girl so put together when her own life felt like it was crumbling around her.

"You two have a story."

Severine raised a brow at Emilia's probing question. This was how she said *hi* to someone? Severine drummed her glove-clad hands on the table. "Yeah. Doesn't everyone have a story?"

She raised a brow, and Tosha shoved her face close. "I told Severine you were a people watcher."

"Severine?"

"No. Seh-vreen." The correction rolled off her tongue. It was by habit.

"A beautiful name for a beautiful girl." Emilia's enigmatic words came out slowly. How much did she see in Severine?

"Mmm...thanks," Severine said uncomfortably.

"That guy that ran away all coward-like...is he your boyfriend?"

A laugh burst out of Severine's mouth. It was brittle. "Ah, that's a big no."

"So he made a mistake?"

"You tell me, Watch-Woman Emilia. What did you see from our exchange?"

"I saw a guy wanting your attention. I noticed a girl who looked broken, but strong at the same time." Emilia paused to flip her hood up. "By the way, any girl that can hold her own is a friend of mine." She held her small gloveless hand out in between the two of them. Severine felt as if she had passed some test. She removed her hand from her coat pocket and firmly shook the girl's hand.

It seemed stupid. But Severine felt an alliance with

Emilia.

Severine shook her head and replied firmly. "Tosha said you're thinking about going here next year?"

"I'm not thinking about it. I am coming here." Briefly, she looked around as a tiny smile played on her lips. "This place is going to offer me so much more."

"Yeah? Bitter temps or better people watching?" Severine teased.

Emilia smiled and her own hidden secrets shown in her light brown eyes. Even observers had their own story.

Chapter Twenty-nine

"What took you so long?"

Severine hurried to where her friend sat and removed Lily's bag from the chair. "Sorry. I met some new people."

"New people?" Lily smiled hopefully.

Severine raised a single eyebrow and draped her coat on the open chair next to her. "Relax. They were girls."

"Still. The word *new* is good!"

Severine nodded, but her concentration was focused on the menu. Lily plucked it from her fingers and placed it on the table. "I ordered for you already," she explained.

"Was I that late?"

"No. When you decided to change where we eat every day, it cuts my eating time. I have to go clear across campus. So I'm on a slight time crunch."

"Are you going to quit on me?"

"Please." Lily rolled her eyes. "I wish I could. I'd save myself some gas money."

At the front counter an order number was called. Lily hopped up from her seat and scurried over to grab their food. Lily bit into her pickle as she walked back to their table.

"Hungry much?" Severine asked with a smirk.

Lily made a face and placed their tray in the middle

of the table. "I'm starving."

Severine opened up her sub sandwich, stared at the yummy B.L.T. and slammed it down. "Ah! I just want to flip out on something."

"Please don't flip out on the sandwich that cost me almost six dollars." Lily said with her mouth full.

Severine thought briefly of her conversation with Macsen and looked at Lily. "I talked to Macsen before I came here."

Lily lowered her sandwich. "You did?"

"It was nothing big, I just..."

"You got nothing figured out," Lily supplied sympathetically.

"Nothing," Severine confirmed. She bit into her food, pissed that the taste was gone for her.

"What happened?" Lily asked gently.

"I wanted to know why. That's all I wanted." Severine looked down at her food. "He couldn't even give me that," she said bitterly.

"You'll probably never get an explanation past 'Uh, I'm sorry. I messed up,'" Lily projected in her best male voice.

Severine raked a hand through her hair. It wouldn't leave her brain. Whenever she took one step forward, Macsen came up beside her and she went ten steps backwards.

Just let it go. Move on.

Her conscience could echo those thoughts as much as it wanted. It was the right thing to do. But her biggest strength was also her weakest flaw. Severine couldn't walk away from something when she didn't know the answer.

Macsen had been a first for her on so many levels. Most importantly, he was the first to break her down. She didn't want to back away.

"I think you need to burn off some stress," Lily declared. She wiped her hands off with a napkin, and lightly smacked her hands together. "Didn't you work out with Anne and beat the dummy to a pulp?"

"She told you?"

"No, Ben told me," Lily supplied. "The dummy looked like Gumby and had to be replaced with a brand new dummy."

"I didn't know that," Severine admitted slowly. "I'm surprised I wasn't charged for it. How much does one of those stupid things cost? Hundred bucks?"

Lily smashed her trash together in a small ball. "Try a few thousand."

Severine's mouth dropped open. "Poor Bill."

"Thayer covered for you. You know, after your punch and run." Lily snickered at her own joke.

Severine stared at Lily like she had two heads. "Thayer?"

Lily shrugged her shoulders. "It's not a big deal when you know the starting center for the basketball team."

"God." Severine smashed her forehead against her palms. The thought of Thayer helping her for nothing in return was a hard thing for her brain to wrap around. "I give up."

"Why? I'm confused. Where are you going with this?"

"Because I thought I had everything pegged. I could've guaranteed you that I knew exactly who Macsen was, along with Thayer..."

"And now?"

Severine looked up at her friend, her trusted companion. It wasn't hard to admit defeat to her. "I think I fucked it up. I think I had impressions of the two of them before I knew everything."

"I think you're completely accurate," Lily gently stated.

"Not helping."

Lily smiled weakly. "Sorry. I love you if that makes you feel any better."

"You have to say that. You're legally bound with a contract." Severine joked lightly—anything to keep her thoughts from focusing on Thayer's kind gesture. It was more than kind.

Lily laughed loudly just as Ben walked up to their table. More and more bodies were starting to fill the small building. Soon there'd be a line practically out the door.

He sat down and immediately kissed the top of Lily's head. When he glanced over at Severine his expression was almost cautious—like she was contagious. "Hey, Severine."

Severine nodded and smiled sympathetically at him. He was probably still scarred from her sobbing her eyes out after her breakup with Macsen. "Benji."

"So, I was thinking..." Lily interrupted quietly.

Both Severine and Ben stared at her suspiciously.

"Why don't you come stay with me?" Lily asked perkily.

Severine quickly looked at Ben. He nodded his head in agreement. Although, he'd probably agree with everything Lily had to say just to make her happy. "Sure. It'd be cool," he confirmed with a firm nod.

"Benji, you live with Tim. I don't think even I could handle him right now."

"I'm happy to report that he is moving out after this semester. Going to his frat house."

"I'm sorry for your loss," Severine added dully.

"Don't be. I almost did the fucking worm, I was so happy."

Severine glanced between the two and laughed. "So it's just the two of you? Aww! You're like a little married couple." Even though Severine was kidding, it was fun to see Ben choke on his sandwich. "Relax, I'm just kidding, Benji."

Ben cleared his throat and chugged down his water before talking. "To clarify, I'm getting a new roommate at the end of Christmas."

"Cool." Severine nodded her head, but she had already stopped listening.

Lily and Ben talked quietly to themselves, and Severine polished off the rest of her sandwich. God, it'd be amazing to be one of those girls that couldn't muster the strength to eat after heartbreak.

There was no better payback than looking amazing in front of your ex. Instead, Severine ate everything in sight. She was an emotional eater. Always had been, always would be. She paid the price by occasionally stepping foot in the gym.

Lily snapped her fingers in front of Severine. "You never answered my question."

"What? About staying with you guys?"

Lily anxiously nodded her head.

"You don't think that will be awkward for everyone?" Severine asked. "You guys canoodling in the next room would be the last thing I'd want to hear."

Lily threw the rest of her pickle in Severine's direction. "Why do you still call it that? I hate that word."

"I love that word."

For a moment, Lily paused and pursed her lips in thought before she flashed her blue eyes at Severine. "Do I need to pack your stuff up?"

"Eh. It would be great not to be stuck alone in the dorms," Severine disclosed thoughtfully.

"You'd be closer to the gym and all the restaurants," Lily said in a luring voice.

"That's great. The last thing I need is the torture of greasy food."

"The best thing of all? You'd be next to me."

It seemed like the opposite of what Severine should do. Going to a friend's house because she was lonely? It was what she wanted, but Severine knew it wouldn't work in the long run. This whole problem was something she needed to face by herself.

Chapter Thirty

Severine hopped back and forth anxiously. It was seven in the morning, on a weekend. She should be studying for finals, creeping on Facebook, calling her mom. Instead, she was pounding on Anne's door.

After Severine's tenth pound, she answered. A blanket was tossed around her shoulder, part of her black hair was sticking straight up, and she had a serious case of morning breath. "What. The. Hell. Do. You. Want?"

"Go to the gym with me," Severine said anxiously.

Anne groaned and leaned her body against the doorframe dramatically. "Screw you, Severine. It's what, four in the morning?"

"It's seven."

"What's the difference?" Anne grumbled.

It was time to be in bed, sleeping the morning away. But Severine needed a breather—from everything. "Can you just get dressed and go with me?"

"Why now? Are you Rocky? Are you training for a boxing match?" Anne peered closer, and checked Severine's eyes. "Did you take speed or something? No human should be awake at this time."

"I agree, but I finished studying a few hours ago, and I can't sleep."

Anne nodded groggily. "You know you're screwing

up my REM cycle, right?"

"Meet me downstairs."

"Bite me, Severine."

* * * * *

Severine had never been a good runner on a treadmill. Was it just her or did everyone feel at some point they were going to fall off the damn thing and bust their ass? It made her nervous.

Next to her was Anne, who was walking as slow as a snail. She said she was walking off her sleep hangover. Severine wholly believed her. But Anne hadn't complained once the entire two hours they had been there. Anne knew why Severine was up. They didn't have to say anything; she was just there for her.

The screen flashed: *three miles*. For once while working out, it was a fast three miles. She slowed the machine to a cool down and stared up at the flat screen mounted in front of her.

Her muscles burned in pain. It was helping, though. The anger rolled off her in waves and down to her feet, pounding away all her hatred. Severine pressed stop and chugged a bottle of water.

"I thought you were gonna run the belt off."

Severine kept her expression neutral and turned around. In front of her, Thayer stood in a pair of basketball shorts and a cut off. He looked at her with no sympathy. Severine could've kissed him for that.

"You feel better?"

She shrugged her shoulders but smiled. "I'd feel better if I could rip your brother's eyes out."

His lips went into a thin line. "Ben told me that Lily wants you to stay with them."

Severine walked in step with Thayer. "Benji has-"

"Oh, don't worry about me," Anne shouted behind them. "I'm okay over here!"

Severine turned back to look at her friend. Her head was inches away from Thayer's bicep. Even sweaty, he smelled good. "I'm waiting for you!"

"Hardly. I'm gonna head out early. I think you kicked your anger right in the ass. Adios, Severine." Anne halted in front of Thayer and craned her neck up to his face before looking at Severine. "No one should look this good after a workout." She walked away but shouted out, "No one!"

"So, Anne still likes me."

"Anne likes no one. And why would anyone dislike you?"

"Because of the whole..."

"You didn't cheat on me." Severine looked around the gym as she waited for the awkwardness to kick in or for Thayer to find an excuse to leave. It never arrived.

"Have you talked to Mac?" he asked quietly.

Severine motioned for him to follow her. "Barely. When I do, none of my questions get answered."

Thayer nodded his head. "So you're really not going to take him back?"

It was the tone of his voice that made Severine stop walking. He stopped with her but stared ahead with a frown on his face. "No, I'm not. Do you find that hard to believe?"

"Maybe I do."

"I can't persuade you to believe it. There's really nothing left to salvage."

He opened his mouth, looking like he wanted to say more, but he quickly shut it. "I don't think he's going to give up, Blake."

Severine looked down at the ground. "Does it really matter anymore? Besides, it's not like we were together for years or even a year. Hell, Thayer, it was only a few weeks. Kids in middle school have longer relationships."

"People fuck up, though."

Severine looked up him at sharply. "Are you

standing up for him?"

"I'm the last person that will stand up for him. But what are you going to do in your next relationship? What if the next guy does something stupid?"

"Simple. I'll just stick to my serial dating. My graphical chart has proven that going on a few dates and moving on has been a statistical success."

"Because you get to know none of them," Thayer muttered.

Severine huffed and placed her hands on her hips. "Really? You're going to give me advice? You do the same thing."

He smirked, but his eyes were serious. "Because I know from date one who's worth my attention and efforts."

"You can tell that quickly?"

Thayer snapped his fingers. "Just like that."

His face was pensive as he waited for her to speak. Severine thought over her words and avoided his gaze. "I think you're right about one thing." Thayer merely raised his eyebrows. "I'm realizing that I knew nothing about Macsen. I thought I knew who he was, but there's another side of him that I've never seen."

"You have no idea," Thayer said seriously.

She wanted to suddenly blurt out how sorry she was for judging him so quickly. Funny how she saw the side of Thayer no one ever did. How much she preferred it to the snarky, quiet one that every girl sighed over and loved.

"I didn't, did I?" Severine asked him. "That's my mistake. I won't make it again."

Thayer looked at her and stepped closer. "He's one guy, Severine. Don't place the rest of us in that light."

"I won't." Severine didn't know if she could keep true to her words. Once you've been burned, it was possible to forget, but a scar would always be there, reminding you of the one mistake.

"Hey." Thayer nudged her lightly on the shoulder. A part of Severine wanted him to keep his hand there. "You looked like shit running on the treadmill."

"Thank you for that."

"That's why I wondered if you'd want to run with me upstairs."

"Upstairs?"

"Above the court, there's a small track for people to run."

Severine automatically looked up to the ceiling. "Since when?"

"Since forever. Follow me—it's on the opposite side. You would've noticed before, by the magic of sight…"

Severine aimed a kick at his calf, and he dodged out of the way with a boyish smile playing on his face. "Come on, Blake." He grabbed her hand in his, without asking, and without caring what they'd look like.

Severine held tight and followed him to the opposite side of the building. When they reached the basketball court, sure enough, a set of stairs was right next to the entrance. They walked up the stairs, and Severine's legs were already cringing in pain. "So this has been here the whole time? Am I the only one that has been clueless about this?"

"Nah. If you venture this far you'd notice it, but you're not a true gym rat."

The small track came in sight. Only one other person ran quietly. It was a perfect place for Severine to run off all her stress in silence.

"So you want me to go? I'll run with you."

Severine riveted her gaze at Thayer.

He shifted forward on the balls of his feet. "If you want me to. You just seem…" his eyes glanced at her thoughtfully, "lonely."

She was, completely and wholly. "Yeah, I'd like that."

Severine watched him nod and look away. She didn't

miss the slight smirk on his face as he went to stretch. She was finding more reasons to count on Thayer—more reasons to depend on him when she wanted to break down and fewer reasons to care about having feelings for him.

Chapter Thirty-one

"Severine!" Her mom shouted. "Severine, can you see me?"

Severine cringed. "Yes, I can. You don't have to shout, Mom. Is this your first Skype call ever?"

Severine watched her mom nod and smile. "Actually, it is. Your Aunt Rachel helped me download it."

Rachel shoved her face close to the screen. "Your mom knows nothing about technology. It's scary."

"You're preaching to the choir. I've tried to get her to Skype with me forever."

"Well, now she has it. There's no excuse." Rachel moved away from the screen and dragged a chair up next to her mom.

"Severine!" her mom shouted. "I'll be back. My casserole is almost done."

"Okay."

"Rachel will keep you company."

Aunt Rachel winked at the screen as her mom moved out of the computer chair and out of the room. "Soo," Rachel drew out, "your mom mentioned a boy...

The wound was healing, but it still hurt to think about. "Ah. That didn't go too well. We broke up a few weeks ago."

"I heard about that. But I'm not talking about that

scum, Severine. I want to know about this other guy."

"The other guy," Severine pronounced slowly.

"Severine!" she hissed out. "Are you with his brother already?"

Her eyes bulged wide. "What the hell? No, no." Severine shook her head wildly. "No, I'm not with him."

Even with miles and miles separating them, she could sense her aunt's interest. She was watching Severine's every move, every fidget, and blink, and it was all taken in account. Sometimes she read into everything Severine didn't want people to see.

"Okay...you're not with this dude-"

"Thayer," Severine interrupted.

Rachel raised her eyebrows. "Sorry. You're not with Thayer, but I've seen that look. Hell, I remember having that look. He must be something to have you squirming like that."

Severine groaned and placed her forehead against her keyboard. "If I say anything, you're just gonna judge."

"I can hardly judge. Last week I went out with a guy name Ceecee. I thought I could get over the name. But clearly, we can see that didn't go anywhere."

Severine glanced up at the screen and smiled. "Ceecee?"

"It was a nickname, okay! I'm not judging, you don't judge. That's the deal here."

Severine nodded. "What are you asking? Am I attracted to him?"

"Yes. But remember, I'm your aunt. I want to give you advice, but give me the clean version."

Severine batted her eyelashes playfully at the screen. "Why yes, I'm attracted to him. Just last week we were at the gym, and I wanted to jump his bones."

"TMI!"

"I'm just kidding." *Not really.*

"So how badly do you want to jump his bones?"

Rachel asked with narrowed eyes.

Severine held both of her hands in front of her, palms up. "Macsen and I," she lifted her right hand slightly. "Visions of Thayer and me," the left hand pushed itself high in the air.

A grin played on her aunt's lips. "A little attracted then, are you?"

"Oh, just a little," Severine said back dryly.

"You really wanna know what I think?"

Severine stalled for time and crossed her legs. "Depends," she finally uttered.

"I think that you need to stay away. Sounds like you have a major spark with this one. And if I were betting, I'd say the feeling is mutual. But he's Scumbag's brother, Severine. Imagine if you dated or were together for a night. It would change many things. And you're bouncing back from a breakup, which let's admit, is not the best feeling in the world."

Severine knew that. Those reasons had popped up in her head more than once. Every time she'd agree with those thoughts, they'd quickly start to fade away. Every time she talked to Thayer on the phone, at the gym, or walking across campus, those warnings faded until there was absolutely nothing holding her back.

With her head pressed close to her screen, Severine whispered, "I don't think I can stay away. It's messed up."

Rachel nodded and whispered back, "Then go for it."

"Okay," her mom announced breezily, "I'm back."

Rachel gave a subtle nod of her head. Severine knew their conversation would be between the two of them. "So, Severine," her aunt called out conversationally, "before we got on here, I was trying to talk your mom into taking a trip with me."

Severine raised her eyebrows. "A trip, eh?"

Clacy scoffed, and Severine smiled at her mom's discomfort. She wasn't a traveler. In fact, you never wanted to travel with her mom. By the end of the vacation, you'd lose the will to live.

"Rachel, we all can't have your...free spiritedness. I can't just take time off from work."

"Sure you can! This will be amazing!" Rachel chirped out.

"When is this trip?" Severine asked.

"Well, that's the thing," Rachel paused uncomfortably. "It's during your break."

"And you want me to go, or you don't want me to go?"

"No!" Rachel rushed out. "We want you to go. The two of us just doubted whether you'd want to spend time with two middle-aged women while they ogled the cabana boys."

Severine laughed at the thought. "No, it's not exactly on my to-do list."

"Severine, I won't go if you want to spend Christmas with me. I know you're still hurting from Grandma's loss. If you want me to be home, I will be."

"You need to go," Severine said instantly. The mention of her grandma urged her to encourage her mom to go. She'd miss her grandma forever, but knew her mom and aunt suffered from the loss even worse. If this trip with her sister would cheer them up, they should do it.

"But-"

"So," Severine interrupted her mom quickly, "where do you want to kidnap her?"

Rachel answered instantly, "Scotland."

Severine's jaw dropped. "There'll be no cabana boys there. You know that, right?"

"Okay, so guys in kilts. Same thing."

Not even close. Severine let it slide. "Mom, do you even own a passport?"

"Yes. I just don't see the need to travel all over the Earth."

Severine frowned, and Rachel supplied an answer to Severine's confusion. "Since your mom was a teenager, she has refused to travel overseas. I think she thinks the ocean will swallow her whole or something."

"No! That's not it. I will remain in the good ol' US of A!"

"Come on, Clacy! I've seen the grandmas on those Norman Rockwell pictures live more wildly than you! Severine, tell your mom she should go."

"You should really go." Her mom gawked at her, and Severine explained her answer in greater detail. "I think we've gone on two vacations my *whole* life, and the entire time you whined."

Rachel squealed and hugged her sister. "You see? You need an adventure. It's only for a week! It will be amazing!"

Severine saw the indecision on her mom's face but knew she was cracking slowly. "And you're okay spending all of your Christmas break alone?"

"I'm okay staying by myself. It will be great, actually. I was planning on a crazy party this weekend. Now I won't have to worry about you getting in the way."

"Cute, Severine," her mom said, giving her the eye.

Severine laughed. "I think you guys will have an amazing time. When are you leaving?"

"In a few days. I figure we can arrive in time for Christmas and celebrate New Year's!"

Her mom groaned loudly, "A trip with you? What am I thinking? I think I need to stock up on some Percocet."

When her mom left the room, Rachel watched her walk away and anxiously moved toward the screen. "What are you really gonna do during your break?"

Severine shrugged. "I don't know. I just found out I'll be alone. I'll figure something out.

"Don't meet up with that Thayer guy," Rachel sharply demanded.

"You mean it's probably a bad idea to have his love

child?" Severine joked.

"Use sarcasm all you want. I think you're biting off more than you can chew." She shifted in her seat and looked closer at Severine. "He's a male version of you. You sure it's a good idea to involve yourself with him?"

Severine didn't want to talk about the truth. She didn't want to talk about what she wanted anymore. What she wanted was off limits. "I don't know anything anymore, Aunt Rachel."

"That's what scares me, sweetie."

Severine looked at her earnestly, making sure to keep her answer vague. "You don't need to worry about it, though. I'll be fine."

Rachel didn't respond back.

Chapter Thirty-two

"Are you shoving it in right?"

Severine brushed away the flakes from her hair and glared at Lily. "No. I'm doing a few roundhouse kicks over here. That's not what you wanted?"

"Severine. Shut up, shut up, shut up!" Lily groaned.

"Wait...you didn't want me to go full-on ninja?"

"I love you, but I will reach over there and kick your ass."

"Said the Polly Pocket," Severine mumbled.

Lily looked close to ripping her hair out. Severine toned down the sarcasm and walked around Ben's Trailblazer. "Is this whole Christmas at his parents' getting to you?"

"Yes!" Lily pressed her face into Severine's shoulder, making her words come out muffled. "I think I drank a whole bottle of Pepto-Bismol."

Severine hefted a piece of Lily's luggage into Ben's SUV. "Why are you freaking out so much?"

"Because, I've never visited the 'family,'" Lily said with air quotes.

Severine dusted off her gloves, and walked with Lily to the passenger door. "That's a good thing! No guy would ever do that if they weren't interested."

"I'm just really nervous. Will they be judgmental?

Not like me?"

"Lily, let me say this as kindly as I can." Severine placed her arms on Lily's shoulders and smiled. "You grew up in the world's strictest home and around people that judged everyone—even on what they were wearing. I think you're good."

"What if they're like my family?"

"Did Ben ask you to bring a pair of culottes?"

Lily shook her head.

"Then you're golden."

Lily started to relax and smiled widely. "I left all my pairs at home."

Severine grinned. "In case they do ask, you can use my favorite excuse—the one I used when I went to church with you."

"They're in the wash?"

"Exactly! You can't go wrong with that one!"

"Babe!" Ben shouted as he came running toward them. "Are you ready?"

Lily nodded her head and turned to Severine. "You gonna be okay by yourself?"

"I think I'll be fine. I'm not a six-year-old."

"It's just...it's..."

"Christmas?" Severine supplied.

"Yeah. You're supposed to be with family!"

"You're spending your entire break with Ben's family," Severine pointed out.

Lily rolled her eyes and opened the passenger door. "I spent all of Thanksgiving break with my family. I've met my quota." She slammed the door and rolled down the window. "Be safe. I'll see you later, friend!"

Severine watched them pull out and walked to her own car. She should feel lonely, but oddly she was ready for a breather...from everyone.

*   *   *   *   *

There's something to be said about having alone time.

Severine had never felt so revitalized. Even though she was essentially trapped on campus, Severine felt a happiness that hadn't been attached to her name in a while. Being away from everything gave her time to think, to regroup and to decide what she really wanted from her life. This year was ending on a mountain of regrets and pain. Severine didn't want the same outcome for the next year.

The promise of a new year and a fresh start put a smile on her face.

With the blinds open, she watched the snow fall softly to the ground. Christmas had come and gone. That was the only time Severine became sad. She had Skyped with both her mom and Aunt Rachel. The smile on her mom's face was perfection. It wiped away any doubt that her mom should've been with her. Maybe her mom needed a break of her own.

A few days after Christmas, cabin fever started to set in. She had spent too much time indoors. Severine needed a breath of fresh air.

She slid on her new brown leather boots, courtesy of her dad. The snow would probably ruin the distressed leather. It was hard for her to care, though, when she felt this très chic.

Her fingers ached as she finished her waterfall braid. When she glanced in the mirror, Severine loved what she saw. With her hair away from her face, her green eyes stood out more. This wasn't a day for blush—going outside for more than a minute would tinge her cheeks pink instantly. She still put some on. Old habits were hard to break.

She grabbed an off-white jacket to put over her tan sweater as she walked to her car. She had nowhere important to go. All that mattered was how she felt.

Fresh snow molded underneath the tread of her tires

as she backed out of her parking spot. Winter weather always made her nervous. Looking at the snow while indoors was great; driving in it was like the devil's playground—she loathed it.

Severine granny-drove toward the middle of town and finally found what she was looking for. When the McDonald's sign came within sight, Severine smiled widely as she slowly made her way into the turn lane. It was a 'clog your arteries with grease and fat and enjoy the whole damn meal' kind of day.

Her feet felt light as she walked across the parking lot. And if she wouldn't have looked like a dumbass, she might've twirled around in a complete circle. How long had it been since her mind felt this extricated from pain?

Simple: before the Sloan Brothers.

A strong amount of wind picked up and slammed into her face. Her eyes watered at the feeling. She didn't notice it. As the air whispered against her ear, all could she hear from it was that something great was coming in her direction. She could feel it. She could-

The door slammed into her, and Severine grunted over the impact.

In front of her stood Macsen.

Her something great was him? Really?

"You have to be fucking kidding me," Severine mumbled angrily. It was official, she was never listening to her conscience again. It was defunct—a glitched bitch.

"Shit," Macsen mumbled quickly. "Sorry, Severine." His hands were filled with bags as he moved closer. The only consolation prize to being bitch slapped by a clear glass door was seeing how shitty Macsen looked.

His dark hair wasn't combed; a flannel shirt was his sorry excuse to brave the bitter outdoors. His skin was now covered in facial hair. Severine would like to think he had given up on life all together and became a hobo, but knowing his luck he'd be on the streets for one day and be discovered by a modeling scout. The next thing she'd know, Macsen would be on every magazine and billboard to torture her. He'd show her, 'Hey, I screwed you over! I got away with it!'

"It's okay." Severine pushed away from the filthy wall and walked away from him. She could feel Macsen's breath on her neck.

"Sev, just wait."

She practically ran.

"You know I've been trying to talk to you."

"I know," Severine said on a deflated sigh.

That's why today was a celebration. Today felt different and free, because there was nothing from him. The minute she wanted to brush him away from her life, he'd leave a text or voicemail. It'd be impossible to move forward with him still within reach.

"Are you ever going to answer?"

"No. I'm not."

She watched as he clenched his jaw and gripped his hair tightly in his hands. "God! What else is there to do?"

"There's nothing to do."

"So nothing? You're finished," Macsen stated sharply.

Her heart gave a lurch, because she still remembered what it was like to be around him, what it felt like to trust him. But when that trust is based off nothing but lies, it was useless.

When she glanced up at him, it wasn't the cold wind that made her eyes well up with tears. "We are. You and I shouldn't talk, shouldn't communicate. At all."

He said nothing, but his eyes showed just how crushed he was by her words. He saw the truth.

Severine's good mood was destroyed. She glanced at him once and opened up her car door.

"I can make this better, Sev," Macsen said softly.

She looked over the roof of her car and shook her head. No matter how hard she looked at him, Severine realized that she had never known much about him. "No,

I don't think you ever can."

Her car started up immediately. Severine stayed rooted in her seat and held her hands close to the vents numbly. What made the word love so great? Her conscience gently told her that maybe, maybe what she had hadn't quite been love. Affection, lust, friendship—all of those, perhaps. But if she had to question the feelings that came with that four-letter word, maybe it was never hers to begin with.

She wanted to purge him out of her life. Now that it was done, it burned. Even when someone needed to wither out of your life, you were still left with the blisters of their decisions. To attain your soul, it hurt.

Severine dug through her glove box and searched for a Kleenex. Instead, she found a wadded up Subway napkin and wiped underneath her eyes.

Her cup holder started to vibrate awkwardly. The noise made Severine jump, and she snatched her phone swiftly. A number she knew perfectly flashed on her screen. For a second, she paused, "Hello?"

"What are you doing, Blake?" Thayer playfully asked.

"I'm sitting in a McDonald's parking lot."

I just saw your brother. And everything feels so final. I want to cry and celebrate at the same time.

"That sounds completely depressing."

"It is." Severine drummed her hands on her steering wheel and cleared her throat. "What are you doing?"

"I'm getting ready to leave for my dad's."

"Yeah?" A pathetic tear fell down her face. Her mom was in Scotland, staring at dudes with kilts, and she was sitting here, freezing her ass off, alone.

Alone. She hated the damn word.

"He has a cabin in Tennessee. About a two hour drive from campus."

"Neat."

"I wanted to say good-bye to you."

"Why?" Severine laughed out.

"Because..." he stopped talking. Severine strained to hear what he had to say. "You make tears look exquisite, but...they're not meant for you."

Severine turned her head every which way in the car. When Thayer knocked on her door, she screamed and dropped her phone. Thayer grinned at her as she quickly opened her door.

Minutes before, she had been with his brother and had felt crushed by their conversation. Severine was fighting to keep control, but for that bastard, she could fall to her knees and let all her efforts dribble away for him.

His hands were tucked tightly into his back pockets as he stood close to her. The intensity of his focus could've been rude. Those impossible gray irises that normally drove her to lunacy were trying to solve her pain. Severine wanted him to successfully work it out for her, it was conceivable that Thayer could make it better.

"Your brother was just here," Severine uttered with a scratch in her voice.

"I know." His eyes never left hers. "You okay?"

"My day has gone to shit, but I'm fine. Maybe you can tell me why I'm seeing both Sloan siblings at McDonald's? Craving some tater tots?"

He shook his head. "I was going to order some food for the road."

"For Tennessee," Severine reiterated.

Thayer nodded. "Yeah," he drew the word out slowly, stalling for time, "you wanna know something insane?"

"No."

"Good. I'll tell you anyway." He shifted away, but not before she saw all of the frustration. Severine just didn't know how it got there.

"I want you to come with me," Thayer eventually blurted out.

Insane was the perfectly matched word to describe what he was thinking. And what was even more outrageous was Severine's urge to say, 'Let's go right now.'

Rather than voicing her wish, she backed up against her snow-covered car. The cool liquid of the snow melted through her jeans and reminded her that she could miss this chance. She could regret this later. Already, too many maybes and whys had occurred in this year. Severine wanted to know she chose a situation with her heart fully in mind.

"Do you think Macsen is going to be there?" Thayer challenged.

Severine put confusion into words, "Am I off-base thinking families celebrate holidays together?"

Thayer looked back at her, just as confused. "He really told you nothing about the dysfunctional family we share, did he?"

Her response would be the opposite of no. That was more humiliating than Severine wanted to admit. Thayer gave her a free pass and kept talking. "No. He won't be there. Just our older brother Mathias, my dad and stepmom."

Stepmom. Severine really knew nothing about these brothers. She was still curious, still wanted to find out the truth.

Was she a victim of amnesia? Her past with the Sloan brothers could be transcribed into one word: disaster.

"Do you want to come along?" Thayer offered. "Or, do you want to stay in your dorm all lonely and emo?"

"How do you know I'm alone?"

"Aren't you?"

They could play hide and seek with their words all day long. Severine was already tired of games. "Yes."

"Just come with me."

Severine ignored his words and pressed forward. "Your family won't find this weird?"

"They won't. You'll be with me."

For once, Severine didn't analyze. She let her want slip free. "I'll go."

Chapter Thirty-three

For the longest time, Severine was scared to swim. When she was a kid it was the deep end that scared her.

She'd use her tiptoes and walk through the chlorine clear water until it reached her lips. Her foot would drag across the bottom. Back then, it seemed like the deep end just plunged into the lowest depths of the ground. It would swallow her whole.

She was diving into the deep end right now. The minute she opened her mouth and agreed to go with Thayer, her entire body sunk to the bottom. She couldn't breathe. Her heart rate was out of control, and her lungs felt like they were on fire.

Her feet hurriedly guided her around her room. Fear tried to bite into the heels of her feet. Her emotions kept her going further. If she stopped, all those fears would completely drown her.

Severine grabbed random garments and tossed the clothing into her suitcase at a frantic pace. She was doing something for her heart for once. She'd become a repeat offender if she could always have this sensation.

"You ready?" Thayer asked by her door.

Severine nodded and grabbed the straps of her bag. "Let's go."

She already knew she was smashing into a moment.

She couldn't write it off later. Her compass pointed straight at him. Repentance could chase afterwards.

"You're a fast packer."

"I'm excited," Severine admitted, as they walked to his truck.

"You're excited to travel with me?"

"You're not that bad."

Thayer tossed her bag into the backseat. "Neither are you."

For the first thirty minutes of the trip, Severine bounced her legs up and down nervously. What the hell was she doing? She went through so many feelings, but none of them involved Thayer taking her back.

"So your parents are divorced," Severine stated.

"You want the story?"

God, did she ever. Severine toyed with the radio and shrugged. "Sure."

Thayer rested his arm on the console in between them. Severine visualized him resting on her. "Our parents have been divorced since we were little. My dad remarried. My older brother, Mathias, and I went to stay with him. Macsen stuck near our mom."

"You say that like it's a death sentence."

Thayer's laugh was ominous. "Because it is. My mom's a piece of work."

"Well, that's kind of you," Severine said slowly.

"If you ever meet her, you'll get it."

Severine skipped to another question quickly. "So do you get along with your dad and stepmom?"

"Yes, I get along with Dad and Jayni just fine." Just by saying their names, his voice perked up.

"It's my turn. And you...let me guess, you have the perfect family," Thayer said confidentially.

"Nope. My parents married and divorced when I was only a few months old. I have a stepbrother named Rennick, and my dad travels around Europe. I'm pretty sure he lives in Czech right now."

Thayer whistled. "You're pretty sure?"

"He was never around. I get money on holidays, birthdays, and when he feels like it. I saw him after my grandma's funeral." Severine shifted awkwardly in her seat and set her gaze out the window. "We don't see each other a lot, and when we do, it's awkward."

"What's in Europe?"

"He says work, but I think he likes to think he's more European than American." The subject of her dad was never talked about with anyone—save Lily—but opening up a part of her life to Thayer surprisingly felt okay.

Instead of probing more into her past like she thought he would, Thayer asked the one question she didn't expect him to ask. "And that's why you have a foreign name?"

"My mom wanted Elizabeth...something classic and pretty. My dad wanted Severine. He was on a French kick back then."

Thayer glanced at her once and whistled. "That wasn't what I was expecting to hear. Interesting little background to you, Severine."

"Touché."

Severine's legs stopped shaking as she stared at Thayer's self-assured smile. Maybe all the rules didn't have any relevance when it came to Thayer. Because sitting next to him and talking to him could become a dangerous habit; a habit that had a high possibility of distorting her strength and making her greedy desires known. At this point, her heart didn't care.

"Are you going to get all quiet on me?"

"No." She glanced at his profile and smiled, stating, "I'm enjoying the scenery."

"Severine, you haven't looked out the window once," Thayer pointed out.

Severine notched her head in his direction and lowered her Ray-Bans. "Really? You can see through my sunglasses?"

Thayer changed his focus from the road to her. "I can see through a lot when it comes to you."

Around him, around them, they would always provoke each other.

"Focus on the road!"

Thayer only glanced up once and directly stared at her again. "You seem tense."

"I don't want to die," Severine shot back urgently.

"Relax, Severine, I know this road like the back of my hand."

Severine grasped the dashboard, like she could control the movements of the truck, and looked out the window. "It's snowing."

"And you're incredible, even when agitated. Are we done with observations?"

Thayer could never say his words gently. It was either at full force or nothing at all. It never failed for Severine—she felt every word.

He relented, as Severine remained quiet, and slowed the truck toward an off ramp. "You're still alive, Blake."

"Barely," Severine murmured.

*   *   *   *   *

"This is going to be awkward," Severine blurted out.

She watched as a wood cabin came into sight. It stood on a slight hill, making the house stand out, but behind it, the view of the mountains and tall trees made it all connect together and create something beautiful.

Seeing something else other than tall trees and green was a relief. It seemed like they had been driving through the forest and on the winding road for hours.

Thayer put the truck in park and laughed quietly. "If you make it awkward. Macsen isn't here. And the rest of my family is fairly normal."

"Fairly?"

Thayer opened his door and looked back at her.

"We're here. I'm not taking you back."

"Maybe they don't want a guest."

Thayer shrugged, uninterested in Severine's protest. He walked to her door and opened it. "Don't be spineless."

Severine's eyes flashed and realized by his slow smile that he was goading her. "I'm anything but that."

"You're right," Thayer agreed, "but right now, you're acting like it." He took his sunglasses off and leaned over to put them in the glove compartment. His shoulder brushed against Severine's knee and when he glanced at her, his smile was wicked. "You need me to carry you?"

Severine clutched the belt buckle across her lap with both hands tightly. "I'm good."

"I can. If you need me to, I will."

"But I don't."

He said nothing in response. Severine watched him get out of his side and walk toward her door. When he opened the door, he ducked his head past the doorframe and pressed his face close to hers. "Why are you here, Severine?"

Her hands blindly reached to unbuckle her seat. The whole time she kept her gaze on Thayer. "To have fun?"

The way he stared at her lips as she talked made Severine shut up immediately. His lips kicked up in a confident grin. "And that's the exact reason why I asked you here."

"No." She was free from her seat belt, but Thayer blocked her from moving—from avoiding the situation. "You asked me here for things to change,"

"Everything. I want everything to change. Remember, this is why you said yes."

One, two, three...

Seconds could pass so fast when you're fighting your heart's urges. Thayer stared at her, daring her to move closer. Severine wasn't made to conform. She wouldn't shift her position. Thayer's eyes narrowed as he saw her resolution.

Four, five, six...

"Thayer!" A female voice yelled out happily.

The two of them turned, and Severine wanted to take a deep breath of relief as she watched a woman wave excitedly from the deck.

Two men walked out the front door. Thayer was true to his word. Macsen was nowhere to be seen. She jumped out of the truck and watched his family watch her.

Thayer's hand splayed against her back. It felt like he was close to swallowing her completely.

"You're here!" A tall, older man walked down the wooden steps and inspected Thayer and Severine.

"I am."

He stopped in front of Severine and Thayer. "With a girl."

"This is Severine." The way Thayer spoke her name made her seem much more than 'just a girl.' Severine wasn't the only one to notice. His dad merely raised his eyebrows and held his hand out. If he knew anything about her previously, it didn't show. "Owen Sloan."

Severine kept her smile in place, as she returned the handshake. Inside, she was a huge fucking mess. In front of her was an older replica of Macsen. This whole entire situation felt like a disaster.

Thayer's fingers pressed into the flesh of her back, encouraging her to lean into him. He knew what Severine saw. She repositioned herself closer to him as the rest of his family walked closer to her.

"Severine, this is my brother, Mathias."

She shook hands with his older brother. He stayed silent, reminding her of Thayer in his demeanor. Both stood tall in height and had the same dirty blonde hair. One thing was different—Mathias's pain rolled off him in waves. He was a damaged soul.

"And I'm Jayni, their mother."

Thayer's stepmom stepped forward with an all-embracing smile on her face. She didn't say stepmom; she owned the word *mother*. It's possible she was all Thayer and Mathias knew.

A face could show you so much about a person. Severine could tell from Jayni's wrinkles that flowed away from her eyes and curved around her cheeks that she was complacent in life. Her blonde hair was cut to her chin, and her fine hair was styled with waves to give it more body. A pair of black-framed glasses perched on her nose. But the one thing that held Severine's attention the most was her brilliant smile. Instantly, she felt soothed. Severine could let her armor down around Jayni.

"It's nice to meet everybody."

Mathias smirked at Severine's discomfort, while Jayni oozed happiness. Owen was the only one that seemed to focus solely on Thayer. "Are you guys hungry?"

"Yes," Severine blurted out. Macsen had ruined her McDonald's run. Her stomach had rumbled the entire trip.

"Come with me. We were just getting ready to eat lunch." Jayni was a few inches shorter than Severine, but she directed Severine toward the house like a mother in charge. "We're having something light. Owen and I are going to a New Year's party, and-"

Severine kept up with the conversation, nodding her head when she needed to. Before they reached the steps, she turned back around and found all three males staring at her.

What did they know that she didn't?

Chapter Thirty-four

Severine took in the guest bedroom. The decor was shabby chic and nothing she would've expected for a cabin in the woods. Like the rest of the house, it was dominated by a woman's taste. And while Severine enjoyed the light colors and pale blue of the walls, it was doubtful Thayer or any other male would.

Her legs paced the wooden floor. Severine was ready to give up, until her aunt answered the phone. "Hello?" Her voice was out of breath, but happy.

"Hey. You guys busy?"

"For you we aren't."

Severine glanced out the window and tapped her forehead against the cold glass. "I wanna tell you something."

Rachel paused. "Do I need to get your mom? Did you just find out you're pregnant, and you don't know the baby daddy?"

"No! And you really need to lay off *Sixteen and Pregnant.*"

"It's a train wreck. You wanna look away, but you just can't," Rachel said in defense of her reality show obsession.

"Moving on," Severine drew out. "I just want to talk

to you."

"Why?" Rachel asked suspiciously.

"I'm with Thayer."

"Ohh..."

"I'm at a cabin in Tennessee...with his family."

"Is this an early April Fools' joke?"

"Does it sound like I'm laughing?" Severine asked dryly.

"Is the other brother there?"

Severine released a deep breath. "No."

"Good. Now, on to my next question, what the in the eff are you doing there? Were you kidnapped?"

Severine groaned and pushed away from the window. "I'm here on my own free will. Believe me. I ran into Macsen at McDonald's, and it wasn't the best feeling," Severine explained.

"And then you randomly decided to go on a trip with Thayer. What do you even know about this guy?"

So much more than I ever knew about Macsen.

"It was on a whim. I'm going against everything I think is right."

"Yes. So what are you still doing there?"

"What do I know about right?"

"Severine-"

"I mean it," Severine rushed out. "How do I know what is really right for me?"

"And right this second, are you regretting your decision?"

Her answer was absolute. "No. This is the opposite of wrong."

"Then it's exactly right." Rachel cleared her throat. "I'm gonna get off here, but be mindful of everything that's happened before this."

"I will," Severine promised.

Their call ended, and Severine stared down at her phone in thought. She could suffer through doubts of how wrong this was. But after lunch and watching Thayer with his family, she wanted to stay. Severine wanted more.

A rap on the door made Severine toss her phone onto the bed like it was poison. Thayer opened the door and peeked his head inside.

"I'm not naked. Clearly, you can come in."

"I knocked too quickly then," Thayer shot back. He stood in front of her dressed in jeans, kept in place with a belt and a simple, solid white crewneck long sleeved shirt.

He said nothing and walked around the room taking in the decorations. When he moved past her, Severine could smell his cologne. She sat down on the edge of the bed and watched him turn around to look at her. His hair was cut short but left longer on the top. He dragged his fingers through his hair, making it messy.

He didn't even have to try. The outer shell of Thayer was lickable. It was what he hid from the elements that had Severine curious and searching for more.

"Get dressed," Thayer insisted. It was one decibel away from demanding.

Severine scrunched her lips to one side and patted her arms and stomach. "Dammit. I could've sworn I put clothes on this morning."

"Put..." Thayer paused for the right word, and finally shrugged, "whatever on. Hell, wear that. We're going out."

"Where to?"

"I have a couple of friends here that I grew up with. They're here for a few days to celebrate New Year's. I told them we would meet them in an hour."

Severine heard his explanation, but she could only focus on the one thing that stood out to her. "You grew up here?"

He didn't tense up or walk away. Thayer nodded his head. "From first grade to sixth."

"Hmm," Severine responded back. Macsen at least

told the truth on one thing.

"You have forty-five minutes to get ready."

Severine moved toward her suitcase and searched frantically for a dress. "You could've told me earlier!"

Thayer stood to her right and watched as she moved her clothes. His scent, his arm pressing close to the side of her ribs, made her close to being completely enveloped by him. "Don't you always look like that?"

"All the time," Severine said dryly. "Every day I wake up with my hair done and lipstick in place."

"I really wanna see if that's true."

His innuendo was transparent. Blindly, Severine grasped the edges of her suitcase. The material briefly warped. "Let me get ready."

He nodded and walked out the door. Severine waited until she heard his footsteps retreat from the door and ran to her bed.

Lily answered on the second ring, "Yes?"

"Quick. I need you to help me find a dress," Severine asked hurriedly.

"Really!" Lily suddenly became interested. "Where are you going tonight?"

Severine avoided the question. "Just help me."

"Fine. Umm...what about that cute sweetheart dress you have?"

Severine didn't bring that with her. She shifted her eyes between the two dresses in front of her. "I'm giving you two choices. My cowl neck dress in plum or a tight sweater dress in silver."

"The sweater dress with a deep v in the back?"

"Yep."

"One last question."

"Shoot."

"What the hell is a cowl neck?"

Severine groaned as she put the phone on speaker and took her shirt off. "Look alive, Lily! It's a neckline that's draped around the shoulders."

"Ahh! Gotcha. Next time just say that. I don't speak *Vogue*. Since I can't envision that dress, I'm gonna go with the sweater dress."

"Good," Severine said. "I'm putting it on as we speak."

"What shoes are you wearing?"

"I only brought a simple pair of black pumps."

"Brought? Where are you?"

Severine paused long enough to adjust the hemline of her dress. "I'm with Thayer...in Tennessee."

"Shut up."

"Can't."

"Hold on. I need privacy to hear this," Lily muttered. A door closed, and Severine heard Lily moving things around. "Okay. You need to spill everything. Right now."

Severine plugged in her curling iron and cranked up the heat. "He asked me to go with him. And so I did."

"By yourself?"

"No, his family is here. Don't have an ulcer."

"Macsen's there?" Lily sputtered.

"Do you think I'd come if he was here?"

"Good point. So where are you going?"

"It's New Year's. We're meeting his friends."

Lily sputtered before she finally said a coherent sentence. "I can't wrap my brain around this...are you with him?"

Severine stared at herself in the mirror and wrapped a strand of hair around the hot metal. "We're nothing."

Lily read in between Severine's pauses. "But you want to be."

"I have no clue," Severine confessed honestly. "This is spontaneous, something I didn't expect. I want to enjoy it."

"Have fun! Just call me tomorrow."

"Gotcha. Oh, how's Benji's family?"

Lily sighed and spoke quieter, "It's going good now. But it was kinda awkward at first. Now I think they're coming around more to me."

"Does he have any siblings?"

"Yeah. Three sisters. They picked me apart during the first hour."

"And what's the final verdict for you? Are you enjoying them?"

A contented sound of relief escaped from Lily's mouth. "They're all great. But I need to go before they think I'm taking a massive shadoobie in here."

"Uck. Go. I'll talk to you later."

"Adios."

Severine turned back to the full-length mirror, and double-checked her make up. Her nerves raced ahead of her as she gathered her coat and purse. She was ready to be released from her indecisive thoughts.

Her feet were sure in their steps as she walked down the stairs. Thayer walked through the front door at the same time. He briskly rubbed his hands together to create warmth and paused as he took in Severine's outfit.

"I'm ready."

His brows rose, and a smirk tilted his lips upward. "I can tell."

Severine buttoned up her coat, as Thayer stared at her. She could feel his regard all over. If she looked away from her jacket, what would he read in her eyes?

In her mind, she had to reaffirm over and over that this was the breakthrough she was determined to have. Severine had no idea what path she was on. No guide was available to point her in the right direction—she was lost in a whole new continent. It gave her a course of energy and made her step forward toward the one person that was just as astray as her.

Chapter Thirty-five

"Do you really need your purse?"

"Let's just say I've seen one too many Lifetime movies."

She shut her door before walking in step with Thayer. Severine could hear the pounding of the music nearby.

"What do these Lifetime movies teach you?"

"That the stalker shows up out of nowhere and is always friendly and nice at first. It quickly turns vicious after that."

He glanced down at her. "Then carry some Mace with you."

"I do," Severine patted her clutch. "It's in my purse. The same purse you were pressuring me into leaving behind."

Thayer looked away, but Severine saw a small smirk lingering on his lips. In the past few hours, Severine had discovered more things about Thayer than she had ever known about Macsen. For once, she pressed her body close to Thayer as they walked into the club.

"Follow me," Thayer shouted above the noise.

Severine went to answer, but stopped short when Thayer grabbed her hand tightly in his and guided her past the warm bodies around them. There was no weaving around people. Thayer towered above everyone, giving him free rein to demand space as they made their way to a couple waiting by the bar.

"Thayer Fucking Sloan!" A guy yelled from the bar.

Thayer's shoulders moved up and down from laughter as he did the 'bro hug' that had been around for ages. "You guys been waiting long?"

The black haired guy laughed and reached a hand out for the small girl next to him. He was around Severine's height. An infectious grin spread over his lips as he wrapped an arm around the girl next to him, bringing her closer. She had on a cute black dress with red heels. They made her come up to Severine's chin. It was dim in the club, but Severine could make out the smokey eye makeup and red lipstick. Her blonde hair was layered around her face in a cute style that Severine would never be able to pull off.

Severine's bitch-o-meter wasn't flying through the roof, and that was a good sign. Time was always the best thing when it came to getting to know other females.

"Severine," Thayer draped an arm around her, shrouding her to his side. "This is Dan and Morgan."

Severine's smile was wide. It was all from Thayer. "Nice to meet you guys."

"How much did he have to pay you to come with him tonight?" Dan teased.

Severine kept a solemn expression on her face as she answered him. "Nothing. He kidnapped me from the local McDonald's."

Thayer guffawed at her response. "What she's trying to say is that we go to the same college."

The mention of school made Severine's back stiffen. Not here, not now. She didn't want to think about it. Thayer noticed her tenseness and started to rub his hand up and down her arm. Both Morgan and Dan watched the movement.

"Are you going to stand here all night?" Morgan

directed her question toward Dan. "Chop, chop, and get us some drinks!"

He walked away, and she slapped him on the butt.

"You want something?" Thayer asked.

"Ahh…" Severine couldn't concentrate long enough to think of anything good. "Just get me a White Russian."

He nodded and followed behind Dan. Severine was left with Morgan. The two of them awkwardly stayed silent. Sometimes it was easy to connect with someone. Other times, it took a little more work. Severine was willing to put in the effort for tonight. "You wanna go find a table?"

Morgan smiled quickly. "Yep. Let's find something far away from the bar."

"Why?"

"It's fun to listen to Dan complain. He's my bitch," Morgan teased.

Severine laughed as she helped Morgan search for a table. One finally became open, and Severine practically tackled someone to get to it.

"Have you been with Dan very long?"

Morgan turned to look back at the bar, where Thayer and Dan stood. A bright smile lit up her face.

"For about five years. It's all really, really romantic. He told everyone in eighth grade that it looked like I drank a bottle of self-tanner, and I baked him a plate of brownies with laxatives laced in them."

Oh yeah, Severine could get along with Morgan. "So true love really does exist."

"And the plus side is I never have to bake for him!"

"Have you known Thayer long?"

"God, yes." Morgan rolled her eyes in thought. "I grew up alongside both him and Dan."

"Really now." Severine leaned across the table anxiously. "Do you have any really embarrassing stories about Thayer?"

Morgan smirked deviously. "I have hours worth of

stories."

"You know you have to tell me one," Severine demanded with a sneaky grin. "Right now!"

Morgan smiled back and scooted closer to Severine. As she settled in her seat, she glanced behind her. Severine looked at the same time, noticing that Thayer was watching her with a slight frown. "Uh-oh. He knows I'm going to say something," Morgan snickered.

"Ignore him," Severine said quickly. "Now, tell me, tell me, tell me!"

"You remember school field trips, right?"

"Of course."

"In the fourth grade, all three classes took a trip to the Arch. It's a long trip on a bus, a really long trip..."

"What did Thayer do?"

"Oh, nothing on the bus. He was probably being a dumbass with Dan. But, after the bus ride there, after visiting the Arch, after everything...that's when things got interesting," Morgan said cryptically.

"Okay."

"We were all getting ready to get back on the bus to go home. But the teachers and chaperones wanted a picture. So we all lined up on these stairs. At the time, I was hitting a growth spurt and had to stand next to Thayer in the back. Well, after the sixth picture, Thayer was getting a little antsy, started mumbling that he had to pee," Morgan paused dramatically.

"Uh," Severine screeched out, "don't tell me."

"Yup, he pissed his pants."

"This might be the greatest moment ever."

"Dan dared him to drink an entire liter of Surge. Even at the age of nine, they were idiots."

"This is amazing. I officially want to make love with this moment."

"Oh, it gets better. All of it is captured on camera. So the first few shots are okay. But then you get to the last three, and it shows me looking horrified while looking down at his pants. Thayer's face is contorted in relief."

Severine laughed until her ribs ached. "I take back what I said earlier. I want to divorce the other moment and marry this moment."

"Shh!" Morgan hissed out. "He's walking over. Play it cool. You heard nothing from me."

Severine nodded and kept her face neutral as Thayer placed her drink in front of her. Her hands immediately reached for the straw, and she sipped erratically.

Thayer leaned his arm on Severine's chair and notched his head in Morgan's direction. "What were you two talking about?"

Morgan shrugged and stirred her drink. "Nothing."

"Nothing." Thayer nodded his head and took a long drink of his Heineken. He tested the boundaries and shifted closer to Severine. His thigh touched her knee, and she raised her eyebrows at him expectantly. "What were you guys really talking about?"

Severine smiled slyly. "Nothing..." Thayer nodded his head and looked away, just as she finally finished her sentence. "Huggies."

He slammed his beer on the table and pointed in Morgan's direction. "I fucking hate you, Morgan."

She shrugged her shoulders while Dan choked on his beer next to her. "Suck it, Thayer. That's for telling everyone during freshman year that my eyebrows looked like the ozone depletion."

Thayer pointed between his eyebrows and smirked. "Good to see you lost your tweezers."

Severine laughed at their banter and enjoyed the moment. Seeing this side of Thayer, for longer than a few minutes, hushed all the worries in her head.

More time sped away as the four of them talked. Thayer's arm moved closer and closer to her back, until it was secured near her hip. After four shots, Severine's peaceful energy was replaced with the crazed feelings she'd had the minute she met him.

Her legs slid to the floor, and she clutched Thayer's hand. "Let's dance."

His smile showed just how pleased he was as Severine led them toward the dance floor.

If Severine concentrated long enough, she would've recognized the song. All she could hear was the beat, as it pulsated around the room. She instantly started to move. Thayer's smile started to fade as he stared at her hips. For someone who was always so smooth, he seemed hesitant. His movements were almost slow, like he was trying to draw out the moment.

He took in every shift of her body. Severine looked him in the eye, waiting for him to relax. Slowly, he started to let go. Severine tilted her head back to look up at him. He couldn't keep the cocky illusion around her. She wanted him like this. Always.

She smiled—it seemed like the wisest thing to do— and grabbed his large hands into hers and held them high into the air. Their bodies were inches apart. They had been thigh to thigh moments ago, but now the air had shifted around them to something more intense.

Any space between them was closed off as Severine lowered their hands and touched the muscles on his hips. Her fingers splayed on his stomach. Severine felt his muscles twitch as she moved them up his chest, around his shoulders.

Thayer's eyes took on a feral look. His hands moved down her hips. He tightened his grip and pulled her close enough for her to feel how hard he was. Severine's response was to push further. She knew she was playing with fire. But right now, she was getting a glimpse at how sex would be with him. Every boundary would be pushed. Neither one would pull away and admit defeat.

The heat of the room made every move even more acute. Everything he felt, she could feel too. Severine didn't ignore what was building around them. She took what she wanted, wrapped her fingers around his neck and guided his lips to hers.

Unknown territory should be a terrifying thing. His tongue crept into her mouth, just as his fingers dragged down the length of her hair and pulled lightly for Severine to tilt her head.

Kissing Thayer bordered on wicked. Severine could become greedy after this.

Lust would set in and she'd want more. Her pride would always be with her, but she'd beg for this again.

Severine wanted him closer. She wanted relief.

Everything about this kiss enticed her to take as much as she wanted. By the time they pulled away, Severine knew she had to have more.

"I wanna go."

Thayer's chest moved up and down as he absorbed her words. His eyes never moved from her face while he nodded his head. "Let's go."

Chapter Thirty-six

"You have fun?" Thayer asked as he opened up the door to his family's cabin.

Severine smiled. "I did." *And I will.* "Your friends are awesome. I want to hang out with them again."

"Why? So you can hear more embarrassing stories about my past?"

"That...plus Morgan reminds me of Lily. You can never have too many Lilys in your life."

Thayer laughed as he shut the door. "You're a poet when you're drunk. Anyone ever tell you that?"

Severine shrugged off her jacket and placed it on the banister. When she turned back around Thayer stared at her with a hungry expression. "Tonight was amazing," he said slowly, like it was painful for the words to come out of his month. "I liked having you to myself. Am I fucked up for thinking that?"

Severine shook her head. "No." He still stood awkwardly by the door. "You can come closer."

His steps to her made the distance seem like nothing. When he was in front of her, Severine craned her neck back. "Even with heels, I still have to look up."

Thayer grinned darkly. His hands settled underneath the curve of her butt. He picked her up, and easily set her on the kitchen counter. The granite counter was cold beneath her exposed thighs.

"You still tower over me. We're supposed to be eye level."

He remained silent. Everything was always silent with him. He moved his hands onto her thighs, and Severine flinched at the action. His smirk was now a smile as he lifted her legs and motioned for her to wrap them around his waist.

She gulped, and he lowered his arms. He moved his head closer, until their faces were inches apart. "I think this is better."

Severine nodded her head in agreement. Thayer seemed composed and relaxed. Her heart was slowly dying. It'd be in pieces before the night was over.

She wasn't used to being this off-kilter. It caused all of her actions to be unsure.

Her hands moved up his arms, and she gripped his biceps painfully. All she wanted was for him to feel her agony. Severine was completely within his reach.

She couldn't run away fast enough. She couldn't get close enough.

His hands took over her face as he looked at her closely. There it was—that smirk. "Look at them."

"What?"

He rubbed his thumb across her cheeks. "Your freckles. You can barely see them from far away." His grey eyes clashed with her own. She stared back. They mixed a new shade for the world. It'd never fit, though. Together, they'd never fit.

One of his hands reached behind her and touched her hair. Her eyes widened but not out of pain. They wanted to close, and she was afraid what would happen after that.

Thayer brought his hand back and held her face once again. His nose connected with hers. As he spoke, his lips touched hers. "You're right. Eye level is much better."

Severine leaned closer, but Thayer retreated. She

wanted to groan. He was building her up.

"What about now? Am I wrong to be this close, Severine? Do you think this is too much?" His eyes glinted with a challenge. "Are you going to call it a night?"

Blood was thicker than water. The two of them both knew how fucked up this was. Severine had the potential to collapse two brothers deeper into a hatred that had already pulled them apart. She didn't want every action to focus on that. They could consist of something further than that.

Presently, Severine didn't care where Thayer belonged, or who he was connected to. It didn't matter. She just craved a place with him.

His skin felt like fire as her fingers dragged down his arms and to his back. He moved closer, still waiting for her to answer. He stopped moving away and settled his mouth on hers. Her lips moved persistently, trying to show him exactly what she felt. Severine wanted him to know how badly she needed this. His right hand touched the side of her cheek as he pulled away and placed his head on her shoulder. His breath came out choppy, and Severine placed her hands on his back. The muscles flinched, and he groaned.

He lifted his head enough to look down at her. Millions of questions were in his eyes, but he stayed silent and stared. Severine's lips curved in a half smile, and Thayer followed the action with his eyes.

"Is this too much, Thayer? Are you going to call it a night?" She turned his words around on him; her voice barely let the words pass. He looked a little afraid. Unsure. His true emotions were showing.

"Just another kiss, Thayer." Her lips were on his as she spoke the last of her words. "That's all."

He nodded and lowered his face again. They both knew it was a lie.

This time, they clashed together. All of their

turbulent emotions came to surface. She felt completely out of control. Every part of her was desolate. With a simple kiss, Thayer could encompass all of her. Lightly, he bit down on her bottom lip. Severine moaned and her fingers dug into his neck as he lifted her off the counter and staggered toward the stairs.

His steps were rushed as he hurried up the stairs. Severine guided her fingers back to his face and crept her tongue into his mouth.

Her feet touched the surface of the second floor, but her lips stayed connected to his. Thayer backed up into her room, and Severine followed. Their positions changed as Thayer directed her away from the door. Too much was between them. Severine tugged at his shirt with antsy fingers. He pulled away impatiently to pull his shirt from his body and came back for more.

Her eyes looked at his body with greed. Her cool fingers touched the skin of his stomach; it was hot to the touch. Slowly, she drifted her fingers down the ridges of his stomach and toward the edge of his boxers. Thayer sharply inhaled, and Severine smiled.

The laughter was sucked out of her the minute she felt his hands push her dress up and away from her skin, and over her head. She stood in front of him in only her panties and bra. There wasn't a thought to cover herself. She wanted Thayer to see every part of her. If she was going to be altered by this, she wanted to make sure he was too.

So much was being manipulated and warped in this moment. Her legs wrapped around him before she could think twice. He reeled backwards, and his shoulders slammed against the door loudly. He craned his head up to keep their lips in place. And with her hands placed on the door above his head, she moved higher. Severine moved against his dick, and he groaned harshly. It sounded painful.

Thayer abruptly dislodged their lips and placed his

forehead against her chest. "Shit, Severine." His words came out rough. She leaned her forehead atop his head.

"What the hell are you doing to me?"

She breathed as heavily as him, and it scared her. She never felt this wild, this free. "I need control of this."

"You want to control me? Then do it." His words came out instantly. "No other girl can say that. Only you, Severine."

She looked at him blankly. His hands reached up to grab her face, but all she felt were his words. They cradled her closely.

The two of them held each other's stare. Severine moved her hands away from the door and linked her fingers at the back of his neck. He lowered her slightly, and their faces were level.

No one wanted to feel weak. Right now, Severine felt completely broken. She shifted, and Thayer let her slide down his body.

He was challenging her. All Thayer wanted from her right now was to admit that she wasn't in control of anything between them. Part of her realized it.

She barely nodded her head, and Thayer pushed her toward the bed. She fell back and watched as he took off his belt and jeans. It was only for a moment, but he paused and stared down at her body. Goosebumps broke out across her skin, and the process followed wherever his gaze went.

He finally lowered himself and hooked an arm around her waist before his skin connected with her own. Her fingers inspected his arms and back. He inhaled a sharp breath but kept his face above her body, watching her every reaction. When his fingers moved toward the clasp of her bra, Severine abruptly shifted positions and straddled his waist.

"Severine," Thayer heaved out her name. It made her lose control.

Her fingers moved to the clasp of her bra, and slowly

she parted the material. He watched the action without blinking. Severine held her finger out to the side and dropped the piece of lace to the floor.

When she settled her arms next to his shoulders, Thayer reached a hand out to touch her. Severine moved backed. "Thayer," Severine cooed. "Do you want this to go slowly?"

He lifted his hips in the air as he spoke. "With you? Yes."

Severine settled her fingers on the edge on his boxers and lowered them enough for her to touch the one part of him that was guaranteed to make him lose his control. "I'm not patient," Severine breathed out.

The two of them stared at each other. She wasn't walking away from this now. Nothing was going to stop her. She lowered her face, and her hair curtained around them, closing them off from everything. When she looked at him, she knew he couldn't see her expression, or the truth in her eyes. "With you, I want to be."

Thayer said nothing back. He nodded his head, moved them across the bed and covered her. His head drifted to her chest. Severine glanced down and watched him lick her nipple. The contact was dangerous. When she moaned loudly, she didn't care. Everything right now felt within her reach, and control. A part of her brain warned her that she was close to losing the power that she always held tight.

For now, she'd relish the feel of having him close.

Thayer pushed down her underwear and looked up at her from underneath his eyelashes. She swore he did it deliberately. There was nothing blocking them from touching. Barriers of clothing that normally hid everything back were shed. His skin touched hers at the same time his lips devoured her own. Severine groaned harshly and gripped the muscles in his back.

When Thayer pulled away, his actions demanded attention. Severine complied. He hovered above her, close to losing himself as much as Severine. Nothing else would give her relief—except him.

"Do I have all your thoughts tonight, Severine?" Thayer asked.

Severine wasn't given the time to answer the question. He entered her before she had the chance.

Delirium was setting in. He paused completely inside her. Severine glanced up wildly and realized he was waiting for her to answer. She didn't have the willpower to sit still.

Shouldn't her body answer how much she wanted this? How much she wanted him? A frenzy was building; she wanted this moment with him. They hadn't even started, and her body was already losing its mind.

"Yes! You do!" Severine finally screamed.

When he moved, the abatement she needed placated through her body. Her eyes clenched tightly together, and Severine relied on feelings. Everything was by touch.

Her legs wrapped around his hips. His fingers wrapped behind her neck.

Everything built quickly around them, as Severine moved her hips. Thayer went further, and she moaned. Their movement drifted far away from her as she screamed and dug her fingers into his back.

"Fuck! Severine," Thayer hollered. His words touched her skin as he collapsed on her.

Severine's eyes stayed rooted on the ceiling. Her body felt at peace, but her mind was already running, already in a panic.

Thayer moved his body and covered their bodies with the blankets at the end of the bed.

His large hand branded her hip and tugged her close. She didn't have the option of moving away.

The sun slowly started to rise. It gave enough light for Severine to see the light gray eyes in front of her, staring at her with possession. "I'm not leaving."

Severine moved her hair away from her face and

stared back. "I didn't ask you to."

He nodded, and Severine laid her head on the pillow. The warmth the two of them created lulled Severine close to the brink of sleep. "Maybe you should know this now." Severine's eyes blinked open, and she felt his words vibrate from his chest. "I want you for more than a day."

Chapter Thirty-seven

Not even emotions could remain loyal. At one point, they'd betray you and leave your soul open to all harm. Severine left her feelings to roam alone. She stepped away from them like a coward and took no claim to them. It made her heart ache to think that sooner rather than later, she'd have to come to terms with Thayer's words.

"*I want you for more than a day.*" Severine shuddered at what those eight words did to her.

Her eyes drifted from the crisp sheets underneath her body and traveled to Thayer.

He lay on his side, with his head buried next to his left arm. His right arm still clung to her hip.

Severine didn't want this moment to vanish. She wanted to keep it safe from the outside world, from everything that was waiting for them back at campus. If she did move closer to him, it wouldn't be by choice.

Quietly, she shifted away and lifted her naked body out of bed and toward her suitcase. Her fingers rifled through her clothes until she found a baggy t-shirt.

Her skin was already forming icicles. She turned back to look at Thayer and stared longingly at the open space next to him.

Connected to her bedroom was a guest bathroom.

Severine brushed her teeth and stared at herself in the mirror. She didn't look forever changed. No. Staring back at her wasn't a girl with a glow to her cheeks, with happiness painted in her eyes. Severine looked afraid, anxious and alone.

She switched off the bathroom light and opened the door. Thayer hadn't moved from his spot, and Severine hurried across the room, ducking underneath the covers to bury herself next to him.

Her body was pressed tight to him. With her mind screaming to get away as far as she could, and her heart pounding in her ears, it became impossible to think clearly.

But this feeling with him...Severine closed her eyes and drank the moment in.

Some things didn't come naturally for Severine. Yet, right now, it all flowed perfectly. This moment was written before it had ever begun. It was meant for her.

He groaned in his sleep, and Severine kissed the side of his pec. From last night, she knew his body by heart. Her hands could tell you what his muscles felt like, and how warm his skin was. And laying next to him the next morning, wrapped against him, Severine knew she was giving him a piece of her heart, just by not leaving.

With her lips still touching his skin, she glanced up and found him looking at her. "Sleep well?"

"Best sleep I've had in a long time," Thayer said in a deep voice. A morning voice had never sounded sexier.

He scratched the side of his head and placed his hands behind his head. His arms flexed, and Severine wanted to have him again. If there weren't scratches on his back now, she'd put some there immediately.

"I'm surprised you're here."

"You thought I was going to run on you?"

"I counted on it."

Severine raised a brow and turned to lie on her back. "I'm still here, Thayer." I have no idea why. Her head moved against the soft pillow to look at his profile.

"The rules don't apply to me?"

Severine nodded, "Apparently not."

His laugh was brutal to her already tender soul. Thayer needed to give her time. Her wound was still fresh. He was close to ripping her thoughts apart. "I want today to be fun. Without thoughts of anything else."

"I want that, too," Severine confessed.

He sat up, and Severine saw the scratches from her nails clearly on his back. Her stomach clenched at the brand she'd left.

"Get dressed in a few minutes. I have something fun planned."

"Fun?"

Thayer smirked in that teasing way that came so naturally to him. "I mean it. Meet me outside."

* * * * *

"Umph!"

Severine was hit hard in the back. She looked over her shoulder at Thayer's borrowed ski jacket, and at the big, wet spot on it. "Really? That was a cheap shot."

Thayer tossed another snowball in the air and grabbed it in the other hand. "Put your game face on, Blake."

Severine adjusted the ski cap on her head. Her cheeks felt raw from the cold air, and her eyes watered from the strong winds. "I don't do outdoors," she admitted.

"That's because you've never done it with me," Thayer winked in her direction.

His words brought the vision of him strained above her last night, shouting out her name. It was her fault for still wanting him. "I think I proved that wrong last night."

He nodded and kneeled next to her. "So, are we

going to pretend that we didn't fu-...have sex last night?"

Severine kept her head down and firmly patted the snow in front of her. "I planned on it." Her head slowly lifted to look at him. "I don't think it should be a big deal, do you?"

Thayer's eyes flared angrily, "Shit, Severine!" he said heatedly. "You're my brother's ex-girlfriend, not another fucking girl!"

"So do you regret what we did because of Macsen?" Severine asked slowly.

He leaned closer and if Severine really inhaled him, she'd be able to smell his scent. Her mouth was inches from his neck, and all she wanted to do was lean forward and bite him there. "I regret nothing, you know that," Thayer said darkly.

Severine's hands paused above the mountain of snow she was forming. "But are you going to later?"

Thayer moved his face closer. His warm breath felt like a caress against her freezing cheeks. "No, I'm not going to."

Her eyes traveled to the scenery in front of her. "I don't think people plan on regretting something. It just kind of happens and before you know it, you're in too deep."

"I'm not thinking those things. None of them," Thayer said with firm resolve. His gray eyes held hers. "Are you?"

"No." And honestly, she wasn't. Her fear was that she would later on.

"You need to tell me what you're thinking. I'm not a mind reader."

Severine's eyes flashed to his. "I have only been broken up from your brother, who cheated, for a few weeks. Call me crazy, but I think I'm going to tread lightly in the romance department."

"Because of which? Macsen? Or him cheating?" he asked seriously.

Her jaw clenched, and she looked at him directly. "Both."

"So you need time to think."

His comment sounded flippant, but Severine felt his eyes. "No, I don't."

"Then what is it?"

Her words made her a walking contradiction.

"Hmm..." he said thoughtfully. Severine finally looked his way, with curiosity plain on her face. "I think you're feeding a lot of bullshit to create a huge clusterfuck of miscommunication."

Severine knew she was. She couldn't push forward from last night. It was more than a replay. It was torched on her skin. Every action of Thayer's brought on a vision that she wanted so damn hard to forget. What would it be like going back to campus? Did she have a chance in hell staying away from him?

"We don't have to be together," Severine dragged out. The words came out forced—almost choked.

"You want that?" Severine's heart squeezed at the intensity in his voice. Thayer kept pressing the issue. "Tomorrow, you want to drive back to campus and pretend none of this happened?"

Severine shook her head. The wind tangled her hair, covering her face. Severine was grateful for the block. It was a thin veil that covered her pain. "No."

His fingers brushed her hair away as his lips kissed the corner of her mouth. "I'm not my brother."

She was starting to see that he was so much more. It terrified her. When she opened her mouth, she blurted out the thoughts running through her head. "This is why you don't sleep with someone who plays the same game as yourself. We both know each line, excuse, and exit."

"So you know I'm not bullshitting you when I tell you I'd take you any way I could."

"Even if it's with me hesitant and scared?"

He smiled teasingly at her. "In spite of that, yes."

Severine's lips kicked up in a small smile. It was with instinct that she moved closer and wrapped her arms around his neck. Thayer only raised his brows. "How are you going to complete tonight?" she asked.

"I'm taking you out."

"Somewhere fancy?"

Sitting in the snow, with his hands resting on his knees, and a huge smile on his face, Thayer looked so happy. "You want that?"

"No," Severine admitted with a wide grin. She didn't know what page they were on, but it didn't really matter. Right now, she still had him. For the next few hours, she could pretend that she had everything figured out.

"Good." Thayer lifted the two of them away from the snow. "We're eating with my family. Does that bother you?"

Severine was going to be given a glimpse into his life. Her cheeks ached from her smile. "Not at all."

"Good, because they're close to crapping a brick to get the chance to talk to you. And I kind of need to see them once."

His hand wrapped around hers felt natural. "Why are we leaving tomorrow again?" Severine asked.

"I'll be asking the same thing tomorrow morning."

Chapter Thirty-eight

"Severine, tell us more about yourself."

When Severine lifted her eyes to Jayni's, she was met with an anxious smile. "Umm..." To give her more time, she held the straw to her lips and sipped slowly.

Around them people talked in quiet tones and ate their food. The local steakhouse wasn't a dress-in-your-little-black-dress kind of place. It was a nice restaurant for people to unwind on a Friday, or for a parent too stressed out to cook. The whole environment was relaxing.

It wasn't the same where Severine sat. The meal with Jayni, Owen, and Mathias had been less painful than she expected. It was still tense. But the questions shot at her were not at a rapid pace, and she was given enough time to deflect them.

"Well-"

Thayer cut in impatiently. "She's from Iowa, has one sibling—a brother named Rennick—and she's fantastically tall." He paused long enough to take a bite of his steak and gave her a long look. "Severine also has a pumpkin spice frappe addiction."

Severine tried to give him a creeped out face but failed. She leaned close to him and smiled. "Have you been stalking my every move?"

"You're a creature of addiction."

"Is my brother your new addiction?" Mathias asked, his words completely humorless.

Severine wanted to groan in frustration. Did she truly believe he'd make anything easy for her? Of course not. He was a Sloan. Any other way, and it would've been an impersonator. For Severine, it was impossible for a Sloan to not get underneath her skin. The worst tragedy was his looks. Severine could skip past the attitude; he was harsh because of the world's doing. Wasn't everyone?

No, it was the green sweater and dress shirt layered underneath that made him seem serene. The minute his brown eyes looked in anyone's direction, freezing temperatures would fill the air. Those irises were cold and distrustful of everything

He shoved up the sleeves of his sweater. His attire was all for appearance. Inside there was a creature waiting to attack.

Severine ignored his brutal stare. "No. Do you think I'm gonna eighty-six him?"

"Look at you!" He flung his hand in the air making her feel like she was an errant piece of lint on his coat. "Of course, you're gonna toss him out."

Owen shut his eyes and snapped his fingers in the air for the waiter. Severine turned her attention back to Mathias. Her fingers drummed repeatedly on the table as she stared at the protective brother sitting next to her. "I'm gonna take the 'look at you' as a compliment. As for tossing him out, that's not going to happen."

Your other brother already used my emotions like a Frisbee.

Mathias didn't look convinced. Severine wasn't going to try and convince him. He could get a brief glimpse into her mind, and he'd know that she wanted to toss Thayer. But it just wasn't an option.

"As always, Mathias, it's good to have dinner with

you," Thayer chimed in.

"I'm okay now." He pointed his steak knife at Severine. She flinched slightly. "I was counting down the minutes until she'd run away to the bathroom and sob her eyes out."

"You know, it's amazing to hear what you think of the female population," Severine dryly commented.

"Don't listen to Mathias," Jayni included herself in the conversation happily. She patted Mathias's back like a devoted mother. "He's the cynic of the family."

"It sounds wike he's a wittle jealous," Severine teased.

"I'm close to him. He's my only brother."

Severine frowned and watched Jayni sadly look down at her plate. Owen muttered a curse and told the worn waiter to bring him another beer. Her curiosity was busting from the seams. To get more information, she'd play dumb. "So it's just you and Thayer?"

Mathias flicked a harsh glare at her. "No, but he's the only one worth mentioning."

It was a direct dig at Macsen. Severine wanted to blurt out more questions. Their family rift wasn't her business, however, Severine kept digging for information. With every cryptic response, she found herself even deeper in their confusing history.

"Let it go." Thayer squeezed her thigh and shook his head no.

Her eyes settled on Thayer's face as he solemnly stared back, not disclosing anything. Severine wanted answers later.

"Severine, have you been to any of Thayer's games?" Owen asked. His question came out as a demand.

"Ah, no. I'm not a sports girl."

Jayni's mouth opened. Her face turned splotchy, as if Severine had told her she was a demon. "You're kidding!"

"'Fraid not. Sports were never on in my home." Severine admitted.

"So you played no sports as a child?" Owen asked.

"When I was a kid, I did. After middle school, I started to lose interest."

The more she spoke, the longer it took for them to wrap their brains around her answer.

Jayni schooled her features and briefly shook her head. "I had just assumed that's how you met him."

"How we really met is an interesting story."

Mathias raised a brow for her to continue. Even Thayer looked at her hesitantly.

"I was just there in my knitting class. I looked up and there was Thayer with a sexy satchel filled with yarn." Severine said as she fluttered her eyelashes dramatically at Thayer.

A reluctant smiled snuck up on Mathias's face. Severine kept score in her mind. The two of them were tied.

"Thayer, I wanna know where my fucking blanket is!" Mathias teased.

"If I knitted you a blanket, it'd look like it got in a fight with a mower."

Mathias slammed his hand down on the table and laughed loudly. "You little shit." His gaze landed on Severine. It was now filled with approval. "Now I know what he sees in you."

"That's a bigger compliment than your 'look at you' comment."

"Hold onto it tightly. You'll never hear another from me again," Mathias quipped.

The check came quickly after, and Severine exited the steakhouse with her face huddled as deep as possible in her coat. Her body shivered as they made it to Thayer's truck. He stopped at the end of the truck bed. Severine wanted to groan that they were spending one more minute outside.

"Thayer, we're still planning on coming to visit in a few weeks." Jayni placed her arm on both Severine and Thayer. "Are we going to be able to see you too, Severine?"

Severine made eye contact with Thayer. They hadn't planned that far ahead. A few weeks for them could be impossible or the easiest thing in the world. Severine nodded her head and spoke her heart's dream, "I hope so."

Jayni smiled and quickly hugged Severine. "I look forward to it."

When Severine shut the door behind her, she looked across the seat to Thayer. "Not as bad as you thought?"

Severine peeled off her gloves and pressed her cold fingers close to the vents. "I don't know what I thought about your family. But this wasn't what I expected."

"What do you think about Mathias?"

"He's protective and terrifying."

"He'd be flattered by the word *terrifying.*"

"Is he always like that?"

"No. Not all the time. There's that one percent...when he's drunk."

"Does he live here?"

Thayer nodded his head. "Yeah. He works for our dad."

"Your dad?"

"My grandpa started a company selling farming equipment. When my grandpa died, my dad took over. Mathias runs the southeast territory."

"Sounds...farmy?" Severine grew up around cornfields. It didn't make her a pro on all things farming. None of it seemed fascinating.

"You look so excited by this information," Thayer dryly said.

"It wouldn't be my dream job."

"It's not Mathias's either," Thayer explained. "But if a farmer has a good season, so does he."

"So your family basically throws their money in the air and rolls around on it."

Thayer shook his head and laughed. "Not even close."

Severine nodded distractedly and stared out the window at the buildings they passed. "Do you think they know about Macsen and me?

For a split second, Thayer clenched his jaw. "No. Trust me, they don't know about you."

"They would've said something to me?"

"No. That'd mean that Macsen had actually talked to them. And that hasn't happened in a while."

"And is that why Mathias doesn't consider him a brother? I don't have siblings, but even I think that's a little strange."

"It is strange. It's completely fucked up. But Mathias and Macsen don't get along for the same reasons I don't get along with him."

"And that's because?"

When Thayer sighed, it exposed all his frustration. "Severine, maybe you'll see Macsen for who he is. Maybe you won't. But my brother is a selfish dick. He's always going to see things his way."

The silence made her ears ring. Her voice came out scratchy. "What did he do?"

Thayer pulled into his family's driveway. His eyes stayed on the steering wheel for minutes, before he looked at Severine with a blank expression. "He did nothing, Severine. And that's what makes him so fucked up."

* * * * *

If I don't get a txt back from u, I'm calling the cops.
Severine stared down at her screen and smirked at Lily's threat. She quickly typed back a response. *I'm good. Call off the hounds.*

It was past two a.m. She should be asleep and ready for the early start she and Thayer would take back to campus. Instead, her heart thumped loudly in her chest, and her legs felt restless. They encouraged her to walk to Thayer's room.

Her feet touched the cold floor. Severine adjusted her flannel sleep pants and creaked open her door. At the end of the hallway stood a small wooden table. On top of it was a picture frame and lamp that was lit for everyone to find their way in the dark. It allowed her to see Thayer's closed door across from her own.

The thumping in her chest sounded loud to her own ears. It sounded like a dozen horses running at top speed. Their hooves pounded against the dirt in perfect rhythm. The rhythm of her heart fascinated and scared Severine at the same time. She'd expected everything to wither away. Once they had their night together thoughts of him would go away—it'd be enough.

That was her first mistake. Because now, if anything, it was worse. Her want spread throughout her whole body and urged her to walk across the hall—to take what she so clearly wanted.

But there was still the fearful side of her heart; the part of her heart that warned her he could do the same thing as Macsen. There was always a chance that Thayer could leave her broken.

She took two steps and halted. Her hand reached out, and she was so close to his door. Close enough to grab the doorknob and turn.

It was her stubbornness that made her turn sharply and silently walk down the stairs. When she got to the bottom floor, she peeked to the left and saw the TV. The volume was turned low, and a late night talk show played. Faint laughter rang from the speakers, and Severine smirked once at the screen. Her eyes turned to the L-shaped couch, and she stopped laughing.

The one person she was trying to keep strong against

lay unaware in front of her. Thayer was stretched out on one side of the couch, with only a pair of basketball shorts on. It was like the world was dangling him in front of her and demanding that she did nothing. Severine was never good at fighting off temptation. The lust inside of her wanted to jump across the couch and take him.

Severine crossed her arms and her fingernails dug into her skin. He gazed dully at the screen, while Severine stared at him from the corner. Light from the TV played across his chest and stomach. She could make out every ridge and definition. Her head wanted to rest against the wall next to her and stay there. But warning bells were ringing in her head; she had already been here too long.

Slowly, she backed up. A floorboard beneath her protested, and Severine froze.

Thayer kept his eyes on the screen as he spoke. "Go to bed, Mathias...I said I'd leave her alone."

His voice was deep. It drifted across the space between them and reached her in a rush. It felt good to know he was thinking about her, that he was fighting the same feelings she was.

She stepped back into the room. "You know it's bad to sleep with the TV on, right?"

At the sound of her voice, Thayer flipped his body over and crashed loudly on the floor. He looked up at her and from where she stood Severine could see his wide eyes. "Holy shit, Severine. You scared the crap out of me!"

Severine smiled and leaned against the back of the couch. "Whatcha doing?"

He stood awkwardly and watched her slowly—with weariness. "Watching TV."

"I didn't know you were a night owl." She walked into the living room and circled around the couch. If he could see her skin, he'd notice that it was prickled with goosebumps. Not from the cold air, it was all from his stare.

"I'm not."

"Then why are you up?"

Thayer tossed the remote away from him and patted the seat next to him. "Probably the same reason you are."

Severine walked over to him willingly and leaned back into the couch. The silence between them wasn't amicable because neither one of them wanted it there. They both had other thoughts on their minds. None of it involved silence.

"I don't want to go back tomorrow," Severine finally admitted.

Thayer nodded and spoke to the floor. "I know. I kind of wish a freak blizzard would hit."

Severine looked down at his arm so close to her own. Her hand reached out between them and with her index finger she traced the veins that led up to his biceps.

She was waiting for him to pull away or tell her that they shouldn't be in this situation. Because if she wasn't thinking right, one of them needed to.

Instead, he grabbed her arms and placed her on top of his lap. She straddled his legs and stared down at the one person that scared her more than anything. Behind them a commercial came on, providing enough light for Severine to see the expression in his gray eyes. He was asking for so much from her. She wanted to give him her trust, but right now, she didn't know how.

Her hands went to the muscles in between his neck and shoulders. They were tense, showing just how apprehensive he was. With his eyes still on her face, he pulled her closer by the drawstring of her pants. "Am I in over my head for still wanting you?"

She could wind up in this position multiple times and never pull away. Even if it was the right thing to do, she'd stay firmly close to him. "No," she finally rasped out.

He looked just as unsure as she felt. He still went

underneath her shirt, he still touched her. When his hands reached the swell of her breasts, she pressed herself closer. Thayer spoke his words against her cheek. "Then what do we do, Severine?"

She pulled her face away long enough to whisper back a response—an answer from her heart. "Just stay close to me."

Even after last night, she still wanted more. So much more. Her hands drifted underneath his basketball shorts and boxers. She touched him, and he groaned. Severine leaned down and whispered two words, "Follow me."

Those words were a simple command, but they held so much power. Anything after this was deliberate and with choice. It'd be impossible to turn back.

Chapter Thirty-nine

Severine could sink her teeth into him. There was no certain sweet out there that was good for you. They were all bad for you. But if you searched long enough, you'd find a chocolate that was sinfully good.

You wouldn't step away with one piece in your hands. No, you'd grab all you could get.

Thayer was Severine's sinful sweet. After him, there'd be no salvation for her. Not when all she could see was absolution. The word gleamed Severine's feelings brightly. Guilt stepped in every time she hurriedly drove to meet him. It'd be forgotten the second she saw him. There was a sense of obligation her body felt toward him and for a few hours, everything would be forgotten.

But her conscience would instantly punish her instincts. Over and over it repeated that she was addicted and that she was bound to get hurt again.

The sneaking around had started the minute he dropped her off at her dorm. She saw him that night. He came to her, pounding on her door without caring if everyone in her dorm heard him.

"I can't give up without a fight." His declaration still gave her chills—still made her heart go into overdrive. After that, everything became a domino effect. It'd probably always be this way.

But it was hard to think of the wrong when something so right lay underneath her.

Her palms glided up his stomach. Thayer smiled and crossed his hands behind his head. His biceps flexed at the action. Severine's fingers trailed across his pecs toward the expanse of muscles in his arms.

Underneath her, Thayer's body jerked. A slow smile spread across Severine's face. "Are you ticklish?"

"What kind of question is that?"

"A viable question when your body jerks around."

"Maybe it's because of you?" Thayer provided.

Severine wrapped her hand around his jaw and kissed him slowly. "You should stop fighting then."

When she pulled her head back, Thayer blinked repeatedly. "I swear, you're gonna fucking kill me," he muttered.

Her heart raced as Thayer's hands moved from her hips up to her waist. His movements were slow, like he was an artist and was trying to trace her figure. If she could halt time from continuing, she would.

Severine let her vulnerability show, just for a second. That was all she could show. She intersected his hands from going any further and linked them with her own. "Add a little poison to your kiss, and you'd be my forbidden fruit."

Thayer arched a single brow. "Getting religious on me, Blake?"

"We both know we shouldn't be here, and yet, we keep meeting." His eyes briefly looked fearful. Severine continued with the truth, knowing that it'd hurt her more than him. She glanced at him and whispered out her response, "Sometimes I think I border on worshipping you."

He slowly nodded his head. They may be alike in so many ways, but there was one thing different about them. Thayer was obstinate. He concentrated over his words with such determination that when he spoke, you knew it was the truth. It made Severine feel heedless—completely out of control.

His eyes drifted down to where they had connected intimately minutes ago. She could go again. Just by him looking at her body, her skin started to tingle with awareness. Severine released his hands, and he immediately cupped her breast. Against her leg she could feel that he was getting hard again. "When we part, what do you feel?" he asked.

It was his eyes she could feel. They traveled across her skin, slowly. He acted as if her body was the map that would lead him to every right direction. Severine's fear was that he'd lead her toward a cliff. She'd plunge into a dark hole and never see the light of day again.

"It's a struggle—a tug of war between my good and evil side."

Her comment was meant to be a joke. Thayer didn't crack a smile. "What do you feel?"

"I feel like I should seize every moment I have with you before it's taken away."

"What does the evil side of you feel?"

Severine shrugged slowly. It was a slash to her heart. Truths weren't something she was used to coming out of her mouth. Unveiling the sensitive side of her soul was a strange feeling. It made her heart race out of fear—fear that he would reject all her answers. "The same thing."

Thayer exhaled a breath and nodded his head. "I think you should listen to both the good and evil side of yourself. They seem extraordinarily smart."

A smile was planted firmly on her face as she stared down at him. When she looked at the clock, her smile dimmed. They'd have to leave soon.

She moved quickly off of him and searched for her clothes on the floor. Severine slipped on her underwear and snatched up the barrette on the dresser. She knotted up her hair and glanced at his jersey hanging up in the corner.

Thayer rolled to his side. The sheet inched down, and she was close to seeing his entire body. "Where are you going?"

She leaned against the wall and crossed her arms underneath her breasts. It was a powerful feeling having Thayer's gaze focused solely on her body. For a quick second, he glanced at his jersey and then back at her exposed skin. "Are you going to my game?"

Her right hand reached out and moved a piece of material away from the hanger. One tiny slip and the rest of the jersey would fall to the ground. Severine caught it with deft fingers and looked down at the letters stitched on the back. It spelled out Sloan. Severine stared at the jersey as she answered him. "I'll probably never go to one."

"Ever?"

"I like the way it is here. People cheering and screaming your name would just be..."

"Too real?" Thayer provided.

Severine let out a deep breath. "Yes."

"Maybe I'll play shitty," Thayer offered. Severine smirked and gripped his jersey tighter in her hand. She knew he wouldn't. "Then you wouldn't have to worry about cheers. It'd be a lot of booing and people yelling at me to get my head in the game. Would that make you feel better?"

"What would make me feel better is if we just stay here." Severine paused and lifted the jersey over her head. When it covered her body, Thayer sat up quickly. Instantly, he was alert.

"Who else has worn your jersey?" Severine asked.

Thayer looked her up and down and smirked. "Just you."

Severine nodded. The wicked gleam in her eyes made Thayer throw his feet over the edge of the bed.

"What about that Vanessa girl?"

"Vanessa?"

"That girl at the club."

Thayer stood and slipped on his boxers. He smiled widely and walked closer. "You seem jealous."

"I am," Severine confirmed. "And I'll probably always be that way. Consider it one of the many perks of being with me."

"It is," Thayer agreed. He stood in front of her, and Severine leaned her head back against the wall to look at his face. His fingers grasped the material of his jersey. He wrapped it around his fist and jerked her towards him. "You know the biggest perk?"

"What?"

"When I play tonight, I'm gonna smell you on me."

* * * * *

Severine could play with the best of them.

Sneaky was her middle name in high school. Her mom used to say that when she was quiet, that meant she was up to no good. Severine smirked and looked down at her coffee. This past week had been filled with nothing but Thayer. It was a good kind of quiet.

"You're here before me." Lily held her coffee in between her hands and stared down at Severine. "This must be serious."

Severine shut her book and scooted over. "We haven't seen each other since school started back up."

Lily shrugged off her jacket and draped it over the edge of the couch. "It's only been a week."

"For us, that's like a lifetime," Severine pointed out.

"That's why you should've agreed to stay with Ben and me for a while."

"That would've been too much."

"So...what's up?" Lily finally asked.

Severine pushed her book aside and laughed at Lily's calm demeanor. "I can't believe this!"

Lily paused, her drink held mid-air, "What?"

"You're not begging to know how my trip with Thayer went?"

A wide smile transformed Lily's face. "My New Year's resolution was to be...less nosey."

"And how's that working out so far?"

Her coffee slammed onto the table in front of them. The brown liquid sloshed over the rim. "I'm dying over here! Just tell me what happened before I piss my pants!"

"It was fun." Severine couldn't keep her grin off her face for longer than six seconds.

"Just tell me, did you..?"

"Did I what? Meet his parents? His older brother, Mathias? Yeah, I did."

"He has an older brother?" Lily's jaw popped open before she tightly shut her mouth and scrunched up her face. "I'll get back to that later. I need to know the good stuff right now. I wanna know about you and Thayer!"

Severine gave Lily a stare that said everything she couldn't and sipped her coffee.

Lily's jaw practically dropped to the floor. "Holy. Shit. If I didn't know you, I'd kind of hate you right now."

"You have Ben, you freak show."

"I'm not blind. That is prime real estate right there."

"Never use that phrase again."

"It's the truth," Lily anxiously stated. "If anyone finds out about this, the female student body is going to light up torches and stand outside your dorm, just waiting to light your ass up! Right now I'm really glad I don't live with you."

"You're not going to say anything. No one is going to know."

"Oh." Lily made a look of disgust. "Ugh. Don't tell me you're going to pretend that it never happened?"

That would be physically impossible. Severine's heart sped up at the thought of pretending. She couldn't go through with it. "Why would I do that?"

"Thank God."

"We're just being quiet about everything," Severine finally admitted.

"And what is everything?" Lily prodded bluntly.

"Just quiet." Lily opened her mouth, and Severine covered her friend's mouth quickly to finish her sentence. "I don't want anything to fall apart. So we're going about this calmly, with both our heads on straight."

"This is all because of Macsen, isn't it?"

"What else would it be?"

A gentle expression crossed over Lily's face. She placed a comforting hand on Severine's leg. "You have to break away from all of that."

"I'm over it."

Lily gave her a doubtful look.

"I mean it," Severine insisted. "It's like that time in fifth grade when Cody stabbed your hand with a pencil. You bitched about it forever.The pain went away, but you were left with a really strange scar."

"I didn't bitch. That hurt. Badly."

It was Severine's turn to look skeptical.

"If you're going to use any of my wounds, use the door slam."

Severine stared down at the floor in thought. When the memory came to her, a look of horror came across her face. "Gideon slamming your hand in a door at church and your nail falling off, is not something I want to think about."

"Now I cried like a bitch over that." Lily conceded.

"Your brother was evil then."

Lily nodded her head in agreement. "I agree. I give him slack now. He's just trying to survive our parents."

"Which brings me to my next point...where the hell were your parents during all your accidents?"

"I'm a church kid. I spent more time running around pews and in Sunday school rooms than anything else."

"You Partlows are psychopaths."

"Enough about my wounds that you weirdly used as an example. I understand that you're cautious. But sneaking around?" Lily looked apprehensive. "How does that help?"

Severine's expression showed her indifference. Nothing was for certain. But there was always the voice in the back of her head that warned her to remain careful. The same thing that happened with Macsen could happen with Thayer. "It doesn't. But the last time I jumped into a relationship, it was a disaster."

"I'll say it again, it wasn't your fault," Lily firmly stated.

"I know that. But you can agree, having any type of connection with someone has the potential to eat you alive."

"Well, yeah. Unfortunately, your past relationship had a nasty appetite."

"It's over, and I'm not gonna think about it." Severine turned her attention to her book but she could still feel Lily's focus on her.

"I can't freaking believe this. I mean we all thought it was going to happen, but I was doubtful."

Severine turned her head back to Lily. "Who's we?"

"You know...Ben, me, Chris. A few other people."

"I'm not even going to ask what was said. You just need to keep your mouth shut and tell no one about this."

"Mmm..." Lily nodded her head and looked away. "Sure."

"Seriously," Severine pleaded, "for now, this stays between you and me. Not even Ben needs to know."

"Is this always going to be a secret?"

"I don't know."

Lily's foot tapped against the coffee table as she stayed silent. "You two can only stay a secret for so long. Someone's going to uncover you. Just don't sabotage yourself."

Severine saw the merit in Lily's words. She gave a

brief nod. "Thanks for listening."

"Anytime, my friend. Anytime." She rubbed her hands up and down greedily. "Now, tell me about this other brother!"

Chapter Forty

Anything that was delicate had a chance of breaking.

Severine kept her mind ready for the time when she and Thayer would break apart.

Only two weeks had passed since Tennessee. It wasn't long at all. Her mind raced forward for the next time they could see each other, but time dragged by like someone stuck in quicksand. There wasn't enough time in the day—not enough moments with Thayer to keep Severine sated.

"You've spaced on me again."

Severine jerked her head in Anne's direction. "Huh?"

Anne exhaled dramatically and dully glanced at Severine. "If you're gonna make me take a walk with you, at least listen to me. Idiot."

"I'm listening now!"

Anne tucked a short piece of her coal black hair behind her ear. "Barely. What's going on with you lately?"

Severine kept her face neutral as she glimpsed at Anne curiously. Her friend could see too much. "What do you mean by that?"

"I'm saying you just seem different."

"I changed face powders?" Severine provided. She'd say anything to keep them off course from what Anne really wanted to talk about. Anything but that. "I think this shade gives me a natural healthy glow," she rushed on, "compared to blending in with walls. I can't wait-"

"I'm not talking about the weather," Anne impatiently huffed. Her breath came out and appeared in the cold air. "Or your makeup products. Your attitude is different."

There was no way to know what her face looked like or what her energy projected. This had been the most carefree Severine had felt in months. Capturing her feelings so they wouldn't show made her heart speed up in protest. "I- I'm just happy," Severine stuttered out.

Anne turned her shoulder to stare directly at Severine. Her eyebrows slanted down in disbelief. "Really happy?"

"Yeah."

"For yourself?"

"Why are you asking me so many questions?"

Anne shrugged and kicked at a rock on the sidewalk. "I talked to Lily today."

"Are you kidding me?" Severine threw her hands up in the air before placing them on her waist. "She can't keep a secret!"

"You might as well have called the local newspaper," Anne calmly said.

"I know she gets diarrhea of the mouth sometimes, but I didn't think she'd flap her jaw over this. Did you get her drunk or something?"

"Nope. We were at the library studying."

Severine looked at her doubtfully.

"Seriously." Anne held her pinky out and smirked deviously. "You want me to pinky swear? I promise we started out studying, and then the last hour we talked about you." Anne's blunt honesty sometimes came in handy. That time was now.

Severine stopped on the sidewalk and tucked her scarf more securely around her neck. "Anything else?"

"Relax. She didn't have a microphone held to her mouth. No one else heard her."

"I doubt that. I know when she really gets into a story, she talks like she's in a stadium." Severine started walking again. Anne's short little legs caught up with Severine's steps quickly.

"Can I tell you what I think?" Anne asked.

"No."

"Well, I'm going to anyway. Then I'll leave you alone."

Severine groaned. "Don't."

"Sorry. I'm going to." The two walked in silence before Anne finally spoke her thoughts. "I don't know if you two together is messed up. Is it awkward? I'd say, probably."

Severine wasn't a crier, but Anne nailed her thoughts on the head. It felt good to have some of her thoughts validated. "But if Thayer knows your true self, and if bullshit comes your way and he still wants to be there, then it's something to really think about. If he wants to invest time with you, to see inside your soul, then I say hold him tight. I can't say I blame you for keeping this a secret. I think I'd do the same."

Severine's smile quivered as she bumped shoulders with Anne. Her words were too accurate. "That was a really thoughtful speech."

Anne snorted, "Don't get used to it. That about took it out of me."

"Thanks."

"Just don't let it go to hell, or I might snatch him up."

Severine laughed while Anne barely cracked a grin. "Totally serious. His voice has the potential to turn even me on. You know, he could make a killing off voice recordings. I'd buy an audio book just to hear him talk. Completely change my nonexistent zest for reading."

"You concern me sometimes."

"It's the truth. You even have to admit that." Anne wiggled her eyebrows and gave a quick wink.

Severine agreed. She was just thinking of him yelling her name.

Anne stopped walking as she glanced ahead. "You know, my ass is freezing and I'm tired of walking. I'm going back to the dorms."

Severine looked in front of them and saw Thayer walking toward them. He smiled and Severine returned the gesture to him. Every step closer made Severine's skin tingle in excitement. She wanted to touch him, wanted to have him all to herself. "You can stay, you know."

"Yeah, right." Anne turned around and hurried in the opposite direction.

Severine stared greedily at Thayer and waited for him to come to her.

She'd never share. Whatever was hers would always remain that way. When Thayer sauntered closer, Severine knew he was strictly hers.

Mine, mine, mine...her mind called out.

She wanted to wrap herself around him and hang tight. It wasn't the place. Not with people walking on the sidewalk around them in the middle of campus. But she was close to not caring.

They stood across from each other, only inches separating them. Thayer smiled down at her and leaned forward on the balls of his feet before moving closer. "I want you to come to my game," he declared.

"A game? Yeah, that's probably not gonna happen."

"You don't want to see me play?" Thayer asked. He knew her answer. He knew every single time he asked.

"Didn't you ask me this awhile back?"

"I did," he confirmed. "But I'm gonna keep asking until you agree."

"I'm picturing all the annoying people and the uncomfortable seats. Sad part is...I think I'd be the person carrying one of those huge bleacher pads around."

"That's okay. You could just tell people you were sore for other reasons."

Severine punched him in the arm. "That's nasty, Thayer." Even so, she couldn't get rid of the thoughts running through her head.

Thayer stopped walking and gave her a double take. He knew what she was thinking. His hands reached out toward her but quickly pulled back. He looked away, and Severine was given a glimpse at his profile. The sharp line of his nose, curve of his lips, the firm line of his jaw—it was all too much. It was starting to feel like torture, standing so close to him and not making contact with him.

"So do I get anything if I win?"

The wind picked up around them, and Severine brought her hood up to block the wind. "Do I have to reward you for playing good?"

He bent down close to her. His cologne wafted toward her, and Severine wanted to bury her face into his neck. With his cheek next to her own, he spoke in a hushed voice. It still rumbled through her and gave her chills. "I'm not above begging. If you don't come to the game, meet me afterwards."

Severine stood on her tiptoes to speak closer, as Thayer leaned his head down to help. One move of her head, and they'd be kissing. His eyes fixated on her lips and Severine could feel her lips tingling. "Where?"

"I'll think of somewhere."

"I'm not meeting you at your apartment," Severine warned.

Thayer's lips thinned slightly. "Hell, I wouldn't ask you to."

"Good, then we're on the same page."

"Our entire situation is messed up. But I'm dead on about one thing—you can't get me out of your head as much as I can't get you out of mine."

Her eyes glinted back at him, and her lips slowly curved upward. "Sometimes I think together we are the worst kind of calamity."

Thayer grinned back. Severine's lips burned. "Then I've never wanted to be destroyed so bad."

Chapter Forty-one

"What does one wear to a game?"

Lily spun herself around on Severine's computer chair. "Well, not a clubbing outfit. I'll tell you that much."

"You're not helping."

Lily stopped spinning and pointed to Severine's body. "Just wear that. It might be Thayer's best game to date."

Severine didn't even bother looking down at her bra and jeans. Her fingers rifled through each hanger as she talked. "You're in a chipper mood."

"Correct! I am. And you know why?"

Severine turned and raised an eyebrow.

Lily hopped off the chair without falling over, "My best friend, who, by the way, has sworn to never attend any sport activities, has now decided to go to a basketball game. It makes me more than curious."

"I never swore not to go to games. I just said I'd rather not."

Lily moved next to her and started moving hangers around. "I think your exact words were that you'd rather watch the *Antique Roadshow* than ever go to *any* game. *Ever*."

"What. Do you record our conversations secretly or something?" Severine asked sarcastically, and held a black turtleneck against her body.

"Uh, please don't wear that. Are you going to a poetry reading after this?" Severine took Lily's brutal advice and hung the sweater back in her closet.

"So you've lifted the ban of attending sports games. You don't think I'm just a little curious?"

Severine silently held out a white v-neck, button up sweater. Lily nodded her approval. "Please. Let's not pretend there's any other reason for me going other than Thayer," Severine finally muttered.

"Wow. I didn't think you'd admit it so quickly."

Severine lifted both shoulders in a shrug and sifted through her makeup. "Well, I'm evolving, ever-changing, if you will."

"And soooo...when the game ends? You're just going to leave the game and be on your merry way?"

Severine shook her head *no* and paused to stare at Lily. "I would tell you, but you flapped your jaw to Anne."

"It was an accident! It came out of my mouth before I could stop it."

"I'm not telling you anything anymore." It was a weak warning. Severine knew she'd tell everything to Lily.

"Okay, okay. I'm sorry. I just need to know what's going on."

Severine sat down on her bed and put on her ankle boots. "He wants to meet after the game."

Lily slowly grinned. "And are you gonna?"

With one shoe still in her hand, Severine pointed a finger at her. "Okay. That! That right there!"

Lily's eyes went wide, and she smiled curiously. "What are you talking about?"

"That smile. When I mention Thayer and me together, you're supposed to tell me that this is completely messed up and that I need to walk in the other direction."

"Maybe I don't think that you should walk in the

other direction," Lily pointed out.

"What do you think I should do?"

"Don't ask me. I'm not a Magic 8 ball. I have no answers for you."

Severine tried to envision a boring night without seeing Thayer. It wasn't going to happen, at least not tonight. "I'm seeing him," Severine said with a quick nod of the head.

"My opinion wouldn't have mattered, would it?"

Severine smiled. "Probably not."

*   *   *   *   *

"Ugh," Severine groaned out. "The noise. I'm already getting a headache."

"Pipe down, will you?" Lily squeezed her body through their row, toward their seats, carrying a pile of candy and popcorn. She tossed the candy at Severine. "I got you some DOTS. I figured that'd shut you up."

Severine caught them with one hand and grinned. "Thanks."

"But I swear, if you complain once, or tell me you wanna go, I'll take them away."

Severine ripped open the box and looked around the building. It was massive. Around them sat thousands of people. And when Severine said thousands, she meant thousands. "Why are there so many people here? There are way too many people on the Earth. And is this seriously a gym where they play basketball all the time?"

Lily made a funny face at Severine. "This isn't a gym, genius. It's an effin Arena. Did the banner above our heads that says, 'Welcome to Rosen Arena,' not tip you off? Also, stop being such a freak. If you keep making odd comments about the world's population, people are going to start thinking you're a Unabomber."

"I'm not weird! This is just so many people. It's too much."

"The game hasn't even started, and you're already complaining."

"Leave me to my DOTS, then."

Lily threw a piece of popcorn in the air to catch with her mouth. It hit the old man in front of them. Lily ignored his glare and ate her food like a normal human. "I'm just familiar with your work. We'll be here for an hour, and you'll be all, 'Oh, my butt hurts, let's go.' Or, 'Why is this so long?' I'm staying for Ben, and that's that."

"No, I've only complained when it came to football. The movie Titanic is quicker to watch than that sport."

Lily nodded her head to the music blaring from the speakers. "So true. Cut an hour off the game and I might watch it."

Severine held her fist out for Lily to hit back. "This is why I love you."

"So does Thayer know you're here?"

"Nope."

"Are you trying to be incognito?"

"Kind of."

"Then you should've thought of that before you chose to sit next to me. We're in the fourth row, my friend. He's gonna notice you."

"He might be one of those really intense players."

"Maybe. Or maybe...shh!" Lily whacked Severine's thigh like she was the one talking. "Warm up time. This deserves my full concentration."

A sarcastic retort was ready to pass through Severine's lips, but she turned her attention to the court and stared along with Lily. On the right side of the court stood Thayer, next to his teammates.

Severine's smile was faint as she watched him stand in line. He moved toward the basket to catch the rebound. He jumped higher than Severine ever could, and firmly held the ball in his hands before passing it off and running to the opposite line. Everything around him was invisible, as his eyes were focused and completely in the zone. With his hands on his hips, Severine took in the long sleeve shirt that had their University on the front and his number, fifty-five. Above it was the name Sloan.

Part of her smile died off when she saw that she wasn't the only one noticing him. A few of the cheerleaders on the side pointed at him. She didn't have to wonder what they were saying. She had probably said it herself. The possessive side of her wanted to stand and point out that she knew more of him than they ever would. She kept still and bounced her legs up and down with anger.

"What's up with them?"

Lily leaned on Severine's shoulder and kept her face on the court. "Who?"

"Those." Severine flung her hand towards the cheerleaders. "It's like slut-a-palooza over there."

"Oh." Lily rolled her eyes. "Yeah, they're always at games. I say we get some male cheerleaders that rah-rah around shirtless with baby oil on their chest."

A random girl in front of them leaned back. "I'd agree to that."

"I'm such a genius," Lily muttered.

A buzzer loudly went off, and the teams went to their side of the court, opposite of each other. Thayer took off his warm up shirt and tossed it on the chair behind him. His back was to her as he listened to his coach speak.

Everyone rose around her. Cheering and shouts rang around the room as the announcer's voice came through the speakers to announce the starting players. Thayer sat in his seat, waiting for his name to be called. Severine wanted to shout out that she was behind him, here to watch him. Instead, she squelched her anxiousness and listened to his name being called.

"And now, our very own starting center forward." The crowd surged with more cheers, and the student body sections jumped up and down. Severine clapped her hands in front of her, slowly getting into the spirit. "At six-foot-nine, Thayer Sloan!"

He ran through the line of his teammates and met the rest of the starting four on the court.

Everyone started shouting and chanting as the refs walked onto the court. Thayer rubbed the bottom of his shoes and solemnly kept his focus on the court.

Severine watched alongside everyone else as the referee threw the ball in the air, between the two players. Thayer caught it with his palm and aimed in the direction of his teammates. Severine stood, without even knowing, for the first time at any game.

* * * * *

"Ohhh." Lily bounced back and forth on her legs.

Severine looked over the shoulder of the person in front of her, to look at the court. She spoke distractedly. "What are you doing, Lily?"

"I have to pee like a freakin' race horse."

"Go to the bathroom."

A teammate of Thayer's made a shot. Applause and whistles rang everywhere.

Lily groaned and squeezed her thighs tightly together. "I can't do that. The line to most ladies rooms is ridic. The line at an Arena? It's nuckin' futs. I'd rather squat down and pee in my cup."

"That's what you get for buying a drink the size of a Big Gulp. You also go pee a lot. Are you sure you don't have a bladder the size of a Skittle?"

"This game can't end fast enough."

"I'm staying for Ben, and that's that," Severine announced in a nasally voice. "Do you remember saying that?"

"That was before my bladder was being crushed like a freakin' pancake."

"Well, there's a minute left. Hang tight, and in the

meantime, think of a waterfall streaming down toward a large ocean."

"Can it!" Lily snarled.

Severine smiled and looked at the basketball court. The whole game she was able to sit back and watch Thayer unaware. It gave her a thrill to see Thayer on the court, to watch him do something with such talent.

A player from the opposite team passed the ball to his teammate. Thayer snatched the ball in mid-air and took off dribbling toward the other basket. When he moved closer, he jumped, turned slightly, and his hands hung onto the rim as the ball went through the net.

Severine stared with wide eyes as he jumped back down. The crowd screamed, and Severine smirked with pride. He turned and pointed his finger straight at her.

Her blood felt frozen, and she felt like she had just been caught.

A smile was on his face as he ran back down the court. Not once did his eyes leave her face. "Uh...is he pointing at you?" Lily asked. Her bladder issue was forgotten as Thayer drew attention away from the game and toward a spectator.

She knew she was the spectator, but the people rows up and across the floor didn't know. Her heart beat wildly, as a woman in front of her smiled up at Severine with a look that said, 'Well, aren't you two just the cutest.' Severine wanted to kill him, but it was a fleeting feeling, not with the happiness rushing through her.

Chapter Forty-two

Severine leaned her body against the pole light, and watched Thayer's tall frame exit the Arena. Dressed in a pair of black track pants and a sweatshirt, he should've looked sloppy. All Severine could picture was him on the court. Grabbing a gray snowcap from the pocket of his hoodie, he put it on and quickly jogged toward her with a wide grin on his face.

People walked around them and to the warmth of their cars. That was where Severine should be, but instead she was looking up at a guy that had earlier made a declaration to her that he couldn't take back. Branding in the bedroom —completely alone—was for their pleasure. They'd know the marks on each other and how they got there. But something so simple as a point...it was more than that. Thayer had just told everyone she belonged to him.

The air was covered in white flakes. They fell around them, and a few clung to their faces. Severine felt one fall on her eyelashes. She still stared up at Thayer.

"That was a good game."

Thayer dug his hands into pockets of his track pants as he lifted a single brow and spoke. "You told me you weren't going to come."

Severine also never thought she'd be craving Thayer

in her bed, but things happen that you don't expect. Keeping her hands busy, Severine slid closer and placed them in a single pocket of his hoodie. "I wanted to see you play."

He enveloped her space and pressed closer. "I saw you after half-time. You were talking to Lily."

"So your first idea was to point at me?" Severine asked.

"You didn't like my acknowledgement?" Thayer asked innocently. Severine knew better. It was all planned out.

"I didn't say I didn't like it..." Severine said slowly. "But now everyone will be wondering what's between us."

He lifted a hand to grasp her cheek. "Maybe that's the exact reason I did it."

"I still want everything kept private...I want you to myself."

Thayer's jaw clenched, and he looked up at the sky. "And you think if people know it will ruin this?"

Severine's extracted her hands from his pocket and lay her head on his shoulder. "Exactly!"

Like everything else in her life, Severine was afraid she'd take all this in too quickly. Thayer tended to surfeit through her. She'd probably never be satisfied with anything in her life. But with him, she was willing to toss out all her theories for the future. "I'm trying my best, Thayer."

He slowly nodded and walked her to his truck, with his arm tightly wrapped around her. They walked in silence, both lost in their own thoughts. Severine finally broke the quiet. "What do you want to do tonight?"

For a second, he played with his keys before he looked at her. "I wanna take you somewhere."

Severine narrowed her eyes as he opened her door. "Where?"

"It's nowhere you'd think."

Severine buckled herself in and looked over at

Thayer's profile. There was just enough light pooling in from the pole light outside for her to see the mischievous smile on his face. "You're freaking me out."

"Are you doubting me?" Thayer asked as he pulled out of the parking lot.

Severine shook her head instantly. "No."

"Good. Trust me."

I trust you with everything.

* * * * *

Severine stared at the scene in front of her skeptically. "Why are we at a park?"

Thayer wiggled his eyebrows and grabbed his gym bag for a pair of gloves. "We're gonna play a game."

"You are?"

"We both are," Thayer corrected.

"I'm in boots with heels, and it's freezing. I don't feel like getting hypothermia."

"You have gloves, and you have a hood on your coat," Thayer pointed out. "When you start shooting the basketball, you won't care."

Severine reluctantly placed her purse on the dashboard. Her eyes were still cautious as she watched Thayer put a pair of gloves on. "I wanna know why we're here in the first place. You just played a game. Shouldn't you be tired?"

"Nope." Thayer grinned happily. Across from her was a man that dominated on the basketball court. But right now, he looked innocent and carefree. "Let's go."

Their doors slammed closed at the same time. Thayer waited for her at the hood of his truck. Tucked tight to his hip was a basketball. His right hand was held out for her to take.

As they walked, Severine peered closer at the small basketball court placed in the middle of the park. Only two lamplights were placed around it, giving enough illumination for the hoops to be seen. A thin layer of snow hid the concrete and painted lines on the ground.

"I'm gonna bust my ass," Severine muttered as they trekked toward the small court. "I can feel it. My ass is already tingling from the contact."

"I'm not making you do full layups," Thayer teased.

"I kind of want to do what you did tonight."

Thayer threw back his head and laughed. "A slam dunk?"

"Yeah. I have the potential." Severine said seriously. She only lasted for a few seconds before a smile crept its way onto her face.

He looked down at her and grinned. "You think so?"

"I know it." Severine couldn't keep her face solemn any longer. She grinned widely as Thayer looked at her skeptically. "You wanna know a super nerd moment for me?"

"Tell me."

"When I was really little, my babysitter let watch *Space Jam*. Remember that movie?"

Thayer nodded and laughed loudly. "Hell, yeah. I think I forced Mathias to watch that with me every day for a month. He still cringes anytime I mention Michael Jordan."

"Well, I loved it. That was when I used to think everything was possible.

The two of them walked onto the snow-covered court. Thayer dusted the snow away with his shoe, making the free throw line apparent.

He turned to the hoop and shot the ball. It connected with the hoop and slammed down to the ground. Thayer ran after it and beckoned Severine to come closer.

"I'm not moving," Severine warned. "I'll just shoot from the free throw line."

Thayer smiled and passed the ball to her. "I'm surprised you know what that is."

Severine rolled her eyes. "I was actually good at

basketball."

"How good?"

"Good enough to kick your ass," Severine teased. He gave her a funny expression. "I enjoyed it a lot." She twirled the basketball with her fingers and after years, she did her best to keep the form correct. It hit the rim and veered to the right.

"Not bad, Blake."

Severine laughed and ran after the ball. "Not bad? Kids on youth leagues can shoot better than me."

"You haven't played in years." Thayer pointed out. He was just being generous. They both knew she sucked.

Severine tsked at Thayer and tossed him the ball. "It's so easy to give advice when you're on top."

With one hand, he aimed at the hoop. It was a swish. Back and forth they went. Severine mostly watched from the side.

"You wanna call it quits?"

"Nah." Severine looked down at her boots that were undoubtedly ruined from the snow. She was having too much fun to leave. "My feet are past the frozen stage."

Thayer laughed and shot the ball and then retrieved it. The process continued for a few more minutes. Severine finally interrupted the quaint silence between them. "So why did you bring me here tonight?"

He lifted his shoulders and shot the ball. "I wanted you to see a part of my life."

"Didn't I see that tonight at the game?"

The ball landed on the concrete waiting to be picked up. Thayer stayed put and stared at her. "That's just a game. Privately, when no one is around, it's a chance for me to focus and clear my head."

"It's therapeutic." Severine said quietly as she looked at him.

Thayer picked the ball back up and shot underneath the basket. "Exactly."

Severine walked up the to the free throw line. Thayer

joined her and stared at the basket. "When I was I kid, all I had was a basket attached to a barn."

Severine peeked a look at him and let him speak.

"It was the crappiest thing. The barn was close to falling apart. It had a caved-in roof, the red paint of the building was past chipped and faded. At one side of the barn was the basketball hoop. It was like the barn and barely hanging on. My grandpa and dad took it down, and we painted it white again. In green paint we had my last name, my jersey number fifty-five, and NBA in bold letters. After that, I didn't care what held up the hoop. It was holding my dreams."

"You used it a lot?"

Thayer nodded. "All the time. Winter was my favorite time to play. I'd get off the school bus and go straight to the place that I considered, 'my area,' and play until my bones felt frozen. The sun would set early and I'd watch it go down and keep shooting until the lamp light came on. I didn't really need the light. I knew my shot by heart."

"Weren't you ever told to go inside?"

A small smile came onto Thayer's lips. "All the time. I'm crazy, though, I loved the winter air. My lungs felt clean afterwards. Everything felt refreshed."

"Did it always stay that way for you?"

Finally Thayer turned to her. A part of his soul was being shared. His gray eyes were raw and fresh with the truth. "Not always. Life got a little better, and a little worse. I don't think I can ever close this door of my life. It will always be an outlet for me."

"Do you want to go pro?"

Thayer shook his head. "No. To get to that point it'd be less of an outlet and more about the game. If I miss a shot here, it doesn't matter. If I make one, well that just surges me further." He turned to her and held the ball out. "You shoot."

Severine clapped her hands together, and Thayer

tossed it her way. The first shot of Severine's bounced off the rim. Thayer tossed the ball back to her. She tried again and missed. Her body was less chilled and her breath hefted out lightly. Severine kept catching the ball from Thayer. Sometimes she'd make a shot, but most times she didn't. But when she did, Thayer was right, it encouraged her to keep going. Severine's cheeks were frozen, her hood had fallen off minutes ago, but she was having genuine fun.

"Your turn."

"You weren't bad," Thayer conceded.

Severine flipped her hood back up and finally asked a question she knew he might not answer. "When you started playing basketball...why was it a hard time for you?"

The flicker of light in his eyes went away. "My parents were getting divorced and were each trying to get full custody of us. My mom won after a nasty battle. I lived with her for a year until my grandpa won full custody of Mathias and me. Macsen stayed with my mom."

She tried to picture both Macsen and Thayer broken apart as children, living in two different households. Sympathy wrapped around her heart. They should've been able to know each other. They were brothers. "That's why you lived in Tennessee as a kid."

He nodded. "During my seventh grade year, Mathias and I finally got to live with my dad. I'd visit my grandparents in the summer. They were like second parents."

"I can understand that," Severine said quietly.

She processed Thayer's explanation of his family life. It answered so much. Her heart ached for him, though. When her parents split, she was too little to notice the change. How could she miss something that had never been there? But to be tossed around between two parents like a hacky sack would've done more damage than

Severine could ever imagine.

"Is that another thing we have in common?" Thayer asked.

Severine nodded and walked closer to him. Thayer rolled the ball away and met her halfway. "I think we're alike in so many ways."

"I liked you watching me play tonight," Thayer whispered.

Her throat felt like it closed; she couldn't get enough air in her body. When he looked at her so sincerely, she forgot everything else. "I liked watching you, too."

"Not at the game. Here. Right now." His honesty projected off him and onto Severine.

She wanted a ladder to climb into his soul and fix everything that had ever broken him.

"My ass is numb and I've lost all feeling in my feet. But I don't care."

"Are you still that cold?" His arms wrapped around her tightly.

"After jumping around and shooting? I'm just chilled now."

His fingers pressed into her hair and the snow falling down around them melted into her dark strands. Severine kept her body still. Pressed against him, she didn't feel the algid temperature.

"The winter sun burns the worst. You know that, right?"

Severine said nothing in response. Her chest was being slammed by a freight train. Whatever he said, she knew it was going to crush her. From the truth in his eyes, she knew he wouldn't be able to take it back.

"No one would really know. Who stays outside long enough to really notice? The air is freezing and harsh. But if you really concentrate, you'll feel the heat." Thayer laughed harshly. It pained him to speak. "I think you're my winter burn."

The war in her mind came at a standstill. There was

no optimism left for her. She wouldn't walk away from him pain free.

Chapter Forty-three

"Are you going to get into trouble for having me up here?" Thayer whispered into her ear.

Her key scratched against the door when Thayer wrapped his arm around her waist. "If you let me concentrate and open this damn door, we won't get caught," Severine whispered back.

The key finally worked, and the door opened widely. Thayer shut the door behind them as Severine took her coat and boots off. The heat was always too much in the dorm room, but right now it was perfect for her chilled body.

Severine walked to Thayer. "What would happen if I came at you with everything I had?"

He raised a brow and leaned against the wall with anticipation. Severine wanted to say that it was all a game, but she was starting to crave these encounters with him. There could never be small portions with him.

"I'd be ready. Hell, I'm ready right now."

Her fingers laced around his neck. Her lips met his softly. Everything in Tennessee was based on greed and the desire to overwhelm. And even though those feelings were still there, Severine wanted slow. She wanted to kiss him at an unhurried pace.

One. She barely pulled back.

Two. Her lips kissed his neck and cheek *slowly*.

Three. Thayer cradled her face. When she looked up at him, she saw impatience in his eyes. His lips landed on her own, soft but demanding. Severine breathed through her nose and stood on her tiptoes.

Her selfish side rose to the surface as she moved her tongue into Thayer's mouth. When he left her room tonight, she wanted his preference to be only her.

His hands would only want her skin. He'd only fit perfectly with Severine.

A moan escaped her lips, and Thayer tilted her head slightly to the side. With more demand in his kiss, Severine's excitement raised a notch.

Thayer guided her back to her bed. Her hands were clenched around his sweatshirt. When she fell back onto the bed, she made sure he followed.

Quickly, he yanked his sweatshirt and shirt over his head. His legs trapped her from moving, as he stood above her quietly. His eyes drifted down to her shirt, and with one hand, he flicked open the lowest button on her shirt. Severine kept her hands firmly on the sheets beneath her and watched his face as another came open.

And another. And another.

Thayer's hands moved aside the open fabric, and he played with the last button. His movements were lazy as he stared at the small object with dedicated concentration. She was going insane, completely losing any rational thoughts. He finally looked at her, and at the same time, the last piece keeping her clothed was broken away. Everything was a defiant challenge between them. All the verbal gauntlets she had thrown at him before seemed to be hitting her straight in the face. She was close to losing this battle.

Maybe he knew she was going to throw a white flag between them. Maybe that's why he moved the thin black strap of her bra aside and kissed the upper part of her breast. Maybe. But it didn't explain why she let him.

She lifted herself up, and Thayer moved slightly away, giving her enough room. He didn't hide his disappointment. He was giving her a chance to leave. Thayer was giving her free rein to call her boundaries between what felt amazing and what was too much out of her control.

Severine stared at the man in front of her. One that everyone thought they knew so well. Thayer looked close to breaking.

With part of her shirt and bra strap hanging down her arm, she moved above him and straddled his lap. Her shirt dropped to the ground, her bra chased quickly after. Thayer's hands wrapped around her waist making her feel delicate, craved...

His lips made contact with her skin. Finally, it felt good to lose.

*　*　*　*　*

It was four a.m. Severine covered the clock and looked at Thayer. He was supposed to leave last night. She grabbed hold of his shoulder and slightly shook him.

"Mmm?" He groaned.

"Thayer, it's four. You should probably go," Severine whispered against his back. He tensed up and finally nodded.

Severine moved away first and went to her closet for a robe. For the first time, she'd use it.

"I can't even move, I'm so tired."

"You can stay here. But it will be a bitch to sneak you out tomorrow."

"Nah, I'll go now."

His body was covered, and he stood to his full height. "I don't like leaving and sneaking around."

Severine nodded. "I know."

He dug through his pockets for his keys, and with a gruff voice, he spoke, "I can't wait forever, Severine."

All breathing after that comment was out of the realm of possibility. She gave him the truth. "Maybe I'll never be able to trust," Severine admitted.

Thayer nodded and combed a hand through his hair. "You're better than that, though. You're way too fucking durable to run away from us."

Severine knew his words were bait for her to latch onto, but everything she was saying was the truth. What if she really couldn't trust again?

He looked almost disappointed. Severine sat on her bed and clutched the front of her robe close to her heart. "This all makes me ache."

His eyes dissected every move. "Then don't run."

"It's not that easy, Thayer."

"I can't keep walking away from this like nothing is happening."

"I'm not bulletproof." Severine stood and wrapped her arms around his waist. She leaned her cheek against his chest. Through the layers of clothing, she could feel his heart beating wildly. "If I was, I would've never been hurt by Macsen. I just need time."

Chapter Forty-four

"Read pages thirty through fifty-five. If you don't, it's not my problem. Class is dismissed." Severine shut her laptop and slid it into her messenger bag. Everyone around her shuffled about and gathered their belongings. She took a glance at the door and almost groaned.

"You seem preoccupied," Tosha commented beside her.

"Because I am," Severine rushed out. Her mind was foggy, and her head was begging to touch her pillow back at the dorms. After Thayer left last night, sleep became impossible, and she was left with a grand total of three hours of beauty sleep. But she was still alert enough to double-check the doors of the classroom one more time. Maybe her luck would change and there wouldn't be anyone waiting for her today. It hadn't. Macsen waited at the door, staring at her from across the room.

Nothing about his expression was friendly. His green eyes were sharply looking at her, taking in her every action. This happened every day and most of the time he'd back off once he realized that Severine wasn't going to respond. Today was different. The look in his eyes was all off.

Tosha noticed the exchange and raised a brown brow. "Things still awkward?"

Not at all. I just slept with his brother last night, but things are great. Severine grabbed her bag, slung it over her shoulder, and gave Tosha a bright smile. "With him? Not at all. We hardly talk."

"It looks like that's what he wants to do."

Severine walked slowly down the steps with Tosha. Her feet settled on each step. They had their own story. Every footstep whispered out his betrayal. It should be so easy to let something go. But as she walked closer to Macsen, all that filled her mind were his lies. It didn't matter anymore what she thought they could've been. Her hatred had dimmed down to pity. It was only a matter of time until she had nothing left to feel for him. He'd be a complete stranger walking down the street; just a stranger that had once broken her trust.

"Yeah. This is weird, I'm gonna go," Tosha muttered. She slid past Macsen just as Severine was getting ready to open her mouth.

Severine held her head high and followed Tosha's lead.

"I need to talk to you," Macsen said behind her.

If she stared forward and looked unfazed, Macsen would look like he was talking to air. He called out her name more persistently, each time more harsh and demanding after the next. When she was close to the door, he yelled at her.

"I knew he liked you!"

Everyone around them paused to stare at him, then at her. Severine gripped the handle of the door so hard her circulation felt cut off. She didn't want to have a conversation with Macsen, least of all in a building surrounded by students. The pain would never pull away, not when he kept luring her back with strange comments like that. Her finger unclasped the door handle, and on second thought she barged through the door and hurried down the steps.

"I saw him at that party! I watched him look at you,

and it drove him fucking crazy that you didn't notice!" Macsen yelled behind her.

Severine stopped walking and quickly turned back around. Her gaze narrowed on Macsen. She grabbed him by the jacket and didn't stop until they were behind the building, away from everyone.

Macsen's bag dropped to the ground, and he approached her slowly. Her lungs felt compressed as he walked closer. "I had something he wanted, Sev. You were talking to me, you were flirting with *me*!" He grabbed his shirt and wrapped it tightly around his fist. "You loved me first!"

"Shut up!" Severine screamed. She clutched her hands tightly to her ears, hoping to block out everything he said. But it didn't. It ruined everything. It ruined what she thought some form of their relationship had been. It ruined her heart.

"I have nothing to lose. All the fucked up mistakes I've made, everything wrong about me, you're seeing right now." Macsen stepped closer and peered at her with an expression that ached. His eyes implored her to see the truth. "What do you know about Thayer? Hmm?"

Severine repeatedly blinked her eyes. "I know all I want to."

"You know nothing."

"Or I could know everything."

"You wanna take that risk? Take a chance like that?"

How much pain could someone sustain? Severine gritted her teeth together. "I think the worst chance I ever took was on *you*."

Macsen flinched, but he kept talking. "I heard you were at Thayer's game yesterday."

Severine turned around slowly. "Yes, I was."

"You hate basketball games," Macsen pointed out.

"I hate cheaters too, and oh look, I'm talking to you."

"That's fucking low, Sev."

"No. It really isn't. I'm going to keep calling you out

on it until it's out of my system. Until-"

"Until what?" Macsen interjected. "Until I'm out of your system?"

Severine stared up at him, hating that he was getting underneath her skin. "When you have to work so hard for something to leave your memory, shouldn't you wonder why it refuses to erase itself?"

He stood in front of her. They hadn't been this close in so long. He was close enough for her to see his light green eyes wide with caution, his black lashes were wet from the harsh wind. All it did was make his irises stand out. It drew her back to the moment she first talked to him, the memory of spending time with him at the library. She remembered how she felt safe around him; how everything felt easy and carefree with him. It still hurt that those memories were now tainted.

"If you close your eyes, you'll remember us. You'll remember how we were together." Macsen was close enough that Severine could reach her hand out and touch him.

Her eyelids wanted to close so badly. She wanted to adhere his words and just listen for once. But she couldn't. If her strength was anywhere, it laid with Thayer. His face flashed into her mind and her heart instantly. She used to think Macsen was authentic—that there was no one like him. She knew nothing about him. Chances were, she never would.

There was nothing to say after this. She had been pushed off their cloud of happiness months ago. Macsen's feet were just now touching the ground. Pain smeared his features, and Severine stepped away.

"I gotta go."

"You know I love you. That has to stand for something!"

Severine peered back to look at him. "And when it's ruined, it stands for nothing. Before you screwed up, you had no idea how you wore me."

Confusion showered his face. "What are you talking about?"

Severine looked up at the clear blue sky. When she looked back at Macsen, her voice wavered, but stayed sure. "My heart was on your sleeve, waiting patiently. You shrugged it off. You didn't care. You didn't realize."

Macsen stood speechless. It felt like Severine was going back to the same place—a place of despair over Macsen—one too many times.

Slowly, she walked backwards, gazing at him sadly. "I think I'm just now realizing that now."

There was a tiny spot for her to turn around and tell him that they could try again, but in this situation, it was too late. Severine had broken him down. It didn't feel good. She knew firsthand that sometimes people had to be at their lowest before things ever let up. None of this was Severine's problem. He wasn't hers to build back up.

She walked across campus like everyone else. No one looked at her twice as she walked to her car. She felt broken, but she kept repeating she was fine.

But she wasn't fine. She wasn't okay. Now she was in so incredibly deep. Macsen's betrayal made her doubt every direction. But the pain she was in now created new lacerations on her already cut up heart. Now she was like Macsen, she couldn't let go of Thayer. She was greedy and selfish all wrapped up with a pretty little bow on top.

Chapter Forty-five

Severine was in a pattern—running around in one big circle with no way to get out. Her feet didn't step out of the boundaries once. As much as she liked to complain to herself, she didn't plan on leaving, no matter how chaotic her cosmos were becoming.

Her feelings for Thayer were her guilt—a want that never seemed to be filled. Even when she went after what she wanted, she still ended up making mistakes.

She slammed the door harder than necessary and crossed the parking lot, toward the sidewalk. Her fingers rapped once against the door. Thayer opened it quickly. The door wasn't even shut before Severine wrapped herself around him and kissed her pain away.

Thayer didn't question. He took all her pain in and gathered it as his own. Reaching across the space, she laced their fingers together. They were getting to a point where kissing, and being together in the closest way possible, wasn't enough.

Tightly, she kept her eyes shut and let his tongue in her mouth. Her confusion. Her guilt. Her pain. It stretched upward. Soon it'd consume her entire body.

Thayer pushed himself away and stared at her face. "Are you okay?"

"No," Severine's lips shook as she spoke. Her heart

raced as she stared up at Thayer and told him the truth. "I just saw Macsen."

His eyes narrowed slightly, but that was the only reaction he gave.

She didn't want any miscommunication with him. Severine didn't want a situation to cause them to drift apart. Thayer deserved the truth.

Thayer's lips thinned slightly. "You need to tell me what's really bothering you." He waited for her to speak.

"I feel stupid for being here...after everything that happened. It's like I'm repeating my past."

His smile was sardonic. "You gathered that all from your conversation with Macsen?"

Severine stepped closer. "What am I doing here?" Her question was strained with so much confusion.

"Maybe you need a hideaway?"

Severine frowned. "You're more than a hideaway."

He said nothing in response and simply held out his hand. Something was hidden in his eyes. But Severine still took his hand and walked down the crammed hallway. Thayer walked in front of her and already things were starting to feel off balance.

When they entered his room he shut his bedroom door and turned to look at her. "What did Macsen say to really scare you?"

His hands reached down to take off his shoes. Severine watched him and leaned against the door. "He told me he saw how you looked at me."

Thayer smiled down at the carpet. He dug through his back pocket and dumped his wallet onto his dresser. "That's it?"

Severine shook her head and slowly took off her jacket. Her feet easily slid out of her ballet flats. "He said it drove you crazy that I didn't notice."

Thayer didn't confirm or deny. He flicked open the snap of his watch and placed it alongside his wallet. His arms reached to his back and he dragged his shirt away from his body. He unbuttoned his jeans but paused when he realized Severine wasn't moving. His brow lifted, and Severine kept looking at the strong V that disappeared under his jeans.

"That's it?"

Severine jerked her gaze back to his eyes. There was no sound between them. Severine leaned down slightly. Her eyes stayed connected with Thayer's as she slid off her black tights. Her body didn't seem to be her own. Thayer watched her skin come into sight. It was his entity. "He said that I talked to him first...that I loved him first."

Something seemed final about this moment. Her fingers hesitated on the zipper of her dress. It was the way Thayer stared at her with determination that made Severine for the first time, nervous.

He came upon her slowly. He only stopped when Severine's shoulder blades touched the wall behind her. When his hands grasped her shoulders, he clutched the fabric of her dress and guided it away from her skin. His face showed everything. After this, absolution wouldn't be given. "Is it true?"

His arms were a cage. She was the gilded bird that was trying to think fast—fast enough to get away from his enclosure. Her hands reached out to touch the firm muscles above his hip. He gripped her hands before they could make contact with his skin. "I had a glimpse of you before him," Severine slowly confirmed.

In between them, her hands were still held by his. She felt bound together by a piece of rope with no way to become free. "I recognized things about you that I didn't want to. I saw too much, and that's why I went for Macsen."

"But you're here with me." His hands reached up and looped underneath her bra straps. He pulled them down and Severine let him. "You're in front of me to touch." One hand tightly clasped her wrists together, the other trailed from her stomach to her breast. When Thayer claimed, it became his property. No matter what it was. It hurt to admit that her body was starting to recognize him as its dominion. "Are you mine, Severine?"

It was first instinct to pull away. That option was impossible. "I'm not going to answer that."

He kissed her neck and gave it a quick nip. Severine jumped at the contact. "Too much to ask?"

She knew the answer, Severine just wasn't going to give it to him. "No."

"I could take you right here."

Her anger rose at his cocky demeanor. He was trying to show her he had the power. Severine jerked back, but that only seemed to make Thayer hang on tighter. "Don't push me, Thayer," she warned.

"I'll take you right here," Thayer repeated again. This time, his fingers dipped into her panties.

Severine's eyes briefly closed. When he took her over, her eyes opened back up wildly. He stared down at her with a confident smile. "What are you trying to prove, Thayer?"

He lifted her higher against the wall. It only took one quick movement of his hips and he was in her.

The hand holding her wrists roughly guided them above her head and to the wall. Severine's breath was coming out faster. "When you leave here, I want everything to be obvious. If these walls around us are going to speak, they're going to shout out that you're mine."

"Is...this about possession?" Her head slammed against the wall as he moved inside her.

His free hand gripped her hip tightly, and guided her away from his body, and back again. "We can't go back from this, Severine."

She itched to wrap her arms around him. Her hands jerked, and he put more pressure on her wrists. "You don't own me."

"I think it's too late to say that," Thayer smirked and moved a finger up and down the curve of her waist. "Look at your skin. It's already branded with my name."

Her body was a traitor. It moved against him, agreeing with every surge and movement from him. "Are you mine?"

Severine heard him. She was choosing to ignore him. Thayer pushed her hips up and pulled her back down slowly. "Answer me."

"Yes!" The pressure was becoming too much.

"Yes, what?"

"I'm yours!"

"See, I don't think you want to be in control," Thayer groaned out. "I think you were wanting someone to test you in every way."

Severine tried to tilt her hips, anything to prove that he was wrong. All he did was smirk at her attempt. "Who's in control here, Severine?"

"You..." It pained her to say it. "And me."

"No." Thayer's clash of opinion was instantly spoken. "Who's the only one that possesses you?"

Severine's head fell back. Her fingers were clenched tightly against his grasp, as he squeezed back. At this point, she'd say anything. It was hard to feel atonement when she felt this good. She moved her head to look down at Thayer. When she shifted her hips, his knees almost buckled.

"If I'm going down, I want you to say the truth." The grip on her hands was starting to become painful. Severine realized he was desperate for the truth.

"The truth?" Severine gasped out. Her heart dropped down to her stomach as her mouth opened up. It warned her to keep the gut wrenching truth to herself. She shifted her hips again, and she watched his face go slack. Some women forgot the power they could hold over a man. Every woman possessed it. Some were just too afraid to use it. Severine wasn't.

"Fuck." He stumbled back. Severine smirked at his loss of control.

His back landed on the bed. Severine stayed on top. His jeans abraded against her legs but she kept moving. Her fingers landed on his stomach and she knew if she pulled away, there'd be marks on his skin.

Something similar to a groan slipped out of his mouth. And in the position she was in, Severine watched him.

His eyes widened and he said the one thing she never expected, "I love you!"

Her heart kept beating wildly as she tried to slow her movements. His hands slammed tightly against her hips. Their breathing came out in gasps together. His stomach muscles clenched as his movements became quicker and quicker. When she came, he trailed after her.

Her body collapsed against his, and her breathing came out in uneven pants.

His words were still being whispered in her ear.

*   *   *   *   *

Severine guided her feet into her black tights and stared down at her body. Her muscles quivered and her heart hammered in her chest. It gasped with each breath that it wanted more of Thayer. She rubbed a hand where her heart laid. No longer could she say it was her own.

"My parents will be here tonight."

Severine froze while putting on her jacket and glanced at Thayer. "Are they here for your game?"

His shirt covered his head. It straightened down his torso, and his face was back in view. "Yeah."

"When are they getting in?"

"Soon."

Severine wanted to see them, but she had already been here too long. Already she could picture Macsen walking through the door and ruining the moment. She walked out into the hall as she spoke. "I better get out of here."

"You're still hiding from him."

Severine turned, and he was behind her. "Because the three of us together in the same room would be weird!"

"If you let him get in the way."

"We try to make it work..." Severine stared at her hands before she spoke. "He'll always hover above us. That can't go away."

He processed her words, and it slowly sunk in. If she expected him to lie down and retreat, she had the wrong Sloan brother.

He was Thayer. She expected a battle. "*If* you want him there. *If* you allow him to."

"He always will be!"

"Because you want him to be. You're fucking scared," Thayer accused.

"Of what?"

"I don't know. Tell me. Tell me and I'll help." He cornered her, crept into her personal space like no other. "What terrifies you so much?"

For once, she was honest. "This." Severine pointed between the two of them. "Us—terrifies me."

She knew with certainty how she wanted her heart handled from now on.

"Why? Because it's a challenge? Because it's not easy?"

She pounced on his words. "You're right! Everything was easy with him!"

"He didn't challenge you! Macsen was there, but he never consumed you!" Severine opened her mouth, and Thayer quickly cut her off. "Don't tell me it was different than what I just said."

"It's not supposed to be this way!" Severine screamed. None of it was. The sneaking around, the fear of getting hurt...

"What do I know? I've only loved you!" Thayer shouted back. Everything in his expression showed his panic. He didn't want to admit it, just as Severine didn't. He paced around the living room before finally choosing to stand in front of her. "Severine, don't you get it? Everything should be mad between us." She wanted to seize back his words, but he kept talking. His words advanced on her and wouldn't let her breathe. "Everything we do together is fucking phenomenal!"

Severine didn't have to wonder. Every single moment with him was stuck in her brain. All the barbs thrown back and forth, his smile, how he kissed her. He was right. Together they were phenomenal.

The balance of their relationship was shifting into something Severine couldn't control. She didn't want to run. She wanted to fight. Thayer was worth it. That thought scared her the most.

A minute passed with no words between them. Tears gathered in her eyes as Thayer shook his head over her silence.

"You're going to say nothing," he accused.

What they had together was beyond Severine. She couldn't say if it was love. Maybe compassion, anger, lust, captivated trust.

She trusted him.

Severine's heart was willing to trust again.

Inside her world, that wasn't enough. Her heart was a sacred place.

"Just give me time," Severine pleaded.

"Give me eternity."

Severine backed away. "I don't kn-"

"Say you love me. Give me eternity, and I'll give you all the time you need."

"We're gonna break," Severine's voice cracked.

"Then make all of this go away!" Thayer shouted. It was loud, an outcry of pain. Severine flinched. He rubbed a hand over his face, a face that looked tortured. "Get the fuck out if you're done!"

Severine stood firm. They both knew the truth.

He finally looked at her and gripped his hair tightly in his hands. "Just go," he bellowed.

Her head moved back and forth. Where was all her quick wit now? She had no coherent thought. Nothing she was thinking could slip out of her mouth and be said right. It was all a mess.

Thayer rushed toward her and gripped her arms painfully. She stood her ground, and kept her eyes rooted in spot, staring at him boldly.

"You know you can't walk away. I got closer than you ever wanted!"

Severine pushed back, but he stayed in place. "You're not letting me think!"

"Come on!" Thayer taunted. She snapped her head up to look at him. He pushed away the hair that was tangled in her eyes. "Lay me down if you're finished! If you can walk away, then go!"

He provoked. He pushed. He stalked until it became too much. "I can't. I love you!" Severine screamed before she could think the words through.

Her breathing came out in gasps. She wanted to wrap her arms around her body, huddle close within herself—away from the pain she was feeling. Thayer's grip became gentle, and she looked up at him with confusion. "This is painful! You and me together scares me! Everything between us is passionate. How do we know if this is really true?"

"You're looking for something you already have."

Severine nodded and held onto his arms. The cards that had been dealt to her weren't expected. The harsh realities of the world would never be a welcoming experience.

"I don't want us closed."

"I don't want that either. I-" Her head jerked to the door when she heard voices. Sooner than later, she'd have to face Macsen with Thayer next to her. Sooner than later, he'd have to see what was reality and what could've been.

In the doorway stood Jayni and Owen. It should've been a time for Thayer and Severine to greet them. But to the side stood Macsen. The expression on his face was impossible to translate.

Jayni stepped forward with a nervous glance between Thayer and Macsen. "Severine. It's great to see you again."

Severine nodded and accepted the hug. Behind Jayni's back, her eyes pleaded to Thayer, for him to get her out of here. She returned the hug with complete distraction. When Jayni pulled away, Severine smiled apologetically. "I should get going. Let you guys have some family time."

Her breath felt shallow, as she looked everywhere else but at Thayer and Macsen. She had to leave. Now. Slowly, she retreated toward the door that was becoming higher ground compared to the reality in front of her. It was all starting to sink.

Macsen stepped away from the wall. With his arms crossed, he stood next to Thayer. It was the closest Severine had ever seen them together. "Dad, Jayni. I never had the chance to introduce you to my ex." He swept a hand in Severine's direction. It was a spotlight no one would crave. "This is Severine...the bitch that has tortured my every thought since I met her!"

Severine's back stiffened. It wasn't his words. She could take the word bitch. Most times she could hold that title above her head like a trophy. Her strength was something to covet. When it came from Macsen's mouth, it was pronounced in the lowest form. It felt vile. It transformed him into a person Severine didn't know.

Thayer shifted to look at Severine. It only took one glance for him to see her anger and pain. He turned away and rushed at Macsen. Disorder erupted as Thayer tackled Macsen to the ground.

Severine stood back with Jayni. A paroxysm of feelings swirled in her veins. Her pain wasn't small; it spread from her heart and numbed her body. Words only went so far. A simple reaction said enough to leave most people satisfied.

With a punch to Thayer's stomach and a quick punch to Macsen's face…Severine cringed with every movement they made.

"Owen!" Jayni yelled. "Get them off each other!"

Owen moved toward the two of them. Macsen slammed Thayer against the wall, and Owen stepped away.

She had to get away from this. Without her coat or keys, Severine walked to the door and promptly ran into Mathias. He stared at her with puzzlement and looked at the commotion behind her.

"Shit," he mumbled. The luggage in his hands dropped. He gripped Severine's shoulders and stared at her point blank. "Stay here. Family time is just starting."

She followed Mathias with her gaze as he shouted out to his brothers. "Curtain's closed! No one gives a fuck about your problems." He clutched Thayer by the shirt and dragged him away. Not once did Mathias glance over at Macsen.

Owen walked into the kitchen and came back out with a roll of paper towels. He threw a few at Macsen and chucked the rest at Mathias.

Macsen heaved out a heavy breath and leaned against the wall. "Finders, keepers, brother!" he taunted out darkly.

Thayer moved forward, and Mathias slammed him back against the wall. Mathias turned to finally look at Macsen. Strangers held more in their gaze than Mathias's. And for a brief second, Macsen's battered feelings came to the surface. Severine saw the guy she first smiled at months ago, the one she believed in. She hadn't seen him in a while. After this, it was doubtful he would be found again.

He momentarily looked at Severine, but the contact did nothing for her. Not anymore.

"What the hell is going on?" Owen bellowed.

Macsen tried to smile. His cracked lip made it impossible. "Thayer wants my seconds."

"Son of a bitch!" Mathias slapped a hand against his thigh and fixed him with glare. "Can you keep your mouth shut?"

Owen finally leveled his gaze on Macsen. His deep voice was clear. "Tell me again what's going on. This time, explain without being a complete asshole. If you say anything about," his finger blindly reached behind him and pointed in Severine's direction, "her, I'll be the one to punch you. You're my son, but you're starting to piss me off now."

In front of Severine was a battlefield. Her heart was drumming to a beat she had never heard. Jayni ran a hand down Severine's arm and patted her shoulder. The arguing erupted in front of her.

Severine didn't want this. It may get better for their family, but that window for Severine seemed to have slammed shut.

Her legs backed up, and Macsen's head shot up quickly. "Stay, Sev!" He sat on the floor, still bleeding, and even battered, he had the ability to wound her. None of this was supposed to happen. "Everyone in my life that's fucked me over is here. Let's all sit and talk!"

"Macsen-" Owen gruffly spoke out.

"Wow! Dad speaks. He has a voice!" Macsen laughed, and it was dark. A chill swept through Severine as she stared down at him. Everything before this moment had been an illusion. An illusion of what she thought she knew to be the truth. The reality was in front of her. It yelled out that this family feud went much deeper than sibling wars. Macsen kept his gaze on her face, and pointed directly at her chest, right where her heart laid. "You want the beginning? Let's go back to the day I met you, Severine!"

"I'm not doing this here."

"I count the times you walk away. You want to know the truth about everything? Then sit."

Severine's animosity rose for him with each word he spoke. A part of her wanted to pummel him with punches for the pain he'd given her. "You want to hash things out in front of your family? Do you really want to do that?" Severine stepped closer. "Tell them you cheated on me with someone else. Tell them all of it, Macsen!"

He leaned his head against the wall, with his eyes in slits, and he looked her over. "Is it any better than you fucking my brother weeks after you left me? And what's worse is you did it behind everyone's back. Who's next, Severine? Hmm? Maybe Mathias?"

His words put the pressure on the trigger. Her anger exploded out of her. She looped around Jayni and went for any part of his body. All she could connect with was his arm—Thayer snatched her back from doing anything else.

Pain was always brought out during the worst of times. Anger sometimes followed. It was the truth that came and snatched it all away. When the truth arrived, the damage would always be far worse. "You never gave me anything!" Severine yelled.

Macsen stood up slowly. His hand reached out, and Severine swore he was in pain. "I gave you everything I possibly could!"

"You're too chicken shit to say the truth about anything! You hide behind it and use it as a fucking excuse!"

"You were with me, but were you ever? I was dragged along while you and my brother snuck looks at each other. So who's the chicken shit? Me or you?"

"That is enough!" Jayni yelled. Her cheeks were

flushed, and her pulse pounded against her neck. Severine blinked a few times before she realized that Jayni was there. Macsen and Severine still had a crowd around them.

Everyone paused long enough to look in her direction. Everyone but Macsen. He snorted and kept speaking. "It'll never be enough until Severine has her truth!"

Mathias rubbed his face and groaned. "Shit. Just stop talking."

Macsen gave Mathias the finger and walked toward the broken kitchen table. His hands wobbled as they grasped a chair that was still intact. "My life became a disaster the minute my mom asked me to testify against Dad during a custody battle."

Everyone stopped speaking.

Severine's eyes widened as he continued. "I lied for her. I was eight years old and believed everything that came out of her mouth. I lied and said my dad had abused me."

Severine's heart dropped to her stomach at his revelation. There was no manipulation in his eyes, just pain. She stepped forward and stood on the opposite side of the table.

"I thought I could keep you without me ruining us. But I fucked even that up. Maybe there is nothing inside of me but a big hole. Maybe I have no soul. Maybe I'm a different breed. My life has been filled with mistakes, and I thought if I kept you away from it, you'd never see that part of me." A single tear fell down his cheek, and Severine's own sadness chased after it. "Everything's better without the truth. Are you happy now?"

"No," Thayer said as he stepped forward, "don't put that on her."

Macsen breathed harshly through his nose. "Don't give her the truth?"

"We hated each other way before she came along."

"Do you ever wonder what we saw in you, Sev?"

She did. Every single day. "No," Severine lied.

"You're a fucking liar," Macsen accused. He knew her well enough to see through her poker face and call her bluff. Both brothers did.

"You were so fucking carefree," Macsen explained. Severine swallowed loudly as he continued. "But you had so much fire in you. After a while, I saw what Thayer saw: a girl that could cut a person down with a look and build them right back up with a smile. I swear on everything that I believed that you wouldn't get to me. I could've guaranteed that your smiles wouldn't make me feel like I could alter all my past fuck-ups and make it better...I tried so fucking hard with you, Severine."

Chapter Forty-six

It was freezing, but Severine stayed outside.

Inside, things were starting to quiet down. Thayer sat at the kitchen table and talked with his dad heatedly. Macsen had left an hour ago.

Severine wanted to follow him and ask him so many things. Every question started with why. His past wouldn't have affected her. What his mom did to him wasn't his fault. He was just a child. She was never given the chance to tell him any of her thoughts.

She gathered her sweater tightly against her and looked up at the sky. It was clear. Stars sprinkled its perfect canvas. Every night, this was a constant. How could she make her life that way?

The patio door opened, and Severine turned her head at the noise. Mathias walked up with his hands in his pockets and flashed his package of cigarettes. "I'm killing sixty seconds off my life." He peered at her. "What's your excuse for being out here?"

Severine hugged her arms tighter around herself and sat on the frigid patio seat. "I didn't want to listen to that."

A cigarette poked out of the side of his mouth. The lighter in his hands brought a flash of light to his face and the dark smirk on his lips. He inhaled deeply, and a trail of smoke escaped his mouth as he lifted his head to the sky. "You mean, not everyone's family is so messed up?"

A wind picked up around them, and the bare branches bent toward the wind's demands. At night, everything was raw, primal, and so completely alone.

If Severine could ever regret her choices, it'd be now. "Tell me something good about your brothers."

His laugh was dark. "I can't." He flicked the tip of his cigarette and stared down at the fixture in his hands. "We're all a fucking mess; each of us in a different way."

Severine shook her head at his cryptic words. "That's a dark thing to say."

"It's the truth. It's what you get for allowing a Sloan into your life."

"You know, I used to think that I could figure it out."

Mathias barely raised a brow. "And now?"

"I'm still just as lost."

"You've started a fire between them," Mathias warned, although the dark smile on his face made it impossible for his warning to be sincere. "It might be impossible to douse those flames." He looked at her sympathetically. "Did you really not have any clue what you were getting yourself into?"

"I didn't want that, what happened earlier," Severine confessed. She needed to tell her feelings to someone.

"I know. Everyone knows." He finished his cigarette and flicked it off the deck without caring where it fell. When he turned back to her, the wind kicked up and tousled his dark blonde hair—so similar to Thayer's. Mathias was too raw, though. He held dark secrets in his eyes and was friendly to no one. "Welcome to the family, tiger." He patted her shoulder and smiled widely. "You've earned your stripes."

Severine tilted her head back to stare back up at the sky. And when Mathias left, Jayni replaced him.

"Hi, sweetie."

Severine turned. "Hi."

Jayni held out a plate of pizza on a plastic plate. "I brought you some food."

"Carbs are dangerous for an emotional girl."

Jayni laughed and sat next to Severine. "I know. I've already had three slices."

She let Severine eat before she tried to start a conversation. Her fingers rubbed in circles against her temple.

"Was what Macsen said the truth?" Severine asked.

Jayni's hand briefly paused, before it disappeared altogether. Slowly, she nodded her head, and the sadness was back in her face. "Severine, have they ever talked about Laurena?" Lily quietly asked.

Severine shook her head. "I didn't know *it* had a name."

"She was never around," Jayni said slowly. Her eyes settled on the tree in front of them as she continued. "Things between Owen and Laurena were a disaster from day one. She came from Germany, couldn't speak a full sentence in English, but she used that to her advantage and roped their father."

Severine stared at her sadly. She was hearing the truth. Before this moment, she would've loved to understand everything. Now, it was painful to listen to a family story filled with downfalls.

"Laurena used the kids as pawns. They were more of a trade-off than her flesh and blood. When they divorced, things got nasty. She wanted everything: the farm, the money. Just for spite, she requested full custody of the boys."

A tear fell down Jayni's cheek, and she wiped it away and smiled at Severine apologetically. "Her love is impossible to see. If you give her what she wants, she'll reward you with attention. But, if you don't, you no longer exist for her.

"Macsen was the youngest. He gave her that attention. She used his love and warped it. Laurena manipulated him to think things. He did what he did to keep her. I don't have to think on it. I know it." Severine felt her stomach crumble over Jayni's explanation. "He was only a kid," she continued, "but lines were drawn after that. Mathias and Thayer ended up living with Owen's father, Eugene, for a few years. They moved to Missouri to live with Owen and me when they were teenagers."

The puzzle pieces came together perfectly. The final masterpiece was horrific. "That's why you have a cabin in Tennessee."

Jayni nodded. "That was Eugene's home before he passed away. We use it regularly when we visit Mathias."

"And where was Macsen?"

"He stayed with Laurena. She was never in one place for too long."

"Why did he stay with her?" Severine whispered. "He could've changed it all."

"Everything that was said in there was the most Macsen has ever said...in front of any of us. None of us knew about you and Macsen, but it's clear you brought something out of him."

"Something dark and ugly?" Severine tried to lightly tease.

Jayni's lips fell out of the flat line they had settled in, and she gave a weak grin. "It's more than I've ever seen from him."

"Why does Macsen go to school here? Why go to the same college as someone you can't stand?"

Jayni shrugged and responded slowly, "We didn't pay for Thayer's schooling. We have good and bad times at the farm. He got a full ride to go here. Macsen is attending with his mom's money."

Severine shook her head and stared down at the ground. This story was crushing her. "The money she got from Owen."

Jayni nodded. "He's not bad. Macsen has good in him. Things are just more twisted for him. He'll never like me because of what Laurena has said. But I think in the past few years, her control has started to wear off. I think he came here to be closer to Thayer. If there was any plan behind Macsen going here, it was to see if he could get his brother back."

"Okay," Severine said slowly. Not everything lined up perfectly. "Why would they live together?"

Jayni sighed. She seemed exhausted. "Owen pays for this apartment. He told them if they were willing to live together and not kill each other, he was willing to pay their rent."

Severine gripped her hair in frustration. Stories were sometimes better left in the dark. The story of the Sloan brothers made everything seem obscured.

Jayni rubbed her back. "I know what I see between you and Thayer. There's something there. Don't let what you heard earlier affect that. None of it stems from you, Severine. Having all four of them together is painful. Someone usually ends up storming away."

Severine would be that person.

People came together. Together, they'd fall apart. And no matter what Jayni said, it wouldn't change the truth that on one minuscule level, Severine had caused a deeper rift.

"I think I'm gonna leave," Severine pronounced awkwardly.

Jayni nodded and stood. "I know this visit started off on an odd note, but we'd love to see you before we leave Sunday."

"I hope." *But it won't happen.*

Jayni accepted Severine's answer and opened up the patio door for them to walk through. Thayer glanced up from where he sat on the couch. He looked severed and blindly pieced together. Fear was in his opaque irises. He held out his hand to her, and Severine's fingers immediately linked with his like a lifeline, a pardon from tonight.

Goodbyes were mumbled and they slowly walked outside to her car. Severine trekked across the parking lot at a deliberately slow pace. She felt as if somehow they were kissing away their future.

"Where do we go from here?" Severine asked finally.

Thayer swallowed and stared down at the ground. That was never good.

Fear took over Severine's body. She gripped Thayer's jaw and forced him to look at her. "Do I give you time? Do I step away?" Her hold from his face disappeared. "Help me out, Thayer. I don't know what to do."

"Neither do I."

His brief response scared her. "Can't we let go of this?"

"What you heard is going to give you doubts."

Severine opened her mouth. Thayer sealed it shut with a kiss. "You can't answer that quickly. It'll be in your head that you started something between Macsen and me, when in reality, it's been like this for years."

Severine anxiously opened her mouth. "Jayni told me. I know everything." Maybe if he knew she had discovered the truth, he wouldn't look crushed.

"Think about it. I'll still be here." His words were like a storm. Its intent was to clean the surface but all Severine felt was the thunder, and all she saw was the lightning striking around her.

"I didn't see you doing this," Severine accused.

A harsh noise came from the back of his throat. His eyes flashed with frustration. He gripped her face in his hands and hovered above her. His lips bore down on hers and wouldn't let go. The intensity was still there. His tongue licked against her closed lips repeatedly. Severine's tears pooled out quickly.

Repeatedly, her hands pushed at his stomach. He

didn't budge; instead, he situated himself close enough to where she couldn't hide from him.

Her mouth opened on a gasp. He consumed every part open to him. And, for once, Severine held back. Her hands shook against her jeans. He was so close, but right now Thayer felt out of her reach.

Severine never wanted the truth to come out. She never wanted her fragile feelings to be exposed. There'd be nothing left of her. But she was close to losing everything. That last bit of armor slowly fell away inside Thayer's apartment.

Her heart was homeless.

All it wanted was a shelter.

Things between them were going to fade and it terrified her.

The truth was, he knew her. He knew every game and every deceptive trick tightly zipped up within her boots, but it was the same for Severine. Thayer didn't have to say anything. His actions showed his desperation. It felt like the beginning of the end.

He wrenched away, long enough to jerk her face up to look at him. "Touch me."

It might be the last time she had him this close. She should've held tight, but she couldn't. She refused to think anything between them was over. Severine's lips shook as she answered him, "No."

His body bowed to hers, and Thayer nestled his nose against her neck. "I need this. I need reassurance that you still want this."

She pushed, and he shifted away. "This is all a big wave off then, no? If you won't be here tomorrow." Severine sputtered out.

"I wouldn't put everything I had into a wave off. I don't think I can do that with you!"

"Then why are you doing this?" Whether he knew it or not, he was crushing her.

He looked just as tortured as her. None of it made

sense. "Meet me in thirty days," he swallowed, "in two months, a whole fucking year. I don't care how long. I'm gonna be here. I'm in love with you."

"I don't need space. You're not giving me a decision in any of this. You're telling me what's going to happen!"

"I've waited too long for you! I want a future with you more than the present. All my family fuck- ups will come back and repeat themselves. That's why I'm doing this. That's why I'm telling you this and giving you a chance to walk away!"

Emotions she never knew she could possess consumed her. Her breathing came out steadily, when inside she was gasping for air. He pulled away and she wanted to plead for him to stay.

She opened her car door and turned back to him. "I love you," Severine blurted out. "You've taunted me from day one. There has always been this warning above your head, that you'd be bad for me, that together we'd be too much..."

He shook his head at her words. Severine continued, "We proved my subconscious right."

*   *   *   *   *

Severine waited until she was back at the dorms to break apart.

The drive from Thayer and Macsen's was normally a short trip. Her lungs felt compressed as she drifted from Thayer. It was hard to regret him. He showed her that love did have a beautiful melody. She wanted to sing out the hymn, over and over.

The shaking in her hands became impossible to constrain. Her grip became tighter and tighter until her circulation cut off. By the time she pulled up into a parking spot, her hands were numb, just like her heart. But feeling would tingle back into her fingertips. It was hard to say when her heart would revive itself back to life.

Bricks weighed her down as she took the stairs up to her room. If dreams existed, she'd fly away from all of this. If wishes could be granted, she'd clench her eyes tightly and make the clock wind all the way back to the moment Lily asked her where she wanted to study.

She'd warn herself. Her shaking hands would grab Severine as she yelled at her to go anywhere else to study—every other place but there.

"Hey, you okay?"

Severine slid her key into the lock and looked up to see Anne walking down the hall with an armful of books. Fibbing about her feelings wasn't an option. She shook her head and glanced back at the door before opening it wide.

Her walls screamed of Thayer.

Anne wordlessly took Severine's hand in her own and guided her into the room. When the door shut, her sadness spilled out in waves. Her back hit the door, and she slid to the ground. Anne followed down the same path.

"I know everything," Severine mumbled out.

Anne kneeled in front of Severine and peered closely at her. "What?"

"Thayer and Macsen. I know everything between them."

A piece of toilet paper dangled in front of her. Severine grabbed it and blew her nose loudly.

Anne sat down Indian style on the cold floor. "It's that bad?"

"It's all a disaster," Severine admitted.

"And where are you now?"

"I don't know," Severine hiccuped. "I went over there for reassurance and left with a mutilated heart."

The tears kept coming. Anne stayed next to her, remaining silent the whole time. Her presence was enough.

When she thought of all the 'almosts,' it made everything worse. Eyes weren't created for sight. They were the portals to someone's past. How could Severine miss the story of the Sloan brothers? Maybe because she expected an anecdote and not a nightmare?

She leaned her head against Anne's small shoulder, and everything gushed out of her soul like a flood.

That night, Severine fell asleep wondering if Thayer would keep true to his word. Because it was known that time separated everything. Time healed wounds. Time made you forget. That's what Severine feared the most.

Three Months Later...

Chapter Forty-seven

What does a heart bleed out when it's crushed?

Its contents could show someone so much of who they really were.

Severine finally understood herself. Her pain screamed to her the truth. It was caustic to admit that she had to search for the sun hidden by shadows. When everything parted, she wanted to discover Thayer. If he could accept her for her faults, then so much was paved out for them already.

Severine wanted that. She wanted a smooth path for them. They needed it—deserved it.

But empathy was something she'd never possess. He told her that when she was ready he'd be waiting. She stayed back. For more than a day. That day spanned into three months.

Her legs moved up and down underneath the coffee table. Lily glanced up at her and barely raised a brow. "I told you this was a stupid idea."

"I think I need to do this."

Lily rose from the table and clutched her magazine tightly to her chest. "No, I don't think you do. But if it's going to give you some kind of closure, then go for it." The bell on the door jingled and they both looked at the entrance. "Well, well, well," Lily murmured near

Severine. She rose to her full height and patted Severine's shoulder as the figure came closer to their table. "I'm gonna look for some books."

Severine nodded and looked at the body walking toward to her. She had already questioned if this was a good decision. When he called, she relented—mostly for closure.

"I can't believe you came."

Severine chose to look first at the baseball cap.

Macsen stood in front of her, dressed in khaki shorts and a gray t-shirt featuring a band she'd never discover. Her gaze traveled up to his face, and Macsen's green eyes, the ones that before could've killed her with a glance, were guarded. There was no way to know what he was thinking.

He pointed to the seat across from Severine hesitantly. It's funny what a few months could do to a person. Time away from Thayer had almost broken her soul in two. Time away from Macsen was a healing process that she had never allowed herself.

She nodded and kicked it out with her leg. "You can sit."

When he settled in across from her, he looked sheepish. "Sorry. I'm still in shock that you actually showed up."

Severine shrugged but said nothing in response.

Macsen tapped his fingers against the table. She watched him repeatedly open and close his mouth.

Months ago, she expected it all from him: the world, his time, and his heart. Severine needed nothing from him now. It didn't give her the agony it once did.

"You deserve something from me," Macsen gradually said. "What I did to you months ago...it wasn't planned. I didn't premeditate any of it."

Severine leaned her elbows on the table and placed her chin in her palm. She was ready to talk this through. "Then why do it?"

He rubbed a hand over his face and readjusted his cap. The discomfort around them rose to a higher decibel. "When I met you, I saw exactly what my brother saw. I thought I had you pegged at first. You turned out to be something altogether unexpected. You gave me everything, and...it overwhelmed me. It scared me."

Severine slowly nodded her head. "It still doesn't explain it."

"Why do you need this explanation?"

"I've gone over it so many times in my head, I've lost count. I need to stand for something. Let me have that one thing, Macsen."

"Why?"

Severine mashed the wrapper of her straw with her palm. When she lifted her hand, it stuck to her skin. Gravity prevailed, and it fell away. Just like Macsen. "I've fallen for so much already. I have nothing left to contribute."

Macsen acknowledged her response with a brief nod of his head. "You seemed to be one step above me, always. When I met Ver—that girl," he corrected quickly, "at the library, I was something to her. I wasn't beneath her, and I didn't have to keep up with her." He took off his baseball cap and played with the bill nervously. "She trailed after me when we were together."

Severine slightly scrunched up her nose at the word 'together.' It would probably be a sore spot for her forever.

"I was funny to her," he continued, "no matter what I said, she'd laugh. She wasn't searching for something with me." His fingers dropped away from the hat, and he looked at her with regret that on most days, Severine could accept. "Our relationship was the opposite of us. I think if I wouldn't have screwed up, there would've been something else to get in between us. I couldn't bounce back quickly enough for you. And when I did, it left me feeling dizzy and unprepared for the next time your brilliance would come my way."

"You could've told me how you felt, what you were thinking..."

"No, I couldn't. I was drinking my delusion and distancing myself from every part of you," Macsen explained.

"You were something to me. At that time, you were what I thought I needed."

Macsen laughed and shook his head at her response. "You never really needed me, Sev. You'll never outgrow the world. But I think I always knew at one point, you'd start to outgrow me."

It was still tense. Severine stared down at the wooden floors beneath her feet. Around them, people talked and laughed. Summer's imprint was everywhere. Skin showed and smiles were in clear sight. Sitting here with Macsen, closing this part of her life was bittersweet. There could've been something there between them. It could've been all-consuming.

Severine was willing to accept that mistakes happened. People could come together after a regret. Most times, when that happened, it showed just how durable a couple could be. From the beginning, Severine and Macsen's durability was stretched thin. Too many things stood in their way.

"Do you ever regret us?" Macsen asked.

"Sometimes," Severine finally said. "I used to all the time. I had this huge idea of what I thought we'd be. We proved that we could have good times, but the bad outweighed everything else." Her fingers picked the flat straw wrapper off the table and smashed it even further. "We weren't made for each other."

Not in the way I am for Thayer.

She kept her thoughts private, and Macsen disclosed his without a care. If only he would've been like this before. "You haven't seen him?"

Severine leaned back in her chair. "We needed time

apart."

His fingers stopped moving, and he flicked his green eyes to her face. "Will you come together after this?"

"I don't know," Severine answered honestly.

"Do you love him?"

Severine paused and stirred the straw around in her cup. "Do you really want to know that?"

He laughed, and it came out choked. "Not really. But a part of me needs to know."

Her nod was hesitant. "Yeah, I do."

At her response, he stood abruptly. His hands settled on the table, and he leaned closer to her. "I'd like to be able to tell you that you should be with him. I'd like to say, if you love him you should go, so I'd know I didn't get in your way."

He slammed his hat on his head. Strands curled around the edge of the cap, and Severine saw the old Macsen again. "I can't say it without lying, though. That'd put us in the same spot as before."

"When did you decide to be honest?" Severine quizzed.

He tucked his hands into his shorts and jingled his keys against his leg repeatedly. "I know I've made a lot of mistakes...in my past, and now. I thought that before you left to go back home, I'd fix this wrong between us."

Their gazes held, and Severine stared at Macsen without blinking. There wasn't much more to say after this.

"I'll see you later, Severine."

"Bye."

He turned to walk away, but Severine saw his eyebrows rise. It didn't look like much, but she noticed the cryptic expression on his face. He didn't have to say anything. Severine knew what he was thinking. Goosebumps rose across her skin as she finally came to the realization that he wasn't done...at least with her.

He turned and walked out the cafe. When the door

lightly closed behind him, that piece of her life and the emotions she had held for so long, fell back into her lap. It was hers again. It was hers to keep close or give away.

A flash of color next to the window caught Severine's attention. She looked up just in time to see a slim girl walk across the room. It was the flash of caramel that hooked her in. The hair color was unique and never seen unless on a hair color bottle. Half her hair was held back with a clip, while the rest fell down her back, almost touching her waist. The girl wasn't immune to the hot weather; her hair was scrunched and styled. But she just made it look natural, almost windblown to look wild and free. Just for that one reason, Severine disliked her.

Severine watched her throw away her drink and turn to walk out the door. Emilia looked back at her and winked. It was on instinct that Severine pulled away.

Her fingers clutched the sides of her chair tightly. Honestly, she didn't know whether to feel shock, or to feel duped. Emilia slung her brown leather bag over her strapless summer dress, and hurried out the door. Her steps were lithe and sure, much like Severine's. When she stepped in front of Macsen and stopped him from getting into his truck, Severine's eyes bulged. They talked with familiarity.

The cold day in winter, when she first met Emilia, she gave no second thought to the girl. She looked like a girl with a story, but didn't everybody have one?

Her eyes narrowed at the girl in front of her. She couldn't help but feel betrayed. "Son of a bitch," Severine muttered in awe.

"What?" Lily swung her bag of books on the open seat, and sat where Macsen once did. Her view from the outside was effectively blocked. Lily dug through her wallet in search of money. "Did you get what you wanted?" she asked distractedly.

Severine nodded her head, slowly. Her eyes stayed on Emilia, and when the secretive girl outside turned, she smirked directly at Severine. "I think so." *Or at least I think so.*

"What the hell are you looking at?" Lily asked.

When Severine looked back up at her friend, Lily was staring distractedly at the door and at Macsen. "Who's that chick with him?"

"Ah...her name's Emilia. I met her a few months back."

Lily narrowed her eyes and peered closer. "Hmm. I don't know her." She paused for a second and her face perked up, "but Melissa would."

"What, are you gonna call her?" Severine asked with a trace of a smile. Her attention was still focused on Emilia, who turned from Macsen and walked toward her sleek, red convertible.

"You need to check your eyes, my friend. Melissa's at the front counter."

Severine pulled her gaze away from the glass window and looked at the counter where Melissa stood. She turned and saw Lily and Severine. Her smile was wide as she walked up to them.

"Hey, I didn't see you guys here."

Lily drummed her wallet against the chair and stared at the window. Severine wasn't going to look.

"I have a question for ya," Lily said with a smile.

Melissa nodded happily and sat down at their table. "Shoot."

"Do you know that girl?" Lily pointed a finger toward the window. Severine looked even though she shouldn't have and saw Emilia getting into her car.

"Emilia?" Melissa repeated back. She tore her straw from the wrapper and pursed her lips.

"Yes!" Severine said triumphantly.

"Then, yes, yes I do know her." Melissa grinned at Severine and Lily's impatient expressions. "I just got done talking to her. She's transferring here for sure, and I was telling her about campus."

"What else?" Lily asked.

"I've only talked to her a few times. All I know is that she's our age, kind of shy, and her last name is Wentworth." Melissa glanced between the two of them and pulled back. "Why are you guys being all weird?"

Lily looked at Severine and pointed a finger in her direction. "Remember that name."

Chapter Forty-eight

Not every relationship would work itself out. Most would fade away into the air, and would join the ranks of all the let downs and disappointments.

Severine adjusted her shorts and stared at the field around her. The urge to bolt and drive back to where she belonged became a tempting thought in her head. If she could, she'd wrap yellow CAUTION tape around her heart, to keep her real emotions confined.

Birds chirped loudly in the trees around her, and the sun started to rise in the sky. It was going to be a clear, sunny day. The weather should've been enough to make her happy. Spring was a runner-up to winter. After a brutal winter it was a necessity. And after the winter she had just experienced, she needed the sunshine. But she couldn't enjoy anything. Her heart was beating too fast.

Right now, in the early morning, it was still chilly. Goosebumps grooved underneath her skin as she waited. An hour had passed and still there were no other people around. Just her. Severine's doubt seeped in, but she stood still and tried to listen for any noise.

Jayni had met her at the front of the farmhouse and had quickly guided her to the back of the farm, toward a red barn. The minute it came into view, Severine smiled widely. Thayer's story played in her mind as she followed the bumpy lines of the name Sloan written across the backboard. Like he had said, his jersey number was up there in faded letters, along with his NBA dream.

Severine walked away from the hoop and stopped where the gravel became faded. A slight indention in the ground was the only indication that someone else had stood there once. As she stared up at the barn, her smile couldn't fade away. Even if she walked away from this journey, she finally got to see where a dream began.

The crunching of gravel was light, but Severine heard it instantly.

Thayer rounded the corner of the barn and halted when he saw her. Dressed in basketball shorts and a t-shirt, he appeared to be a person enjoying a nice summer stroll. Slowly, he approached.

Severine's heart hammered with every dribble of the ball in her hands. Her hands shook, and she knew she wouldn't be able to keep up with the casual attitude for too much longer.

"I've made ten out of twenty-five," she passed the ball over to him, "what does that make me?"

He grabbed the ball instantly. Maybe it was habit, but casually he dribbled the ball in between his legs, as he walked closer to her. "It makes you mediocre."

Standing in front of him without touching him was torturous. Her hands twitched to reach out. Severine instead ate him up with her eyes. The sun rose to his height and made his gray eyes seem almost clear. He stopped in front of her, waiting for her to make the first move.

Severine swallowed and gave him a small grin. "I'm here."

"In Missouri," Thayer observed. He moved closer and grinned.

Severine snatched the ball away from his cocky hands and twirled it between her fingers. "If I have any more time for myself I'm going to explode." She held the ball behind her. "Are you still waiting?"

"I did that for you. So you wouldn't blame me for anything."

Severine's voice broke. "I never blamed you."

"Not now, but maybe you would later."

"You gave me time, and I'm here. I still want something for us."

Thayer scratched the back of his head and looked away. "Even with knowing my family's story?"

"Even with that," Severine conceded.

"And Macsen?" Thayer asked.

"It won't ever be comfortable between us," Severine admitted. "I think the two of us know that, but the discomfort is worth it if I can be with you."

"Why do you want to be with me, Severine?"

Her hand skated up his shirt and rested above his heart. "I like what beats within you. You give a good show, Thayer Sloan. But remember, I saw you first." Severine used his words. The same words he had tortured her with months before.

Thayer's arm looped around her and grasped her back firmly. "You give a good show yourself." His hands curved against her cheeks and between them the ball dropped. Severine smirked. "But now that you're here, there's no other way for you to go."

Epilogue

"These need to be soaked in bleach and lit on fire," Severine commented.

She gathered Thayer's sheets and threw them in the corner, far from where she stood. "When's the last time you washed those suckers?"

Thayer shrugged a large shoulder and rifled through his boxes. "I don't know...a few weeks ago?"

Severine made a face and looked around Thayer's room. "You know what's scary? You had to guess at how long they'd been on your bed. I'm not staying over here if those sheets stay on."

Impatiently, Thayer searched through a box. At Severine's threat, he turned around quickly. "Severine! That's the only pair I have."

Severine smiled cheekily and grabbed the Target bag next to her leg. "I noticed. That's why Lily and I got you a new pair." She glanced down at the new brown sheets and tossed them at Thayer.

He caught them with one hand and looked at the package. "At least they're brown."

"That's it? That's all you have to say? Those are seven hundred thread count, Thayer! Those things will rock your world."

Thayer moved his eyebrows up and down and wrapped an arm around Severine. His hand immediately went under her tank top and gripped her hip. He pressed her closer against him, and through his shorts she could feel he was already getting hard. "That's why I have you."

Severine turned away quickly and went to the opposite side of the bed. She tried to appear unfazed by Thayer's words, but true to form, she was failing.

After a summer together, Severine was still trying to wrap her head around the two of them. She thought she had everything figured out about relationships. Before Thayer, she could've told you what she needed out of life, and what was best for her. Being around him showed her that he was just what she needed. She was discovering that it was okay to be wrong. Because when you're wrong, you discover all the things you should've done.

Things with them would undoubtedly be bumpy. But those times would be rare, and when they didhappen, Severine would be ready, alongside Thayer. They were both too stubborn to back away from anything.

She unzipped the plastic bag and dumped the new sheets on the mattress. "Nuh-uh. Lily and Ben are in the other room. That's weird."

"They live here, too," Thayer said with frustration. "I can't kick them out every time I wanna have sex with you."

"It's just...weird."

"I'm willing to move past the awkwardness," Thayer said playfully. His smile was wide and one hundred percent mischievous.

Severine straightened out the bottom sheet. Thayer grabbed the opposite side and started to help her make the bed. His arms flexed as he tucked in his side of the sheet. A man helping out with making a bed had never been so sexy. "I'm sure I'll get used to it. But it wasn't like Lily and I had guys in our dorms every weekend."

"Do you need to get back soon?"

Severine nodded her head and grabbed a fresh pillowcase. "Yeah. I have a few more boxes to unpack."

Thayer smacked his hands together and Severine tossed the pillow in his direction. He caught it and quickly threw it on the bed. He jumped on the bed, stretched out and his body like a contented cat after a long day of doing nothing. "Are you gonna come over here?"

Severine crossed her arms and smiled, "No."

Thayer moved across the bed. With his feet planted on the floor, he opened his legs and crooked a finger at Severine. She stepped forward and his arms instantly encircled her waist. His fingers hooked through the belt loops on her shorts and when her knees were pressed up against the bed, he slowly lifted up her tank top. He stopped at her bra line, and leaned his head close to kiss her stomach. His mouth moved lower, toward the curve of her hip. She felt him nip her skin lightly and jumped at the contact. Thayer soothed the bite with a quick lick but that only made Severine want more.

He looked up at her with his stoic gray eyes. There was so much more to him than anyone would ever realize. Thayer smiled and his hands moved from her waist and down to the back of her thighs. His journey was slow, as his hands drifted past the material of her jeans and underwear and toward her butt. He was inches away from making her lose it when they heard noises coming from the other room. Severine made a face at the obvious groaning and slowly pulled away. Thayer glared at the wall behind her head.

"Yeah," Thayer drew out slowly, "this is going to be weird."

She didn't want to pull away. Especially when they were just getting started. The longer she heard Lily and Ben in the other room, the chances of her cutting her ears off and throwing them at the wall became higher.

"Take me to my dorm," Severine sighed. She pulled down her shirt and redid her ponytail. "They're not gonna end any time too soon."

"We're gonna figure something out," Thayer said as they hurried down the wooden stairs and out the front door.

Severine laughed as they walked into the humid air. Her shirt instantly stuck to her back. She was already counting the days until the first leaf changed colors, declaring summer was over. "What do you suggest? Maybe we should all make a schedule?"

Thayer grabbed his keys and threw them repeatedly in the air. "That's exactly what I was thinking."

"Maybe we should become celibate?" Severine offered as she hopped into the truck.

Thayer slammed his door louder than usual and glared at Severine. "That's funny—for a minute I thought you were trying to say we should refrain from sex."

"We could try."

"And I'd fail after a day. I'd be like a person left in the desert without water."

Severine snorted at Thayer's example. "I think not having sex for a day compared to no food and water in the desert is a little bit of a reach."

"For me, it's the perfect example because it's exactly how I'd feel."

They passed by a few fast food restaurants. Once the air conditioning kicked in, Severine leaned back in her seat and took a deep sigh. "How did your dad take you moving out of the apartment?"

Thayer shook his head and kept his eyes focused on the road. "He didn't seemed surprised. I think he was more shocked that we put up with each other for as long as we did."

Now that Severine knew the full story, she wasn't surprised either. It would've happened sooner than later, regardless of Severine being in the picture. She was just the catalyst. "So if you're gone, is your dad gonna pay for the rent?"

"Hell no."

"Are Macsen and Chris going to get a new roommate then?"

They slowed down to a stop and waited at a red light. Thayer toyed with the buttons on the vents, and she knew he was slowly starting to become tense. "Probably. Macsen will still have to find a job...fast."

Severine glanced out the window and nodded as they started moving again. "Does he really have to get a job? Can't he just get money from..." Severine stopped speaking. Not sure if she should say Mom or Laurena.

Thayer smiled at her and shook his head. "What? From Laurena?"

Severine nodded.

"That would mean that they'd have to be on good terms. Who knows where they stand."

"Could he even stick it out?"

"With a job?" Thayer laughed at her question. "Who knows? I don't really care what he does."

"Such a close-knit family you have," Severine said sarcastically.

"It's not something you can magically snap your fingers and make better, Severine." He removed a hand from the steering wheel and snatched her hand up. He squeezed once and kept speaking, "And even if there was a chance for things to be better, it'd have to come from Macsen. I don't want to close out my brother. I know he's my blood. I know we'll always share our last name. But that's all we have right now."

Slowly, her emotions gripped her heart. They all deserved a happily ever after. When she picked up a book to read, she read through all the trials and heartache to get to the good part—the part where everything became resolved. None of the endings got old. A small part of her childhood dreams was still with her and would probably always be. The world was filled with disappointments. Why would she want to read about the harsh reality when she wanted to escape from everything? The Sloan family deserved something good to happen. Darkness seemed to follow them everywhere.

"I hope something changes."

Thayer turned into a parking space near her dorm and stared at the window. When he looked at Severine, he had a weak smile on his face. "I do, too."

They both understood that the chances of it happening were extremely low.

"Do you need to unpack anything else?" Thayer finally asked.

Severine unbuckled herself and nodded quickly. She was happy for the change of subject. "Not really. I just need to organize some stuff and then I'm good."

The small reprieve from the heat vanished as Severine opened her door and walked toward her new home.

A few girls were scattered around the front of the building, while many sat in groups of three talking and laughing. Severine didn't know how they were surviving the boiling sun. She let out the deep breath she was holding and glanced up at the tall brick building that would be their home for the next year.

Inside the dorms wasn't much better than outside. If anything, the stairwell was even stuffier. Thayer stayed next to her as they walked up the two flights of stairs and slung his arm over her shoulder. Being next to him still felt right; it still made her heart feel full.

"You ready to live here for another year?"

Severine shuddered and shook her head. "Tiny room and a bathroom not connected my room? Yeah, I haven't been counting down for this moment."

Thayer pushed aside the escaped strands from her ponytail and kissed her neck. Severine wanted to lean against him. "Stay with me for a little bit."

It was a tempting offer. One more second in the hallway with him, and she'd grab him by the collar and make him take her with him. "We left to get away from Lily and Ben's startlingly loud sex-capade. We'd end up here more than anything."

"Good point."

Severine opened her door and made a beeline for her bed.

That is, until the boxes on the floor stopped her from moving any further.

She looked down and teetered back and forth like a Weeble Wobble. Thayer snatched her arm and righted her. Severine's eyes were still on the boxes scattered across the room. "Shit. What is all this crap?" Severine muttered.

Thayer leaned against the wall and took in the clutter. "Looks like you have a new roommate, Blake."

"No, I have a hoarder. Not a roommate."

"I'm sorry," a voice called out behind Severine. "I'll get the boxes unpacked as soon as I can."

Severine almost jumped in shock. But it was hard to move when you were frozen from weariness.

Emilia held a laundry basket filled with small boxes and a laptop case. Her hair was pulled back into a high ponytail, with every strand away from her face or perfectly tucked behind her ear. On a day where sweat would make everyone's face look greasy, Emilia's face looked smooth and sweat free. Her eyeliner was streak-less and her lipstick was fresh. Everything that involved Emilia was elegant: her makeup, her hairstyle. Even her brown ballet flats were scuff-free.

She moved the purple laundry basket and her red, sleeveless blouse came into view, along with a pair of white, high-waisted shorts. She didn't look like she was moving in. Honestly, she looked like she was getting ready to go to the country club and join the rest of the socialites for brunch.

"Uh...am I missing something here?" Severine finally asked.

Seeing her at the coffee shop with Macsen was weird enough. But here? In her room? Severine's belly unfurled with a strange feeling.

Emilia was quiet; she hid so much. That was precisely why Severine was nervous.

She smiled at Severine and let out a deep sigh. To Severine, it sounded fake. "I thought you'd know by now. I'm your new roommate."

Severine gaped while Thayer leaned against the wall and stared between the two of them. He was unaware of the fear running through Severine's mind—the fear of what this girl had planned.

She stared at Severine and Thayer like she was out for vindication. The only problem was Severine had no idea why she was searching for it.

Acknowledgements:

It takes a small country to create a book from start to finish. I didn't know how this journey would go. The people I've met along the making of Every Which Way are amazing talented people and I'm so grateful for their help.

I knew betas would be important, but I really didn't know how spectacular they'd be. They read Every Which Way from the beginning and they've seen it go through so many alterations. I have a rare group of girls that are gems! I love them.

Erin,Janna, Lindsay, Amy- You ladies are NOT afraid to say what you think and I'm so grateful for that. I couldn't ask for a greater group of girls!!!

Chrystle-I knew this girl on goodreads. We shared a love for books and soon she invited me to a book club that she had formed. From there I discovered a group of amazing ladies that were equally as passionate for reading as I was. She was my book soulmate and when I told her I wanted to share my book she was supportive in an instant.
I think my books would still be on my hard drive, for my eyes only, if I didn't have your awesome friendship. Thank you.

Tosha and Stephenie -You two have this passion for Severine's book that completely stuns me. Both you of 'got' Severine and that was the greatest feeling. The support you two have given is just downright amazing.

The both of you were my first cheerleaders outside of my family. I can mark a goal off my list because of you two.

Jessica- How long have I talked to you about my stories? Hours and hours you've had to listen to my ideas. I love that you believe in this story and you're not afraid to tell me what you think. I love our bond over reading and writing!

Sheena- I love that we share a mutual passion for reading and I love your challenge to me when I was a kid: "Read this book and I want you to tell me all about it." It was short and simple, and I don't remember anything about it but I remember the feeling of finishing and the joy I got from reading it. You've been a cheerleader in my corner–always telling me to send more, and more chapters your way. You've known about my dreams for years and you didn't roll your eyes.

Taryn-My amazing Frank. Thanks so much for taking a chance on Every Which Way and for creating an amazing blog tour banner.

Sarah Hansen at Okay Creations. You know I love you. I'm one message away from getting a google alert that you've put a restraining order against me. You have an amazing talent and when you showed me your idea for the cover of Every Which Way I think my heart dropped. My character—a character that had been in my head for so long—was brought to life. It was the greatest feeling. And that's why I adore you and your talent.

Lori Sabin- Thank you so much for editing Severine's story. You're an amazing, talented editor. If I think too long about your help and how generous you've been, I'm liable to start crying. Your way with words is simply amazing. Danke, danke, danke.

My CP, Melissa Brown. I had—and still—don't have an idea what I'm doing. You've held my hand through all of this and I am so grateful for you!! Our friendship completely warms my heart. I love our daily conversations, your encouragement, your advice! All of it. Every author needs a critique partner like you.

My mom and dad for encouraging my love for reading.

Lastly, to Joshua for always putting up with my book talk, for watching the kiddos on your days off and letting me hole myself away to write. Last year, you surprised me with a little writing corner and said it'd be my place to get away and breathe. You've constantly given me support and told me I could do this without hesitation. I write what I know, and I know everything from us.

About the Author

College seemed like too much stress for me. Traveling across the world, getting married, and having three kids seemed much more relaxing.

Yeah, I'm still waiting for the relaxing part to kick in...

I change addresses every other year. It's not by choice but it is my reality.

While the crazies of life kept me busy, the stories in my head decided to bubble to the surface. They were dying to be told and and I was dying to tell them.

I hope you'll enjoy escaping to the crazy world of these characters with me!

For more information on Calia Read visit her blog:
www.Caliareadsandwrites.blogspot.de

Or visit her Author Page on Facebook
www.facebook.com/CaliaRead

Follow Calia on Twitter
@Caliaco22

1261455R00207

Made in the USA
San Bernardino, CA
05 December 2012